SHORTLIST

Paris
2009
WHAT'S NEW | WHAT'S ON | WHAT'S BEST

www.timeout.com/paris

Contents

Paris by Area

Essentials

Published by Time Out Guides Ltd
Universal House
251 Tottenham Court Road
London W1T 7AB
Tel: + 44 (0)20 7813 3000
Fax: + 44 (0)20 7813 6001
Email: guides@timeout.com
www.timeout.com

Managing Director Peter Fiennes
Financial Director Gareth Garner
Editorial Director Ruth Jarvis
Deputy Series Editor Dominic Earle
Editorial Manager Holly Pick
Assistant Management Accountant Ija Krasnikova

Time Out Guides is a wholly owned subsidiary of Time Out Group Ltd.

© Time Out Group Ltd
Chairman Tony Elliott
Financial Director Richard Waterlow
Group General Manager/Director Nichola Coulthard
Time Out Magazine Ltd MD Richard Waterlow
Time Out Communications Ltd MD David Pepper
Time Out International Ltd MD Cathy Runciman
Production Director Mark Lamond
Group IT Director Simon Chappell
Head of Marketing Catherine Demajo

Time Out and the Time Out logo are trademarks of Time Out Group Ltd.

This edition first published in Great Britain in 2008 by Ebury Publishing
A Random House Group Company
Company information can be found on www.randomhouse.co.uk
10 9 8 7 6 5 4 3 2 1

Distributed in US by Publishers Group West
Distributed in Canada by Publishers Group Canada

For further distribution details, see www.timeout.com

ISBN: 978-1-84670-104-7

A CIP catalogue record for this book is available from the British Library

Printed and bound by Firmengruppe APPL, aprinta druck, Wemding, Germany

The Random House Group Limited supports The Forest Stewardship Council (FSC), the
leading international forest certification organisation. All our titles that are printed on
Greenpeace approved FSC certified paper carry the FSC logo. Our paper procurement
policy can be found at www.rbooks.co.uk/environment.

Time Out carbon-offsets all its flights with Trees for Cities (www.treesforcities.org)

Paris Shortlist

The **Time Out Paris Shortlist 2009** is one of a new series of annual guides that draws on Time Out's background as a magazine publisher to keep you current with what's going on in town. As well as Paris's key sights and the best of its eating, drinking and leisure options, it picks out the most exciting venues to have opened in the last year and gives a full calendar of events from September 2008 to December 2009. It also includes features on the important news, trends and openings, all compiled by locally based editors and writers. Whether you're visiting for the first time in your life or the first time this year, you'll find the *Time Out Paris Shortlist* contains all you need to know, in a portable and easy-to-use format.

The guide divides central Paris into ten areas, each containing listings for Sights & Museums, Eating & Drinking, Shopping, Nightlife and Arts & Leisure, and maps pinpointing their locations. At the front of the book are chapters rounding up these scenes city-wide, and giving a shortlist of our overall picks. We include itineraries for days out, plus essentials such as transport information and hotels.

Our listings give phone numbers as dialled within France. From abroad, use your country's exit code followed by 33 (the country code for France) and the number given, dropping the initial '0'.

We have noted price categories by using one to four euro signs (€-€€€€), representing budget, moderate, expensive and luxury. Major credit cards are accepted unless otherwise stated. We also indicate when a venue is **NEW**, and give **Event highlights**.

All our listings are double-checked, but places do sometimes close or change their hours or prices, so it's a good idea to call a venue before visiting. While every effort has been made to ensure accuracy, the publishers cannot accept responsibility for any errors that this guide may contain.

Venues are marked on the maps using symbols numbered according to their order within the chapter and colour-coded as follows:

❶ Sights & Museums
❶ Eating & Drinking
❶ Shopping
❶ Nightlife
❶ Arts & Leisure

Map key	
Major sight or landmark	▢
Hospital or college	▢
Railway station	▢
Park	▢
River	▢
Autoroute	═
Main road	
Main road tunnel	
Pedestrian road	
Arrondissement boundary	
Airport	✈
Church	✚
Métro station	Ⓜ
RER station	Ⓡ
Area name	LES HALLES

Time Out Paris Shortlist 2009

EDITORIAL
Editor Dominic Earle
Proofreader Patrick Mulkern
Indexer Rob Norman

DESIGN
Art Director Scott Moore
Art Editor Pinelope Kourmouzoglou
Senior Designer Henry Elphick
Graphic Designers Gemma Doyle,
  Kei Ishimaru
Digital Imaging Simon Foster
Advertising Designer Jodi Sher
Picture Editor Jael Marschner
Deputy Picture Editor Katie Morris
Picture Researcher Gemma Walters
Picture Desk Assistant Marzena Zoladz

ADVERTISING
Commercial Director Mark Phillips
International Advertising Manager
  Kasimir Berger
International Sales Executive
  Charlie Sokol
Advertising Assistant Kate Staddon

MARKETING
Marketing Manager Yvonne Poon
Senior Publishing Brand Manager
  Luthfa Begum
Sales & Marketing Director,
  North America Lisa Levinson
Marketing Designers Anthony Huggins,
  Nicola Wilson

PRODUCTION
Production Manager Brendan McKeown
Production Controller Caroline Bradford
Production Co-ordinator Julie Pallot

CONTRIBUTORS
This guide was researched and written by Anna Brooke, Alison Culliford,
Jonathan Derbyshire, Natasha Edwards, Iris Mansour, Rich Woodruff and
the writers of *Time Out Paris.*

PHOTOGRAPHY
All photography by Elan Fleisher, except: pages 13, 69 Oliver Knight; pages 14, 25, 26,
29, 30, 56, 63, 64, 70, 74, 76, 82, 95, 98, 99, 100, 108, 109, 110, 112, 113, 116,
118, 121, 122, 132, 133, 136, 139, 141, 144, 147, 153, 156, 157, 158, 161, 164,
168, 169, 172 Karl Blackwell; pages 21, 22, 43, 44, 47, 49, 50, 53, 124 Jean-
Christophe Godet; pages 34 David Lefranc; pages 37, 51, 87, 129 Heloise Bergman;
page 52 N Borel/Jakob & MacFarlane Architects; page 67 L/B, Palais de Tokyo Paris,
2007; page 79 Thomas Bouet; page 85 M N Robert; page 105 Didier Herman; page
125 Hervé Abbadie; page 126 Eric Laignel; page 148 Jakob & MacFarlane Architects.

The following images were provided by the featured establishments/artists: pages 36,
39, 134.

Cover image: Steven Vidler/Eurasia Press/Corbis

MAPS
JS Graphics (john@jsgraphics.co.uk).

About Time Out

Founded in 1968, Time Out has expanded from humble London beginnings into the
leading resource for those wanting to know what's happening in the world's greatest
cities. As well as our influential what's-on weeklies in London, New York and Chicago,
we publish more than a dozen other listings magazines in cities as varied as Beijing
and Mumbai. The magazines established Time Out's trademark style: sharp writing,
informed reviewing and bang up-to-date inside knowledge of every scene.
  Time Out made the natural leap into travel guides in the 1980s with the City Guide
series, which now extends to over 50 destinations around the world. Written and
researched by expert local writers and generously illustrated with original photography,
the full-size guides cover a larger area than our Shortlist guides and include many more
venue reviews, along with additional background features and a full set of maps.
  Throughout this rapid growth, the company has remained proudly independent,
still owned by Tony Elliott four decades after he started Time Out London as a single
fold-out sheet of A5 paper. This independence extends to the editorial content of all
our publications, this Shortlist included. No establishment has been featured because
it has advertised, and no payment has influenced any of our reviews. And, for our critics,
there's definitely no such thing as a free lunch: all restaurants and bars are visited
and reviewed anonymously, and Time Out always picks up the bill.
For more about the company, see www.timeout.com.

Don't Miss
2009

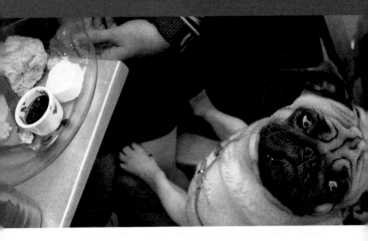

Sights & Museums

Nicolas Sarkozy hasn't been in power long enough to make his mark on Paris in the way that his predecessors François Mitterrand and, to a lesser extent, Jacques Chirac did. Modern Paris has both men's fingerprints all over it: in Mitterrand's celebrated *grands projets*, such as the pyramid at the Louvre (p74) or the Opéra Bastille (p115), and in the Chirac-sponsored Musée du Quai Branly (p127), a museum of non-Western art that opened in 2006 in a building designed by Jean Nouvel.

But fears that Sarkozy would turn out to be some philistine uninterested in the fabric of the French capital were partially assuaged by the speech he gave in 2007 at the opening of the Cité de

l'Architecture et du Patrimoine (p57), a wonderful architectural museum that occupies the eastern wing of the Palais de Chaillot. The President used that occasion to invite several of the world's leading architects, including Norman Foster and Richard Rogers, to brief him on ways of renewing the built environment in Paris.

While they do that, cultural and urban renewal carries on apace. The summer of 2008 saw the opening of 104 (p159), a multi-media arts centre built in premises previously occupied by the city's undertakers, and the Cité de la Mode et du Design (p152), part of the renewal of a strip of run-down warehouses by the Seine in the 13th. And a few months before that, the Palais de la

Palais Royal p11

Porte d'Orée opened its doors to the Cité Nationale de l'Histoire de l'Immigration, charting the history of immigration in France.

Elsewhere, the list of sights worth seeing is almost endless – from defining monuments such as the Eiffel Tower (p124) to lesser-known gems like the Musée Gustave Moreau (p88). All this, and much more that we haven't yet mentioned, in a city that's a manageable size and boasts one of the best transport networks anywhere in the world.

Neighbourhoods

Parisians use two distinct systems when thinking about their city: the named districts – the Marais, the Latin Quarter, Montparnasse and so on – and the arrondissements. The boundaries of the former aren't always clear, whereas the latter are fixed administrative units (there are 20 in all) that spiral out, clockwise and in ascending order,

www . k u b e h o t e l . c o m

from the Louvre. Together they comprise an urban jigsaw that the novelist Julien Green once compared to a model of the human brain. Each piece has a particular connotation or function: the 5th is academic; the 6th is arty and chic; the 16th is wealthy and dull; while the 18th, 19th and 20th arrondissements are riotously multicultural. Residents are frequently assessed, on first meeting at least, by their postcode, and as a consequence often develop a fierce sense of local pride. Indeed, many of them will tell you that Paris isn't so much a city as a jumble of villages, each pungently and defiantly distinctive.

We've divided this book into areas, though not necessarily into shapes that residents would recognise; we've imagined the city as a series of visitor-friendly concentrations of shops, sights, restaurants and bars. The Champs-Elysées & Western Paris section has the famous avenue as its spine, lined with high-end shops and showrooms. It also contains fashion's most glamorous thoroughfare, avenue Montaigne, which is almost matched in lustre and allure by rue du Faubourg-Saint-Honoré. Montmartre & Pigalle has, at its northern end, picturesque Montmartre with its vertiginous flights of steps, narrow winding streets and the massive bulk of Sacré-Coeur (p88). To the south lies Pigalle, famous for the Moulin Rouge and its strip clubs and scuzzy bars (though it's a good deal more salubrious today than it once was). Opéra to Les Halles used to be the centre of royal power in Paris, and you can get a sense of this by taking a stroll around the Palais Royal (p75). Today, however, it's the city's commercial and cultural powerhouse: it's home to the massive Les Halles shopping

complex, the jewellers and fashion houses of Place Vendôme, and to the Louvre, Palais Garnier (p86) and Musée de l'Orangerie (p74).

North-eastern Paris is the area visitors from the UK are likely to see first: Eurostar trains terminate at the Gare du Nord (p96) in the 10th arrondissement. The area is on the up, with its main artery, the charming Canal St-Martin, now lined with chic boutiques and cafés. Further north and east of here is the magnificently odd Parc des Buttes-Chaumont (p96), a warren of cliffs and grottoes carved out of a former quarry. Marais, Bastille & Eastern Paris is barfly territory, especially along rue Oberkampf, rue Jean-Pierre Timbaud and rue Saint-Maur. The ever-trendy Marais itself, which is choked with independent galleries and quirky shops of all kinds, is also the centre of gay life in Paris.

The Islands – the Ile de la Cité, the oldest part of the city and home to Notre-Dame cathedral (p119), and the more elegant Ile St-Louis, with its shops and restaurants – are highly distinctive and an essential port of call on any itinerary.

Undeniably, the main attraction of the affluent (and sometimes stuffily institutional) 7th & Western Paris area is the Eiffel Tower, a universal visual shorthand for the French capital. Its elegant ironwork is most alluring at night, when it is lit up by tens of thousands of shimmering lightbulbs. This is also the best time to climb the Tower, because the queues are at their shortest. For many years, St-Germain-des-Prés was the intellectual heartland of the city, home to Sartre and de Beauvoir. But these days it's more about fashion than philosophy, and the expensive cafés are no place for starving writers. The city's most

beautiful park, the Jardin du Luxembourg (p132), won't cost you a sou, however; and the Musée d'Orsay (p133), though not free, is still excellent value. Due east, the Latin Quarter is home to several of Paris's most august academic institutions, including the Sorbonne. And to the south, Montparnasse, though no longer the artistic stronghold it was in the 1920s, still boasts a number of excellent cafés and restaurants, and the resting place of some of France's most illustrious dead, the Cimetière du Montparnasse (p154).

Getting around

In 2007, the mayor launched Vélib, a free bike scheme that put 20,000 bicycles at the disposal of residents and visitors alike. But if you don't feel up to taking your chances with the Paris traffic, invest in a Mobilis pass and travel around the city cash-free. The Paris métro is one of the oldest public transport networks in the world, and buses are clean, frequent and cheap. Some of the bus routes are worth riding just for the sightseeing opportunities they offer: no.24 takes you through St-Germain-des-Prés and the Latin Quarter; no.69 runs all the way from Gambetta in the east, via the Louvre, to the Champ de Mars in the west; and no.73 connects the Champs-Elysées to the futuristic concrete jungle of La Défense.

But you can't beat walking. Paris is compact enough to be navigated on foot, and this is the best way to hear the heartbeat of the city. This way you'll discover that far from being a 'museum city' suffocating under the weight of its 'heritage', Paris is a thriving capital that looks to the future without ever forgetting its past.

Place Vendôme p11

Rose Bakery p17

WHAT'S BEST
Eating & Drinking

When compared with other capital cities, Paris's dining scene is often criticised for being stuck in a time warp. But that doesn't mean that change isn't happening. Traditional bistros and brasseries may still retain their Belle Epoque cupolas and zinc-topped bars, but the stuff coming out of the kitchen is increasingly modern, with an accent on raw materials rather than elaborate sauces and accompaniments. Technique remains crucial – this is France after all – but at a time when the quality of what we eat is at the forefront of our minds, more

and more chefs are concentrating on buying the finest ingredients, and bringing out the best in them.

This trend is confirmed across the spectrum of Paris's eateries, from low-key *tables d'hôte* such as Granterroirs (p63) to swish seafood eateries such as L'Ostréade (p156), whose oysters and fish dishes stand their ground without extra seasoning, and haute cuisine temples such as Arpège (p127), where Alain Passard presents his puritan beetroot in nothing but a salt crust. Even non-French chefs are jumping on the bandwagon. American Daniel Rose, in his

SHORTLIST

Best new
- Jules Verne (p128)
- L'Ostréade (p156)
- Poussette Café (p92)
- Le Restaurant (p137)

Best value
- Le Baron Rouge (p107)
- Chez Toinette (p90)
- L'Encrier (p108)

Most glamorous
- Alain Ducasse au Plaza Athénée (p61)
- Les Ambassadeurs (p62)
- L'Atelier de Joël Robuchon (p135)
- Café de la Paix (p77)
- Drouant (p77)
- Hemingway Bar at the Ritz (p77)
- Lapérouse (p146)

Bars with character
- Andy Whaloo (p106)
- Café Charbon (p107)
- De la Ville Café (p77)
- La Fourmi (p90)
- Harry's New York Bar (p77)
- La Palette (p137)
- Le Piano Vache (p146)

Cocktail classics
- Le Crocodile (p146)
- Kong (p78)
- Lizard Lounge (p108)

Best for nighthawks
- Le Fanfaron (p108)
- La Perle (p109)
- Au P'tit Garage (p107)
- Le Sancerre (p92)
- Le Tambour (p80)

Regional champions
- L'Ambassade d'Auvergne (p106)
- L'Ami Jean (p127)
- Chez Michel (p98)
- Granterroirs (p63)
- Un Jour à Peyrassol (p78)
- Aux Lyonnais (p76)

16-seater Spring (p93) restaurant, serves an excellent no-choice menu that depends entirely on what he finds on the morning market, and UK-born Chris Wright at Le Timbre (p137), named after the French word for stamp because the dining area is so small, buys his wares from the finest suppliers in Paris, presenting uncorrupted dishes whose flourishes never detract from the main ingredient.

Bistros & brasseries

One thing that will never change, however, is Paris's attachment to its bistros – where locals go to be greeted with a handshake and a smile, where wine comes in carafes and where the dishes make you feel warm inside. Many, like Alain Ducasse's Aux Lyonnais (p76),

BOUILLON
Racine

Located in the heart of the LatinQuarter,
the Bouillon Racine combines art nouveau charm and
exceptionally tasty food.

Open daily noon-11pm
Live jazz 1st & 3rd Tuesdays of the month
3 rue Racine, 6th. Mº Odéon.
Tel: 01.44.32.15.60
Email.bouillon.racine@wanadoo.fr
www.bouillonracine.com

deliberately serve only time-honoured (often regional) dishes, but others are swaying from traditional cuisine, putting a modern spin on French classics. Le Pré Verre (p146), La Cerisaie (p155), L'Ami Jean (p127), Le Temps au Temps (p110), Le Châteaubriand (p107) and Le Bistrot Paul Bert (p107) all push the boundaries of French bistro cooking. Just be warned, though – the chances of getting a bargain nowadays are slim and the task of serving budget food has mostly fallen to the cafés. While many bistros serve three courses for between €30 and €40, prices can easily creep to over €60 a head. Remember that lunch is always cheaper or opt for the prix fixe menu in the evening.

The same is true if you're looking for old-school pleasures in a brasserie. The prospect of sitting amid art nouveau extravagance watching Paris unfurl before your eyes, as waiters in black and white rush between tables serving platters of oysters and choucroute, comes at a price, but is cheaper at lunchtimes. Bofinger (p107), part of the Flo chain, is one of the most popular, pulling in locals and tourists; like most brasseries, you should book at least two days in advance. Other sure-fire addresses include La Coupole (p156).

Posh nosh

To crank it up a notch, you could opt for a spot of all-out luxury in one of the city's haute cuisine restaurants. Many other eateries serve cooking of comparable skill and quality, but nothing can beat the feeling you get when you are treated like royalty. What's more, these high-class establishments are beginning to swap their revered classicism for something more fun. Les Ambassadeurs (p62) in the Crillon is a perfect example. Inside the lavish marble and gilt dining room, chef Jean-François Piège serves a Michelin-starred menu featuring an Explosion de Pizza – a little doughy ball of pizza, on a spoon, that literally explodes inside your mouth. Service remains impeccable five-star, but the dress code is more flexible than in days gone by. Other sumptuous dining experiences are to be had at Le Meurice (p78), Alain Ducasse au Plaza Athénée (p61), and Ducasse's latest acquisition, the Jules Verne (p128) in the Eiffel Tower, which also offers some of the city's finest views (book three months ahead).

If money is an issue, but haute cuisine still appeals (and it's worth trying at least once in your life), reserve a table for lunch when dishes are often half the evening price, or opt for Michelin-starred newcomer Le Restaurant (inside L'Hôtel, p137), where Philippe Belissent creates unforgettable menus that start at just €75.

Café culture

A rapidly emerging trend is the Anglo-style snack shop. Cojean (17 bd Haussmann, 9th, 01.47.70.22.65) and La Ferme (55 rue St-Roch, 1st, 01.40.20.12.12) both serve healthy sandwiches, soups, and salads to eat in or take out. The Anglo theme continues at boho-chic Rose Bakery (p92) where organic soups, quiches and inventive salads have shown Parisians that the British know a thing or two about nosh; and Bread & Roses (p135) is a bakery run by a Frenchman who is passionate about British food, especially cakes.

The ubiquitous Parisian café, where wine is cheaper than water, is still well and truly present, although the iconic, scruffy neighbourhood haunt with its revolting Turkish loo and peeling paintwork is fortunately becoming a thing of the past. Many cafés

have upgraded their interiors and prices accordingly, but their menus (often featuring light bites like omelettes and croques monsieur), remain cheaper than in restaurants. Just a handful of addresses nostalgically cling to their shabby-chic image – generally in the artsy north-east. A perfect example of this is Chez Jeanette (47 rue du Faubourg-St-Denis, 10th, 01.47.70.30.89), which despite the new owner's decision to preserve the 1970s decor, grease 'n' all, has never been busier. If grime gets you down, you still can't beat a chic café experience in the famous (if not inexpensive) Left Bank institutions Les Deux Magots (p136) and Café de Flore (p135), or at Café de la Paix (p77), whose millefeuilles are unrivalled.

If you're after something stronger, the 10th and 11th, especially around Oberkampf, continue to be the most happening areas for bars. Café Charbon (p107), which acts as both a restaurant and pre-club cocktail bar, and L'Alimentation Generale (p106), whose excellent concerts give precious stage space to up-and-coming musicians, are the places to be seen in. Other trendy locals gravitate towards grungy all-nighters like Le Sancerre (p92) or La Fourmi (p90).

For those with money to burn, the city's other party central is the area around Champs-Elysées. Abandoned by all but a 'wannabe' crowd a few years ago, the area has regained favour with the smart set and now boasts some very posh addresses indeed. If you're curious, have a tipple in Le Dada (p63) and count the designer handbags.

Making a meal

It is not unusual for Parisians to turn up at a restaurant without a reservation, but if your heart is set on somewhere specific, or the restaurant is popular, book ahead. Once you're sat at the table, it's yours until you decide to leave (it is considered the height of rudeness for the waiter to bring you the bill before you've asked), except at popular bistros with multiple sittings, where you'll be expected to leave before the next guests arrive. Also remember that tips are usually included in the bill and that you are not expected to leave anything, although one or two euros for exceptional service will always be appreciated.

As a general rule, the closer the tourist site and the better the view, the worse the food – although there are exceptions, such as Les Ombres (p128) on the roof of the Musée du Quai Branly, which affords an exceptional panorama of the Eiffel Tower and serves gastronomic cuisine.

If you are looking for a snack, bear in mind that almost all Chinese *traiteurs* are mediocre, reheating dishes in a microwave while you wait. You are much better off finding a bakery or packing a picnic and saving your cash for a special dinner.

Apart from fast-food outlets, non-French food is increasingly popular. The streets around Belleville (20th) and the southern end of the 13th are crammed with decent Chinese restaurants; the 2nd, around rue Ste-Anne, is flourishing with Japanese eateries, including the very excellent Kai (p78); rue des Rosiers in the Marais is a centre for Jewish cooking; and Italian, Indian, Moroccan and Lebanese cuisine can be found across the city.

Finally, try to avoid anywhere with a menu labelled 'menu touristique' or 'we speak English'. As tempting as it may be, these are sure-fire signs of mediocre cooking.

Rick Owens p22

WHAT'S BEST
Shopping

While a strong euro means that shopping in Paris will not reward your pocket, it is, and ever will be, a sensual pleasure. Whether it is trying on draped creations behind the velvet curtains of Lanvin or tasting cheeses at an open-air market, the joy is in experiencing the pursuit of perfection for which the French are famous. While we have window shopping, they have window licking (*lèche-vitrine*).

It is also pointless these days to shop for pan-European brands in Paris as you won't pay much less for Zara and H&M than at home. The search for something definitively Parisian, however, is rewarded by an ever-growing array of talents now setting up their own boutiques, especially in the Marais.

The concept shop trend, which began ten years ago with Colette (p81), is now a central feature of the Paris shopping scene. Elevating the buyer's job to one of style maker, they not only hand-pick the fashion and objects on display, but frequently collaborate with designers to produce exclusive and limited edition merchandise, crossing the boundaries between clothes, music and product design. The newest of this band, LE66 (p65), makes a brave challenge to the global chains on the Champs-Elysées with its hip and original fashion. Here you'll also find a refreshingly un-French style of service, where the staff are intelligent and enthusiastic about what they are selling.

Paul & Joe

In the luxury market the race is on to create the most splendiferous showcase in town. Spring-summer and autumn-winter 08 fashion weeks were the scene of some of the most extravagant parties Paris has seen for a long time, as brands such as Fendi (who reputedly paid $1m for 40 minutes of Amy Winehouse), Hermès, Yves Saint Laurent, Sonia Rykiel, Givenchy and Roberto Cavalli launched refitted or new stores in the luxury heartlands. And now that France has a fashionable first lady residing in the midst of it all, the spotlight is firmly on French designers.

Luxury mile

The stretch of rue St-Honoré and rue du Fbg-St-Honoré from the Hôtel Costes to the Hôtel Bristol is wall-to-wall fashion boutiques, and during fashion weeks you'll see plenty of outlandish looks teetering along the narrow pavements. With the exception of trash temple Just Cavalli, it's all taste and intimacy, with the new Givenchy (p65) and apartment-style Lanvin (p83) as highlights. The apart-boutique trend was started by Paul Smith (3 rue du Fbg-St-Honoré, 8th, 01.42.68.27.10), and though you can buy his clobber in England, it is worth visiting just to see how cool Britannia must seem to the French in this homage to English eccentricity.

Walking east, rue St-Honoré leads neatly to the Palais-Royal, which is fashionable again thanks to the presence of Rick Owens (130-133 Galerie de Valois, 1st, 01.40.20.42.52) and Marc Jacobs (p83). A newcomer to the district is Kitsuné (52 rue de Richelieu, 1st, 01.42.60.34.28, www.kitsune.fr), long-time purveyor of clubby music compilations, which is now selling its own branded clothing including Scottish cashmere and Japanese jeans. Cult Swedish brand Acne Jeans (124 galerie Valois, 1st, 01.42.60.16.62, www.acnejeans. com) is also a hit here, with a range of soft and fluid casuals.

Avenue Montaigne's headliners include the Roberto Cavalli flagship at no.50 and Fendi at no.22, while, Agnès B joins the more casual crowd infiltrating the Golden Triangle (38 av George V, 01.40.73.81.10, www.agnesb.com).

If you're in the market for an expensive new watch, then you should check out Rolex's first exclusive boutique in Europe (56 rue de Rennes, 6th, 01.53.63. 00.50, www.rolex.com).

Marais style

The northern part of the Marais, now dubbed NoMa – on rues Charlot, Poitou and Saintonge – has sealed its identity as the essential district for hot and hip fashion.

Here you'll find multi-label boutique Shine (p113) and young French label Swildens (22 rue de Poitou, 3rd, 01.42.71.19.12) which boasts Carla Sarkozy as a client. AB33 and No.60 (33 & 60 rue Charlot, 3rd, 01.42.71.02.82/ 01.44.78.91.90) stock a delectable selection of womenswear and accessories, while truly original, one-off and skilfully crafted pieces can be found at Galerie Simone (124 rue Vieille du Temple, 3rd, 01.42.74.21.28). Tara Jarmon recently opened her fourth Parisian boutique here over two floors of a 17th-century *hôtel particulier* (106 rue Vielle du Temple, 3rd, 01 42 72 26 04, www.tarajarmon.com).

The most exciting newcomers, however, are Dolls (56 rue de Saintonge, 3rd, 01.44.54.08.21), stocking cutting-edge labels in an ecologically designed space, and April 77 (49 rue de Saintonge, 3rd, www.april77.fr), offering skinny jeans and faux leather jackets in a beatnik setting. NoMa is also an *haut lieu* of vintage.

The Left Bank

The long-established shopping area of St-Germain tends to be more conservative, but is increasingly offering a mirror image of the Right Bank with brands insisting on a presence on both sides of the Seine. These include Martin Margiela (p84), Paul & Joe (p139) and Vanessa Bruno (p140). Shoe heaven is found along rue de Grenelle with all the top brands. Newcomers include bobo bags in colourful fabrics and denim from the former prêt-à-porter designer Jérome Dreyfuss (1 rue Jacob, 6th, 01.43.54.70.93), Hélène Lamey's French-made nightwear and childrenswear at Bluet (18 rue du Pré aux Clercs, 7th, 01.45.44. 00.26), Shyde's Birkinesque dresses

SHORTLIST

Best new
- I Love My Blender (p112)
- LE66 (p65)

Best souvenirs
- Dyptique (p149)
- La Galerie du Carrousel du Louvre (p82)

Best boutiques
- Agnès b (p80)
- Boutique M Dia (p81)
- Givenchy (p65)
- Lanvin (p83)

Best concept stores
- Colette (p81)
- L'Eclaireur (p111)
- Ekivok (p81)

Best vintage
- Comme On Eline (p111)
- Didier Ludot (p81)

Best accessories
- Alice Cadolle (p80)
- Erès (p81)
- Hervé Chapelier (p138)
- Peggy Huyn Kinh (p139)

Best food and wine
- Christian Constant (p138)
- Fromagerie Quatrehomme (p128)
- Jean-Paul Hévin (p138)
- Julien, Caviste (p112)
- Patrick Roger (p139)
- Poilâne (p140)

Literary life
- Bouquinistes (p149)
- Red Wheelbarrow (p113)
- Shakespeare & Co (p149)

The classics
- Le Bon Marché (p138)
- Chanel (p81)
- Dior (p65)
- Galeries Lafayette (p82)
- Printemps (p84)
- Sonia Rykiel (p140)
- Yves Saint Laurent (p140)

and blouses (28 rue St-Sulpice, 6th, 01.40.26.22.16) and attractive multi-brand shop Kyrie Eleison (15 carrefour de l'Odéon, 6th, 01.46.34. 26.91) with lush creations by Orla Kiely, Eros-Erotokritos, Velvet and La Fée Parisienne. On the luxury scene two big names have revamped their boutiques: at Yves Saint Laurent (p140) opium-coloured walls and lacquered ceilings provide a sumptuous showcase for Stephane Pilati's creations, while at Sonia Rykiel's enlarged St-Germain flagship (p140) black mosaics, smoked glass and multiple mirrors evoke a '70s nightclub.

Food shopping

The new layout of Fauchon (28 & 30 pl de la Madeleine, 8th, 01.70.39.38.00), with different areas (pâtisserie, bakery, fruit and vegetables, etc) and chefs on hand at each to offer advice and recipes, provides an excuse to indulge at this luxury foodstore. Food markets, both permanent and temporary, are found in all arrondissements, and two of the most popular are the historic Marché d'Aligre in the 12th, and the relatively new Marché des Enfants Rouges in the 3rd, which focuses on organic produce. For a full list, see www.paris.fr. Foodie streets include rue de Buci (6th), rue des Martyrs (9th) and rue Mouffetard (5th).

Practicalities

VAT at 19.6% is included in the price of most items. Opening hours are generally 10am-7pm, with some shops closing for lunch. Departments stores stay open late on Thursdays. Many Marais shops and those on the Champs-Elysées stay open on Sundays.

Marché d'Aligre

Coques

Wagg

WHAT'S BEST
Nightlife

Club life in Paris remains something of an enigma compared with other European cities, but beneath the apparently uneventful surface there's a vibrant assortment of venues. Look in the right place, on the right night, and you'll find sweaty dancefloors, dive bars hosting celebrity DJs, boats rocking (literally) from dusk till dawn and some of the most stylish clubs in the world. And when it comes to music – especially jazz, blues and *chanson* – you'll find more than enough going on to keep your feet tapping.

Nightclubs

The Paris clubbing scene has been enjoying a renaissance of late. Among the new wave of clubs, the most exciting are Le Showcase (01.45.61.25.43), located in a former warehouse directly underneath the Pont Alexandre III, and Paris Paris (p84), a cosy basement venue that attracts a cutting-edge crowd to its electro nights and monthly dance classes hosted by concept store Colette. Provided you can get in to either, you'll be rubbing shoulders with the likes of Justice, Sebastian, Mr Oizo, Kavinsky, Busy P and other members of the city's cool clubbing community. As well as the all-out newcomers, a couple of old favourites are back on fine form – the revived Bains Douches (p115) and the reincarnated Bus Palladium (p93). Meanwhile, the Rex (p85) has installed one of the best sound systems in Europe.

The trendy new places tend to produce a constantly changing line-up of electronic music, techno, hip hop, house, disco and even rock – as epitomised by the fashion for 'selectors' rather than mix DJs. Look out for one-offs by such hip labels as Imprime and Record Makers, as well as regular sets from Jennifer Cardini, Laurent Garnier and Miss Kitten.

For the superclub experience, make for the recently opened Djoon (22 bd Vincent-Auriol, 13th, 01.45.70.83.49), a restaurant, bar and club that mixes an industrial setting with baroque frescoes and an electro, garage and house soundtrack, or Queen (p66), a mostly gay club known for its high-octane disco nights. Smaller but well worth checking out, especially for 'after' parties, are the floating Batofar (p152) and Bateau Concorde Atlantique (Porte de Solférino, 25 quai Anatole-France, 7th, 01.47.05.71.03), and the Nouveau Casino (p115). In fact, it's with the 'afters' that things really get going in Paris: there are as many early Sunday morning events here as there are Saturday nighters.

For standard house try Folies Pigalle (p94) and Red Light (p157), among others; for deep, progressive or minimal sounds, make tracks for Nouveau Casino. Straightforward hip hop nights are held at the Opus Café (167 quai de Valmy, 10th, 01.40.34.70.00); and the Rex has a regular hip hop night called Freak Out. For drum 'n' bass the main nights are monthly Massive at Rex and I Love Jungle at a succession of hired venues. Trance and hardcore tend to stay outside Paris, with outdoor events organised by local collectives and sound systems, though a few crop up indoors. Dance music of every stripe gets an outing at the Paris version of Berlin's Love Parade, the Techno

SHORTLIST

Best new/revamped
- Les Bains Douches (p115)
- Le Sunset (p85)

Best bands
- Le Bataclan (p115)
- Café de la Danse (p115)
- La Cigale/La Boule Noire (p93)
- Olympia (p84)
- Le Point Ephémère (p99)

Best sound systems
- Djoon (p27)
- Rex (p85)

All night long
- Nouveau Casino (p115)

Sunday sessions
- Wagg (p140)

Best for sunny days
- Point Ephémère (p99)
- Red Light (p157)

Perfect for posing
- Le Baron (p66)
- Paris Paris (p84)

Best for star DJs
- Rex (p83)

Best for party snacks
- La Bellevilloise (p28)
- Café Charbon (p107)
- Le Sabot (p140)

Best gay clubs
- Queen (p66)

Best for jazz
- Caveau de la Huchette (p149)
- New Morning (p99)
- Petit Journal Montparnasse (p157)
- Le Sunset/ Le Sunside (p85)

Killer cocktails
- Djoon (p27)

Life is a cabaret
- Le Lido (p66)
- Moulin Rouge (p94)

Parade (p34), which takes place in September and draws thousands.

If you like your clubbing cosy, there are hip bars around Bastille, the Marais, Oberkampf and the Grands Boulevards willing to oblige. Traditionalists can find plenty to keep them happy too; swing, be-bop and rock 'n' roll after the jazz concerts at Le Slow Club (p85), and a stream of school disco-type nights where the DJ is no superstar: check out the twice-monthly Bal at Elysée Montmartre (p94). Salsa and world music events are plentiful, with regular nights at Le Divan du Monde (p93).

Paris clubs don't really get going until 2am, and people often hit a DJ bar beforehand. Many clubbers visit several venues in one night and finish their evening at an 'after' on Sunday morning. This can be costly, but there's also quality DJing at free nights in some clubs during the week. Free passes can be found on various flyers; flyer information is available at www.flyersweb.com. Other good sites are www.radiofg.com, www.novaplanet.com and www.lemonsound.com.

Note that the last métro leaves at around 12.45am (1.45am on Friday and Saturday), and the first only gets rolling at 5.45am; in between those times you'll have to get home by night bus or taxi.

Rock, roots & jazz

If you'd set your heart on a late-night gig, think again. Trendsetters may flock to Paris to meet, plan and jam, but many punters complain that the powers-that-be – the people who dreamed up the *lutte contre le bruit*, or noise clampdown – are spoiling the party. Live music often winds up at 10.30pm (sometimes earlier). Venues like Nouveau Casino, La Maroquinerie (23 Rue Boyer, 20th,

01.40.33.35.05) and Le Point Ephémère (p99), all with a varied showcase of contemporary sounds, are fighting an ongoing battle to persuade the authorities that increased sound levels will not bring social meltdown.

Still the *banlieue* raps on, currently to the strains of TTC, La Rumeur and Le Remède; and should you like your Francophonia delivered by husky-voiced ladies, you'll be glad to know *la chanson française* continues to thrive – in places like newcomer La Bellevilloise (19 rue Boyer, 20th, 01.53.27.35.77), founded in 1877 as a socialist cooperative and now a multi-purpose exhibition and concert venue. On similarly solid foundations is the city's rep as an international hotspot for jazz and blues. Venues like the New Morning (p99), revamped Sunset (p85) and Caveau de la Huchette (p149) have been hosting big names for years, and few arrondissements are without a similar cellar.

Paris has a lively world music scene – often Arabic and African – at places like Le Bataclan (p115). US and UK indie acts and rocktagenarians drop by on tour to places like Olympia (p84) and La Cigale (p93).

Listings can be found in the weekly *Les Inrockuptibles*, whose database at www.lesinrocks.com has all that's hot in town. Monthly *Lylo* is distributed free at Fnac (p65) and in bars such as La Fourmi (p90). Virgin Megastore (p66) and Fnac have their own ticket offices. Get to a gig at the time given on the ticket; they usually start on time.

Cabaret

A century and a half after cancan was born, dancers are still slinking across Parisian cabaret stages. The Moulin Rouge (p94) popularised the skirt-raising concept in the 19th century, and since then venues like Le Lido (p66) have institutionalised garter-pinging for ever.

These days, a cabaret is an all-evening, €100, smart-dress event, served with a pre-show meal and champers. Male dancers, acrobats and magicians complement the foxtrots; dancing is synchronised, costumes are beautiful, and the whole caboodle totally respectable. The Moulin Rouge is the most traditional revue and the only place with cancan. Toulouse-Lautrec posters, glittery lamp-posts and fake trees lend tacky charm, while 60 Doriss dancers cover the stage with faultless synchronisation. Sadly, elbow room is nil, with hundreds of tables packed in like sardines. But if you can bear intimacy with international businessmen, the Moulin Rouge,

the cheapest of the food-serving cabarets, won't disappoint.

For space go to Le Lido. With 1,000 seats, this classy venue is the largest, priciest cabaret of the lot: the art nouveau hall's high-tech touches optimise visibility and star chef Paul Bocuse has revolutionised the menu. The slightly tame show, with 60 Bluebell Girls, has boob-shaking, wacky costumes and numerous oddities: courtesan cats meeting Charlie Chaplin, for example.

The newly reopened Bobin'O (14 Rue de la Gaîté, 14th, 01.43.27.24.24) provides a fresh alternative to the usual cabaret. As well as high-powered routines and variety acts, the Bobin'O has a 1,000-capacity lounge and club that hosts glitzy and quirky clubbing alternatives.

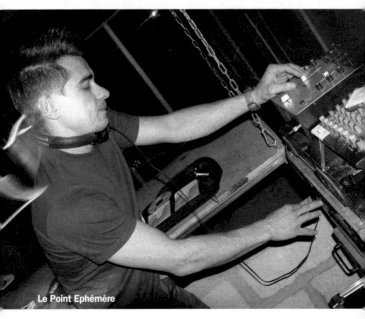

Le Point Ephémère

IRCAM p33

WHAT'S BEST
Arts & Leisure

Paris and the high arts go way back. The city invented the public film screening; classical music and opera have been a vital part of its cultural life since the Middle Ages; its theatrical heritage is world-class; and it has been fertile ground for contemporary dance for decades. Furthermore, new talent is regularly given a stage for expression in venues such as the Maison des Métallos (p115) and 104 (p159). What's especially good about the arts here is the accessibility: there are any number of festivals and discount promotions throughout the year, many organised by the city council, that bring what Anglo-Saxons often consider to be 'elitist' art forms within the

reach and appreciation of the general public. Even the fleeting visitor can reap the benefits.

Film

Cinema going is a serious pastime in Paris. More tickets per head are bought here than anywhere else in Europe, and in any given week there's a choice of around 350 movies – not including the numerous festivals (p34), many of which offer free or discounted entry. The city houses nearly 90 cinemas and around 400 screens, almost a quarter of which show nothing but arthouse. Even the multiplexes regularly screen documentaries and films from Eastern Europe, Asia and South America. This vibrant cinema scene is constantly evolving, with new multi-screen complexes under construction in the north-east, and classic pictures houses constantly under renovation (the art deco Louxor is due to reopen in 2009).

Visiting one of the city's many picture palaces is an experience in itself – from the glorious faux-oriental Pagode (p128) and kitsch excesses of the Grand Rex (p86) to the innovative Forum des Images (p86), which reopens at the beginning of 2009 after a major facelift. In addition to the multitude of retrospectives and themed seasons, there are many Q&A sessions with directors and actors.

New releases, sometimes as many as 15, hit the screens on Wednesdays – when certain cinemas offer reduced rates.

Opera & classical

After years of invigorating the Opéra National de Paris (p115) with his uncompromising programming, modernist director Gérard Mortier will take his final curtain call in 2008-9. Under Mortier's leadership, the Paris opera company has earned acclaim for its daring, innovative productions – even if certain conservatives bemoan the lack of traditional values. Expect fireworks and fun for his final season. The Opéra Comique (p86), meanwhile, continues to capitalise on new financial security following its promotion to National Theatre status by offering an eclectic season of revivals and classics.

Plans are underway to construct a new 2,000-seat symphonic concert hall in the Parc de la Villette for 2012; in the meantime, the city's current largest classical venue, the Salle Pleyel (p69), remains home to the Orchestre de Paris. Elsewhere, director Jean-Luc Choplin provides a populist touch at Châtelet (p86).

SHORTLIST

Wonderful settings
- Grand Rex (p86)
- Palais Garnier (p86)
- Théâtre des Champs-Elysées (p69)

Best new venues
- 104 (p159)
- Maison des Métallos (p115)

Most innovative
- International opera at the Festival d'Automne (p34)

Most romantic
- Candlelit recitals for the Festival Chopin (p38)

Best bargains
- Film tickets at €3.50 during Printemps du Cinéma (p36)
- Free concerts and gigs at Fête de la Musique (p38)

Best alfresco
- Cinéma en Plein Air (p38)
- Festival Classique au Vert (p34)

Best film venues
- Forum des Images (p86)
- MK2 (p99)
- La Pagode (p128)

Best classical venues
- Salle Pleyel (p69)
- Théâtre des Champs-Elysées (p69)
- Théâtre de la Ville (p86)

Best opera venues
- Opéra Comique (p86)
- Palais Garnier (p86)

Best churches for music
- Eglise St-Germain-des-Prés (p130)
- Sainte-Chapelle (p120)

Best museums for music
- Centre Pompidou (p101)
- Musée du Louvre (p74)
- Musée de la Musique (p159)
- Musée d'Orsay (p133)

© Bal du Moulin Rouge 2003/2008 - Moulin Rouge ®

Discover the Show of the Moulin Rouge !

1000 costumes of feathers, rhinestones and sequins,
sumptuous settings, the expected return of the giant Aquarium,
the world famous French Cancan and … the 60 Doriss Girls !

Dinner & Show at 7pm from €145 • Show at 9pm : €99, 11pm : €89

Montmartre - 82, boulevard de Clichy - 75018 Paris
Reservations : 33 (0)1 53 09 82 82 • www.moulin-rouge.com

Contemporary composition remains a strong suit in Paris's musical makeup, thanks to the work of IRCAM, the Ensemble Intercontemporain and the active involvement of Pierre Boulez. It's matched only by the Early Music scene, led by William Christie's Les Arts Florissants, with French conductor Emmanuelle Haïm providing glamour alongside more earnest specialists Christophe Rousset and Jean-Claude Malgoire.

There's plenty going on in churches and other venues, too. Les Grands Concerts Sacrés (01.48.24.16.97) and Musique et Patrimoine (01.42.50.96.18) offer concerts at various churches.

Many venues offer cut-rate tickets to students (under 26) an hour before curtain-up – but be suspicious of smooth-talking touts around the Opéra. On La Fête de la Musique (21 June) all events are free, and year-round freebies crop up at the Maison de Radio France and the Conservatoire de Paris, as well as at certain churches.

Dance

Although the sumptuous ballet productions at the Palais Garnier (p86) and international companies at Châtelet (p86) will always delight audiences, it's in the sphere of contemporary dance that Paris currently shines brightest. Opened in 2004, the prestigious Centre National de la Danse (1 rue Victor-Hugo, 93507 Pantin, 01.41.83.27.27), just outside the city centre, has given France an impressive HQ for its 600-plus regional dance companies, and welcomes international stars – with emphasis on new creation. Every season sees some kind of contemporary dance festival in or near Paris; Paris Quartier d'Eté (p38) and the Festival d'Automne (p34) are two of the biggest.

Theatre

French-speaking theatre buffs have ample choice in Paris: from offbeat productions in small, independent venues to high-brow classics in grandiose auditoriums like the Comédie Française (2 rue Richelieu, 1st, 08.25.10.16.80), whose staples include Molière and Racine.

Fortunately for Anglophones, the Paris theatre scene is becoming ever more international. The newly restored and re-baptised Odéon Théâtre de l'Europe (pl de l'Odéon, 6th, 01.44.85.44.00) offers plays in a number of languages, including at least one per season in English. Maverick, Brit-born director Peter Brook also programmes occasional English-language productions at the Théâtre des Bouffes du Nord (37bis bd de la Chapelle, 10th, 01.46.07.34.50), while Francophile John Malkovich sporadically directs anglophone shows. Meanwhile, the Glasshouse company (glasshouse.monsite. orange.fr) puts on classics from the Anglo-American repertoire, and the Monday at 7 troupe brings to life British plays at the Sudden Théatre (14bis rue Ste-Isaure, 18th, 01.42.62.35.00). Shakespeare in English is performed every summer at the Bois de Boulogne's Théâtre de Verdure du Jardin Shakespeare (08.20.00.75.75) by London's Tower Theatre Company (www.towertheatre.org.uk).

What's on

For listings, see weekly magazines *L'Officiel des Spectacles* or *Pariscope*. When it comes to films, take note of the two letters printed near the title: VO (version originale) means a screening in the original language with French subtitles; VF (version française) means that it's dubbed into French. Cinema seats can be reserved at www.allocine.fr.

Calendar

Nuit Blanche

This is the pick of events that had been announced as we went to press. On public holidays, or *jours feriés*, banks, many museums, most businesses and a number of restaurants close. New Year's Day, May Day, Bastille Day and Christmas Day are the most piously observed holidays. Dates highlighted in **bold** indicate public holidays.

September 2008

2 Aug-21 Sept
Festival Classique au Vert
Parc Floral de Paris
www.classiqueauvert2008.com
Free classical recitals in a park setting.

Early Sept **Jazz à la Villette**
Parc de la Villette
www.jazzalavillette.com
One of the best local jazz fests.

5 Sept-12 Oct **Festival Paris
Ile-de-France**

Various venues
www.festival-ile-de-france.com
The capital's own film festival.

13 **Techno Parade**
www.technopol.net
This parade (finishing at Bastille) marks the start of electronic music festival Rendez-vous Electroniques.

Mid Sept-end Dec
Festival d'Automne
Various venues
www.festival-automne.com
Major annual festival of challenging theatre, dance and modern opera.

20-21 **Journées du Patrimoine**
Various venues
www.journeesdupatrimoine.culture.fr
Embassies, ministries and scientific establishments open their doors.

October 2008

Ongoing Festival d'Automne (see Sept; Festival Paris Ile-de-France (see Sept)

4 Nuit Blanche
Various venues
www.nuitblanche.paris.fr
For one night, galleries, museums,
swimming pools, bars and clubs stay
open till very late.

4, 5 Oct Prix de l'Arc de Triomphe
Hippodrome de Longchamp
www.prixarcdetriomphe.com
France's richest flat race attracts the
elite of horse racing.

**13, 14 Fête des Vendanges
de Montmartre**
Various venues
*www.fetedesvendangesde
montmartre.com*
See box p39.

23-26 FIAC
Paris-Expo
www.fiacpais.com
Respected international art fair.

**28 Oct-2 Nov Grand Marché
d'Art Contemporain**
Place de la Bastille
www.organisation-joel-garcia.fr
Contemporary artists display and sell
their work at this annual arts fair.

November 2008

Ongoing Festival d'Automne
(see Sept); Grand Marché d'Art
Contemporain (see Oct)

Early Nov Festival Inrockuptibles
Various venues
www.lesinrocks.com
Rock, pop and trance festival curated
by rock magazine *Les Inrockuptibles*.

11 L'Armistice (Armistice Day)
Arc de Triomphe
The President lays wreaths to honour
French combatants who died in the
World Wars.

19 Fête du Beaujolais Nouveau
Various venues
www.beaujolaisgourmand.com
The new vintage is launched to packed
cafés and wine bars.

21 Nov-24 Dec Africolor
Various venues in St-Denis
www.africolor.com

African music festival with a spirited
wrap party.

December 2008

Ongoing Africolor (see Nov);
Festival d'Automne (see Sept)

Dec-Mar Paris sur Glace
Various venues
www.paris.fr
Three free outdoor ice rinks.

24-25 Noël (Christmas)

31 New Year's Eve
Huge crowds on the Champs-Elysées.

January 2009

Ongoing Paris sur Glace (see Dec)

1 Jour de l'An (New Year's Day)
The Grande Parade de Paris brings
floats, bands and dancers.

6 Fête des Rois (Epiphany)
Pâtisseries all sell *galettes des rois*,
frangipane-filled cakes in which a *fève*,
or tiny charm, is hidden.

20 Mass for Louis XVI
Chapelle Expiatoire
Royalists and right-wing crackpots
mourn the end of the monarchy.

February 2009

Ongoing Paris sur Glace (see Dec)

Early Feb-mid Mar Six Nations
Stade de France
www.rbs6nations.com
Paris is invaded by Brits and Celts for
five big weekends of rugby.

7 Nouvel An Chinois
Various venues
Dragon dances and martial arts demos
celebrate the Chinese new year.

March 2009

Ongoing Paris sur Glace (see
Dec); Six Nations (see Feb)

Early Mar-Apr Banlieues Bleues
Various venues in Seine St-Denis
www.banlieuesbleues.org

Six Nations p35

Five weeks of quality French and international jazz, blues, R&B and soul.

Mid Mar **Printemps du Cinéma**
Various venues
www.printempsducinema.com
Film tickets across the city are cut to a bargain €3.50 for three days.

April 2009

Ongoing Banlieues Bleues (see Mar)

Early Apr-end May
Foire du Trône
Pelouse de Reuilly
www.foiredutrone.com
France's biggest funfair.

10 Le Chemin de la Croix (Way of the Cross)
Square Willette
Good Friday pilgrimage as crowds follow the Archbishop of Paris from the bottom of Montmartre to Sacré-Coeur.

12 Pâques (Easter Sunday)

Mid Apr **Marathon de Paris**
Av des Champs-Elysées to av Foch
www.parismarathon.com
35,000 runners take in the sights.

End Apr-mid May **Foire de Paris**
Paris-Expo
www.foiredeparis.fr
Enormous lifestyle salon, full of craft and food stores, plus health exhibits.

End Apr-early May **Grand Marché d'Art Contemporain**
Place de la Bastille
www.organisation-joel-garcia.fr
Contemporary artists display and sell their work at this annual arts fair.

May 2009

Ongoing Foire du Trône (see Apr); Foire de Paris (see Apr); Grand Marché d'Art Contemporain (see Apr)

1 Fête du Travail (May Day)
Key sights close; unions march in eastern Paris via Bastille.

1 Jour de l'Ascension

Early May **Printemps des Musées**
Various venues
www.printempsdesmusees.culture.fr
For one Sunday in May, selected museums open for free.

Early May-June **La Fête des Enfants du Monde**

Tour de France p38

Various venues
www.koinobori.org
A Franco-Japanese festival with shows, exhibitions and concerts.

8 Victoire 1945 (VE Day)

Mid May **La Nuit des Musées**
Various venues
www.nuitdesmusees.culture.fr
For one night, the landmark museums across Paris stay open late and put on special events.

Mid May **Festival Jazz à Saint-Germain-des-Prés**
St-Germain-des-Prés,
various venues
www.espritjazz.com
A ten-day celebration of jazz and blues.

Mid May-early June **Quinzaine des Réalisateurs**
Forum des Images
www.quinzaine-realisateurs.com
The Cannes Directors' Fortnight pro-gramme comes to Paris.

End May-early June **Festival de St-Denis**
Various venues in St-Denis
www.festival-saint-denis.fr
Four weeks of concerts showcasing top-quality classical music.

End May **Le Printemps des Rues**
Various venues
www.leprintempsdesrues.com
Annual street-theatre festival.

23 May-16 July **Foire St-Germain**
Various venues
www.foiresaintgermain.org
Concerts, theatre and workshops.

End May-early June
French Tennis Open
Stade Roland Garros
www.rolandgarros.com
Glitzy Grand Slam tennis tournament.

June 2009

Ongoing Festival de St-Denis (see May); Quinzaine des Réalisateurs (see May); French Tennis Open (see May); Fête des Enfants du Monde (see May); Foire St-Germain (see May)

1 Lundi de Pentecôte (Whit Monday)

Early June **Tous à Vélo**
Across Paris
www.tousavelo.com
Cycling tours and activities as Paris's two-wheelers take to the streets.

Early June-July **Paris Jazz Festival**
Parc Floral de Paris
www.parcfloraldeparis.com/
www.paris.fr
Free jazz at the lovely Parc Floral.

June-July **Festival Chopin à Paris**
Orangerie de Bagatelle
www.frederic-chopin.com
Romantic candlelit piano recitals in the
Bois de Boulogne.

Late June **Fête de la Musique**
Various venues
www.fetedelamusique.fr
Free gigs (encompassing all musical
genres) take place across the city.

Late June **Gay Pride March**
www.fiertes-lgbt.org
Outrageous floats and costumes
parade towards Bastille, followed by
an official party and various club
events throughout the city.

Late June-early July **La Goutte
d'Or en Fête**
Eglise St Bernard
www.gouttedorenfete.org
Raï, rap and reggae.

Late June-early July **Paris Cinéma**
Various venues
www.pariscinema.org
Premieres, tributes and restored films
at the city's excellent summer film-
going initiative.

July 2009

Ongoing Foire St-Germain (see
May); Paris Jazz Festival (see
June); Festival Chopin à Paris
(see June); La Goutte d'Or en
Fête (see June); Paris Cinéma
(see June)

Early July **Solidays**
Hippodrome de Longchamp
www.solidays.com
A three-day music bash for AIDS
charities, featuring French, world and
new talent.

Early-late July **Etés de la Danse**
Centre Historique des
Archives Nationales
www.lesetesdeladanse.com

International classical and contemporary dance festival.

July-Aug **Cinéma en Plein Air**
Parc de la Villette
www.villette.com
A summer fixture: a themed season of
free films screened under the stars.

14 Quatorze Juillet (Bastille Day)
Various venues
France's national holiday commemo-
rates 1789. On the 13th, Parisians
dance at place de la Bastille. At 10am
on the 14th, crowds line the Champs-
Elysées as the President reviews a military parade. By night, the Champ de
Mars fills for a huge firework display.

Mid July-mid Aug
Paris, Quartier d'Eté
Various venues
www.quartierdete.com
Classical and jazz concerts, plus dance
and theatre, in outdoor venues.

Mid July-mid Aug **Paris-Plage**
Pont des Arts to Pont de Sully
www.paris.fr
Palm trees, huts, hammocks and
around 2,000 tonnes of fine sand on
both banks of the Seine bring a seaside
vibe to the city. Not only this, there's a
floating pool and a lending library too.

Late July **Tour de France**
Av des Champs-Elysées
www.letour.fr
The ultimate cycle endurance test
climaxes on the Champs-Elysées.

August 2009

Ongoing Cinéma en Plein Air (see
July); Paris, Quartier d'Eté (see
July); Paris-Plage (see July)

**15 Fête de l'Assomption
(Assumption Day)**
Cathédrale Notre-Dame de Paris
Notre-Dame again becomes a place of
religious pilgrimage.

Late Aug **Rock en Seine**
Domaine National de St-Cloud
www.rockenseine.com
Two days, two stages, one world-class
rock line-up.

La Fête des Vendanges

Among Montmartre's brash cabarets and art for tourists is a little known *route des vins*. Today, Paris's very own vineyard, Le Clos Montmartre, sits on the northern side of the Butte. It covers a mere 1,560 square metres and produces an average of 1,000 bottles a year, but its modest harvest is celebrated with a huge party, the **Fête des Vendanges** (p40), on the second weekend in October. During three days of revelry, the streets around the Sacré-Coeur swell with parades, food stands, wine connoisseurs and tourists caught up in a Bacchanalian street party.

A sip of the Cru du Clos Montmartre is rare since almost the entire supply is auctioned off for charity, but its absence is amply compensated for by stalls upon stalls selling wine from neighbouring vineyards and other epicurean delights.

France would not be France without a dose of ceremony to temper the hedonism. One of the most prominent groups to pay homage to the harvest is the wine-tasting brotherhood, the Commanderie du Montmartre, who parade through the streets wearing red and blue, Paris's official colours. Guests of honour include Paris's mayor and the *parrains d'honneur*, the king and queen of the harvest, usually two celebrities who inaugurate the parade.

Montmartre's wine-making past stretches back to Roman times, and wine has been produced on this site since the 12th century. By the 1850s, Montmartre was supplying wine all over Paris. However, a phylloxera outbreak destroyed a significant portion of crop and the introduction of railways meant that wine could be transported from further afield. This particular vestige of Montmartre's wine-making past deserves to be celebrated for its rarity and for its survival.

September 2009

Early Sept **Jazz à la Villette**
Parc de la Villette
www.jazzalavillette.com
One of the best jazz festivals in the city.

Sept **Festival Classique au Vert**
Parc Floral du Paris
www.paris.fr
Free classical recitals in a park setting.

Mid Sept **Techno Parade**
Various venues
www.technopol.net
This parade (finishing at Bastille) marks the start of electronic music festival Rendez-vous Electroniques.

Mid Sept **Journées du Patrimoine**
Various venues
www.jp.culture.fr
Embassies, ministries and scientific establishments open their doors. Get *Le Parisien* for a full programme.

Mid Sept-mid Dec **Festival d'Automne**
Various venues
www.festival-automne.com
Major annual festival for all kinds of challenging theatre, dance and modern opera performances.

October 2009

Ongoing Festival d'Automne
(see Sept)

Early Oct **Prix de l'Arc de Triomphe**
Hippodrome de Longchamp
www.prixarcdetriomphe.com
France's richest flat race.

Early Oct **Nuit Blanche**
Various venues
www.nuitblanche.paris.fr
For one night, a selection of galleries, museums, swimming pools, bars and clubs stay open until very late.

Mid Oct **Fête des Vendanges à Montmartre**
Various venues
www.fetedesvendangesde montmartre.com
See box p39.

End Oct **FIAC**
Paris-Expo
www.fiacparis.com
Respected international art fair.

End Oct **Grand Marché d'Art Contemporain**
Place de la Bastille
www.organisation-joel-garcia.fr
Contemporary artists display and sell their work at this annual arts fair.

November 2009

Ongoing Festival d'Automne
(see Sept)

1 Toussaint (All Saints' Day)

Early Nov **Festival Inrockuptibles**
Various venues
www.lesinrocks.com
Rock, pop and trance festival curated by rock magazine *Les Inrockuptibles*.

11 L'Armistice (Armistice Day)
Arc de Triomphe
The President lays wreaths to honour French dead of both World Wars.

Mid Nov **Fête du Beaujolais Nouveau**
Various venues
www.beaujolaisgourmand.com
The new vintage is launched.

December 2009

Ongoing Festival d'Automne
(see Sept)

Dec-Mar **Paris sur Glace**
Various venues
www.paris.fr

Mid Dec **Africolor**
Various venues in St-Denis
www.africolor.com
African music festival.

Mid Dec-late Jan **Patinoire de Noël**
Eiffel Tower
www.tour-eiffel.fr
Check out the ice rink on the first floor.

24-25 Noël (Christmas)

31 New Year's Eve

Itineraries

Vélib

Pedal and a Picnic

St-Germain-des-Prés may be more Louis Vuitton than Boris Vian these days, but there are still enough small galleries and bookshops in the neighbourhood to ensure that it retains a whiff of its Bohemian past. Aside from art and books, the 6th arrondissement (and its neighbour the 7th) is also a great place to shop for food, since it boasts some of the finest artisanal bakeries and traiteurs in Paris.

And thanks to **Vélib** (www. velib.paris.fr), it's easier than ever to get around the *quartier* in order to stock up. What's more, the standard-issue bike is equipped with a fairly capacious basket that should accommodate everything you'll need for a sumptuous picnic – which we recommend taking in the elegant surroundings of the Jardin du Luxembourg.

Since you'll be deliberating over your purchases each time you stop,

this itinerary will probably take you the best part of two hours. And remember, after the first half hour on Vélib, which is free, there's a sliding scale of charges. Don't bother searching for a station each time you need to stop; just use the chain provided to lock your bike.

START: Station Vélib, 1 rue Jacques Callot, 6th (Mº Mabillon).

Detach your bike from the *borne* and cycle down rue Mazarine as far as the carrefour de Buci. Turn left into rue de Buci and carry on until the junction with rue de Seine. The stretch of rue de Seine between here and boulevard St-Germain is lined with butchers and greengrocers. Ignore the smell of roasting chickens (you'll be getting cooked meat elsewhere), and just buy salad leaves and fruit. Then head back down rue de Seine (it's one way, like many of the narrow streets round here) towards the river.

Jardin du Luxembourg p44

About halfway down, turn left into rue Jacob, a typically well-heeled slice of Left Bank real estate – all furniture shops, galleries, boutiques and elegantly turned-out *femmes d'un certain age*.

Cross rue Bonaparte and take the next left into rue St-Benoît. Pause for a moment to look in the window of the **Librairie Saint Benoît des Prés** (2 rue St-Benoît, 6th, 01.46.33.16.16), which specialises in rare books, original manuscripts, letters and autographs. On our most recent visit, letters written by George Sand and Charles de Gaulle were on prominent display.

Continue down rue Saint-Benoît as far as place St-Germain-des-Prés, where you'll find three venerable St-Germain institutions: **Café de Flore** (p135), **Les Deux Magots** (p136) and **La Hune** bookshop (p138). The Flore and the Deux Magots throng more with tourists than writers these days, though the former is still a favoured haunt of ageing enfant terrible Bernard-Henri Lévy. If you spot a man with a mane of black hair and a white shirt open to the navel poring over a notebook, it's probably 'BHL'. Next door, La Hune, which opened in 1949, is a kind of holy shrine for that nearly extinct species, the Left Bank Intellectual.

But it's not books we're after, it's bread; so pick your way across boulevard St-Germain and follow rue Gozlin round into the rue de Rennes. This is a broad, thunderously busy main road lined with chain stores. There's not a great deal to distract as you bowl south for half a kilometre or so, until you reach rue du Vieux Colombier on the right. You'll have to do battle with buses and taxis in this narrow cut-through which leads to the altogether more charming rue du Cherche-Midi. On the left-hand side of the street, wedged in among the usual expensive boutiques, jewellers and galleries, stands **Poilâne** (p140), the renowned family bakers. You can expect to have to queue here for the famous Poilâne loaf – but it's

Fromagerie Quatrehomme

worth waiting for: dark, firm and distinctively flavoured. The tarts and the biscuits are wonderful too.

Having loaded the bread into your basket, carry on down rue du Cherche-Midi. Go straight across boulevard Raspail. Take the first right into rue Dupin (there's a coffee merchant's on one corner, a fishmonger on the other). Running down one side of this quiet street is a fine, if forbidding, example of 1930s art deco municipal housing.

You'll eventually reach rue de Sèvres. Lock your bike up against the railings here and cross the road on foot to La Grande Epicérie, the food hall in Paris's oldest department store, **Le Bon Marché** (p138). This is a gastronome's paradise, a super-abundant temple to food. Make your way to the traiteurs in the centre of the hall and choose from a staggering array of cooked meats – succulent hams

and pungent garlic sausages in dizzying profusion. While you're here, you can also pick up dressing for the salad and a bottle of wine (and a corkscrew if you need one).

It just remains to buy some cheese, and for this you'll need to get back on your bike and cycle a little further south down rue de Sèvres, deeper into a residential corner of the 7th arrondissement. You'll pass on the right the wonderful art deco entrance to the Vaneau metro station, with its green iron lattices and globe lanterns. A little further along on the same side of the street, on the corner of rue Pierre Leroux, stands **Fromagerie Quatrehomme** (p128). Run by the eponymous Marie, this place is famous across Paris for its comté fruité, beaufort and oozy st-marcellin – all dispensed with winning bonhomie.

Your basket will now be near to overflowing and the smell of the cheese will be making you hungry. It's time to head back into the 6th arrondissement and make for a picnic spot in the Jardin du Luxembourg. Turn round and cycle north back up rue de Sèvres, as far as rue St-Placide on the right, just before you reach Le Bon Marché. Shortly after you pass the St-Placide métro station, turn left into rue de Fleurus. You'll pass the men's and women's branches of the unbearably cool clothing store **APC** (p138), which stand opposite each other. And if you think you need more biscuits or another tart, pop into **Bread and Roses** (p135).

The **Jardin du Luxembourg** (p132) is ahead of you, on the far side of rue Guynemer. There's a Vélib station at 26 rue Guynemer, next to the park entrance. As is usual in Paris, the grass here is not for sitting on, let alone picnicking on. Instead, find a bench in the shade and indulge.

Poilâne p43

River-boat shuttle service

B&TOBUS
PARIS

Tour Eiffel
Musée d'Orsay
St-Germain-des-Prés
Notre-Dame
Jardin des Plantes
Hôtel-de-Ville
Louvre
Champs-Élysées

1 Pass
8 Stops
To discover Paris

Information : ▶ Nº Indigo **0 825 05 01 01** **www.batobus.com**
0.15 € TTC / MN

Moonlit Montmartre

Changing from impossibly
romantic to horribly tacky
in the blink of an eye, the Butte
Montmartre has an amazingly
schizophrenic personality. While
souvenir shops selling Chat Noir
fridge magnets draw tourists like
iron filings, neighbouring streets
can be like silent film sets. This
walk gives you the choice of avoiding
the tourist madness or taking the
road more travelled. Either way,
the Butte is a wonderful place for
a moonwalk, and one of the safer
areas of Paris to wander at night.

START: M° Anvers.

Your route starts with a steep
climb up rue de Steinkerque, where,
by night, the fabric shops of the
Marché St Pierre metamorphose
into sellers of Eiffel Tower T-shirts.
Gangs of American high-school
pupils will be heading down as
you go up, but bear with us. At the
top you get your first view of the

magnificent **Sacré-Coeur** (p88),
all lit up and slightly unreal. Turn
right and skirt round the basilica's
park via rue Ronsard. Suddenly
the crowds are gone, and all you
can hear is the distant beating
of tribal drums from somewhere
inside the closed park gates.

Coloured lights beckon at the
top of the steps on rue Paul Albert
(only in Montmartre can a street
actually be a staircase) and you
come out on the delightful place
Maurice Utrillo with three lovely
dining terraces: those of restaurant
L'Eté en Pente Douce, and of cafés
Botak and Au Soleil de la Butte.
But press on, there's more
enchantment to come. Continuing
up steep rue Paul Albert, now silent
as a winter night, you'll come to
the steps of rue du Chevalier de
la Barre, flanked by earthbound
constellations of fibre-optic stars
leading you, as if in a Disney

Wanted. Jumpers, coats and people with their knickers in a twist.

From the people who feel moved to bring us their old books and CDs, to the people fed up to the back teeth with our politicians' track record on climate change, Oxfam supporters have one thing in common. They're passionate. If you've got a little fire in your belly, we'd love to hear from you. Visit us at **oxfam.org.uk**

Be Humankind   Oxfam

Registered charity No. 202918

Musée de Montmartre

fantasy, towards the ghostly basilica. At the top, turn around and savour the sea of twinkling lights before you: Paris!

Carry on walking, keeping the basilica on your left, and eventually you come down to the parvis with its fabulous view of the whole illuminated city. Unfortunately, everyone knows about this view, and it's thronging with people, bad guitar strummers and randomly strewn bottles, so don't attempt to descend the steps, but go back the way you came (rue du Cardinal Guibert) to join rue du Chevalier de la Barre. Up to the left, past the Irish pub **Corcorans** (51 rue du Chevalier de la Barre, 18th, 01.42.52. 10.57), another great view spreads out before you, this time to the north, at the bottom of the hundreds of steps of rue du Mont Cenlis.

Now you have a choice: if you want to avoid the Montmartre theme park of the place du Tertre, take silent rue Cortot to the left, past the **Musée de Montmartre** (p88), then left up rue des Saules and right to place Jean-Baptiste Clement, before bearing left down steep cobbles to rue Ravignan and rue Gabrielle. This is a bit of a slog, however. The alternative is to cross place du Tertre with its picket-fence terraces and portrait painters, brave rue Norvins, then go down rue Poulbot, which is a pretty enclave with classier restaurants and a good view of the **Eiffel Tower** (which you can't see from the parvis) on place du Calvaire. The steps of rue du Calvaire take you down to one of our favourite bars, **Le Rendezvous des Amis** (23 rue Gabrielle, 18th, 01.46.06.01.60).

Descend the steps at the corner of the bar, then turn right and go up rue Berthe till you descend more steps at rue Androuet and rue des Abbesses, taking you down to place des Abbesses, with its bars that feel a world away from the heights you've just come from.

The walk sounds short, but it's the night-time equivalent of a step class. You'll need a beer: go to **Le Sancerre** (p92), where you might catch some live music and certainly some lively company at the bar.

Batofar p53

Heading East

This walk explores the fast-growing ZAC Rive Gauche in the 13th arrondissement, a long stretch of land between Gare d'Austerlitz and the Périphérique in south-east Paris. If your image of Paris is one of historic monuments, aristocratic stone mansions and Haussmann apartments, then this area, once occupied by railway yards and riverside warehouses, will confound your expectations.

New buildings in a wilful diversity of shapes and materials sprout up by the day alongside rehabilitated industrial buildings, and unlike businessy La Défense, the ZAC Rive Gauche has gone for deliberate heterogeneity. Investment banks, service companies and IT firms exist alongside university faculties, artists' studios, garden squares and residential buildings, brasseries, schools and designer furniture

outlets, a multiplex cinema and riverside music venues. Come on a weekday around lunchtime and you'll find students and office workers; at the weekend, it's more likely to be cinemagoers and families ogling the hamsters at pet and garden emporium Truffaut; while from mid July to mid August, the whole quayside converts into a part of Paris-Plage.

START: Mᵒ Bibliothèque (avenue de France exit).

As you emerge amid pristine new branches of traiteur Lenôtre, supermarket Monoprix and sports equipment store Decathlon, you might not realise that you are actually standing on a massive concrete platform constructed over railway sidings. Cross rue de Tolbiac where you can look through the railings to see the engineering works below. In one direction lies the old Paris of rue de

Piscine Josephine-Baker p53

Chevalaret, in the other brave new Paris, and between the two a bit whose future hasn't yet been decided. There's an even better view from the upper floor of the **MK2 Bibliothèque** (p152), the 14-screen flagship of the MK2 cinema chain.

Behind the cinema, towering over the area is the **Bibliothèque Nationale François Mitterrand** (p150) national library, also known as the TGB (Très Grande Bibliothèque). The last of President Mitterrand's *Grands Projets* was this statement building that kicked off the area's transformation. Dominique Perrault's design with its four L-shaped glass towers seems gargantuan, but once inside the atmosphere is quite different from the windswept expanse above. Despite its size (the circuit around the central well is a sizeable stroll in itself), it's a surprisingly bright, intimate space, with lots of wood and red carpet, and leather chairs for admiring the view of the pine forest in the middle.

Return to the deck by the eastern exit and go down the steps, crossing rue Emile Durckheim into pedestrianised rue Jean-Anouilh between smart apartments. Ahead, across rue Neuve de Tolbiac, you'll see the turret of **Les Frigos** (www.les-frigos.com), where over 200 artists, photographers, musicians and craftspeople have studios in a graffiti-adorned former refrigerated cold store. Happily preserving an arty, anarchic presence amid all the gleaming newbuilds, the artists were the first to colonise the district and have been a crucial pressure group in the campaign to preserve its industrial heritage and social mix.

From rue des Frigos, turn right into rue René Goscinny. Speech bubbles attached to lampposts and in the pavement in tribute to the creator of Astérix prove that even development zones can have a sense of humour. Then turn left back into the avenue de France. Nearby, on place Robert Antelme, big blocks of golden Burgundy

Cité de la Mode et du Design

stone look as if they have been left over from one of the building sites all around you, but turn out to be a sculpture installation, *Hommage à Charlie Parker* by Alain Kirili.

From here there's a good view of the Jardins des Grands Moulins, a new ecological park being created by landscape designers Ah-Ah. When completed, it will reproduce different wetlands with marshy areas and a lily pool, using rainwater collected from adjacent buildings. Turn left down rue Françoise Dolto and right into rue Elsa Morante. Here you are firmly in the university quarter. Cross curious rue Watt – the city's lowest street, which disappears underneath the railway tracks – and enter the Jardins du Biopark, home to a cluster of biotechnology companies, where plants climb up the galvanised steel ribs that cover the buildings. Exit the garden on rue Jean-Antoine de la Baïf. On your right is the pixellated silver façade of the chemistry faculty; on your left towards the river you'll reach the striking steel and red brick Compressed Air Building.

Built in 1890 to provide pressurised air for a network of hydraulic lifts and road junction clocks, it was renovated by Frédéric Borel (who also designed the extension) for the Paris Val de Seine architecture school. Not all industry has disappeared, however. Across the road on Port de Tolbiac, barges still deposit sand for the Lafarge concrete works, a reminder that Paris is also a port.

Take quai Panhard et Levassor westwards. At No.43, a plaque recalls that this was the site of a forced labour camp for Jews interned here before deportation during World War II. Just beyond stretches the massive concrete Halle aux Farines, where flour was stocked after milling and put into sacks, converted by architect Nicolas Michelin into lecture theatres, teaching rooms and a student café. On the ground floor, **Béton Salon** (www.betonsalon. net) puts on experimental art shows and evening performances. Across the grassy esplanade, walk into the imposing Grands Moulins, the former flour mills that now form

ITINERARIES

Passerelle Simone de Beauvoir

the focal point of the university, masterfully converted by Rudy Ricciotti into the university library.

Continuing along the quai, you might want to pause at **Bioart** (1 quai François Mauriac, 13th), an organic café and restaurant. Then cross to the Port de la Gare. On this stretch of river in front of the national library, labour gives way to leisure with a cluster of party boats: southern steamer-style Charlestone (www.peniche charleston.com), red lighthouse ship **Batofar** (p152), and three-masted Chinese junk La Dame de Canton (www.ladamedecanton.com).

Then admire the Passerelle Simone de Beauvoir. Austrian architect Dietmar Feichtinger's fabulously slinky footbridge is designed like two intersecting ellipses, allowing you a choice of routes: back up to the library deck, down to the quayside or across the river by upper or lower levels to the Parc de Bercy. It's worth crossing over just for the sake of it, then return to the quay where you'll find the **Piscine Josephine-Baker** (p152), a floating swimming pool.

Back on quai de la Gare, take rue Abel Gance past red-brick cubic Eglise Notre-Dame de Sagesse back to avenue de France. If you want, turn left up boulevard Vincent-Auriol to detour along rue Louise-Weiss with its row of contemporary art galleries. Otherwise, head right on avenue Mendès-France. This is office territory, although on Place Augusta Holmes a steel and glass aquatic monster emerges from the side of a building and loops in and out of the paving stones before a stairway leads you down to the traffic-filled quai d'Austerlitz.

Below, a bright green wave beckons, where goods warehouses have been transformed into the **Cité de la Mode et du Design** (see p152). Open day and night, you can go for a rooftop stroll, wander round the shops and exhibitions, study fashion at the Institut de la Mode or have a drink or a meal. Finish your walk by hopping on to a boat or continue along the quai to the métro at Gare d'Austerlitz, one of Paris's grand old railway stations, itself set for a little jazzing up by architect Jean Nouvel.

www.treesforcities.org

Trees for Cities
Charity registration number 1032154

Travelling creates so many
lasting memories.

Make your trip mean something for
years to come - not just for you but
for the environment and for people
living in deprived urban areas.

Anyone can offset their flights,
but when you plant trees with
Trees for Cities, you'll help create
a green space for an urban
community that really needs it.

To find out more visit
www.treesforcities.org

Leave
Your
Mark

Create a green future for cities.

Paris by Area

Palais de Chaillot

Champs-Elysées & Western Paris

The Champs-Elysées remains a symbolic gathering place: sporting victories, New Year's Eve, displays of military might on 14 July – all are celebrated here. Over the past decade, the avenue has undergone a renaissance, thanks initially to the facelift – including underground car parks and granite paving – instigated by Jacques Chirac. Chi-chi shops and chic hotels have set up in the 'golden triangle' (avenues George-V, Montaigne and the Champs), while fashionable restaurants draw an affluent and screamingly fashionable pack.

This great spine of Paris started life as an extension to the Tuileries. By the Revolution, the avenue had reached its full extent, but it was during the Second Empire that it became a focus for fashionable society, military parades and royal processions. Hitler's troops made a point of marching down it in 1940, as did their Allied counterparts four years later.

The western end is dominated by the **Arc de Triomphe**, towering above place Charles-de-Gaulle, also known as L'Etoile. From the top, visitors can gaze over the square (commissioned later by Haussmann), with its 12 avenues radiating out in all directions.

South of the arch, avenue Kléber leads to the monumental buildings and terraced gardens of the panoramic Trocadéro.

Sights & museums

Arc de Triomphe

Pl Charles-de-Gaulle (access via underpass), 8th (01.55.37.73.77). M° Charles de Gaulle Etoile. **Open** *Oct-Mar* 10am-10.30pm daily. *Apr-Sept* 10am-11pm daily. **Admission** €8; free-€5 reductions. **Map** p58 B2 **①**

Napoleon ordered the arch's construction in 1809 as a monument to the triumph of his armies, but almost immediately his empire began to collapse. The arch, 50m (164ft) high and 45m (148ft) wide, was only completed in 1836. It is carved with the names of Napoleon's victories, and decorated on its flanks with a frieze of battle scenes and sculptures, including Rude's famous *Le Départ des Volontaires*. The annual Bastille Day military procession begins here.

Bateaux-Mouches

Pont de l'Alma, 8th (01.42.25.96.10/ 01.42.25.02.28/www.bateaux-mouches.fr). M° Alma-Marceau. **Departs** *Apr-Sept* every 15 mins 10am-11pm daily. *Oct-Mar* every 45mins 11am-9pm daily. **Admission** €9; free-€4 reductions. **Map** p58 C4 **②**

If you're after a whirlwind tour of the essential sights and don't mind crowds of tourists and schoolchildren, this, the oldest cruise operation on the Seine, is the one to go for.

Cinéaqua

2 av des Nations Unies, 16th (01.40.69.23.23/www.cineaqua.com). M° Trocadéro. **Open** 10am-8pm daily. **Admission** €19.50; free-€15 reductions. **Map** p58 B5 **③**

Opened in 2006, this aquarium and three-screen cinema is a key element in the renaissance of the once moribund Trocadéro. Many have baulked at the admission price, though.

Cité de l'Architecture et du Patrimoine – Palais de Chaillot

1 pl du Trocadéro, 16th (01.58.51.52. 85/www.citechaillot.fr). M° Trocadéro. **Open** noon-8pm Mon, Wed, Fri; noon-10pm Thur; 11am-7pm Sat, Sun. **Admission** €7; free-€5 reductions. **Map** p58 A4 **④**

Opened in 2007 in the eastern wing of the Palais de Chaillot, this architecture and heritage museum impresses principally by its scale. The ground floor is filled with life-size mock-ups of French cathedral façades and heritage buildings. Upstairs, rooms house full-scale copies of medieval and Renaissance murals and stained-glass windows. The highlight of the modern architecture section is the walk-in replica of an apartment from Le Corbusier's Cité Radieuse in Marseille.

Event highlights The *Elle Décoration* Suite vue par Christian Lacroix (until 4 Dec 2008)

Galerie-Musée Baccarat

11 pl des Etats-Unis, 16th (01.40.22. 11.00/www.baccarat.fr). M° Boissière or Iéna. **Open** 10am-6pm Mon, Wed-Sat. **Admission** €7; free-€3.50 reductions. **Map** p58 B3 **⑤**

Designer Philippe Starck has created a neo-rococo wonderland in the former mansion of the Vicomtesse de Noailles. See items by great designers, services made for princes and maharajahs, and monumental show-off items made for the great exhibitions of the 1800s. The opulent Le Cristal Room restaurant has a two-month waiting list.

Galeries Nationales du Grand Palais

3 av du Général-Eisenhower, 8th (01.44.13.17.17/reservations 08.92. 68.46.94/www.rmn.fr/galeries-nationales-du-grand). M° Champs-Elysées Clemenceau. **Open** 10am-8pm Mon, Thur-Sun; 10am-10pm Wed; pre-booking compulsory before 1pm. **Admission** *Before 1pm with reservation* €11.10. *After 1pm without reservation* €10; free-€8 reductions. **Map** p59 E4 **⑥**

Constructed for the 1900 Exposition Universelle, the Grand Palais was the work of three different architects, each of whom designed a façade. During World War II it accommodated Nazi tanks. In 1994, the magnificent glass-roofed central hall was closed when bits

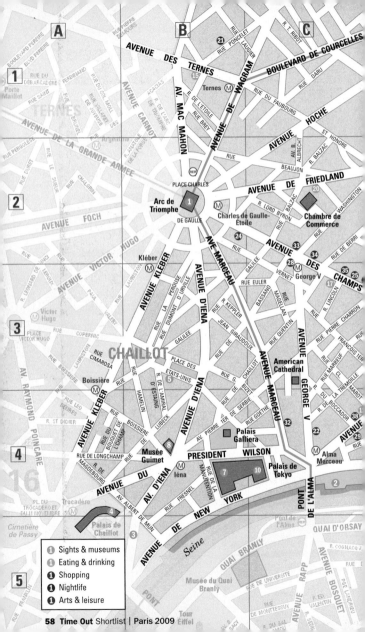

Sights & museums
Eating & drinking
Shopping
Nightlife
Arts & leisure

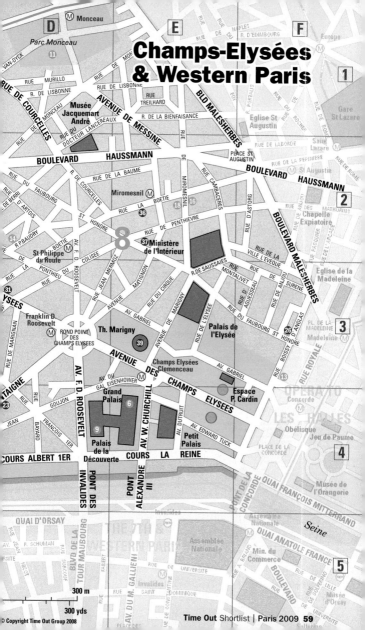

Champs-Elysées & Western Paris

© Copyright Time Out Group 2008

Bateaux Parisiens
The most Parisian journey

Sightseeing Cruises

Café Seine

Lunch Cruise

Dinner Cruise

Private Charters

At the foot of the Eiffel Tower

Port de la Bourdonnais • 75007 Paris
Tel.: + 33 176 641 445
www.bateauxparisiens.com

Bateaux Parisiens

of metal started falling off, although exhibitions continued to be held in the other wings. After major restoration, the Palais reopened in 2005.

Musée d'Art Moderne de la Ville de Paris

11 av du Président-Wilson, 16th (01.53.67.40.00/www.mam.paris.fr). M° Alma Marceau or Iéna. **Open** 10am-6pm Tue-Sun. **Admission** *Temporary exhibitions* €4.50-€9; free-€4.50 reductions. No credit cards. **Map** p58 B4 **7**

The monumental 1930s building that houses the city's modern art collection reopened in 2006 with a Pierre Bonnard exhibition. The museum is strong on the Cubists, Fauves, the Delaunays, Rouault and Ecole de Paris artists Soutine, Modigliani and van Dongen. **Event highlights** La Photographie à Düsseldorf (3 Oct 2008-4 Jan 2009)

Musée National des Arts Asiatiques – Guimet

6 pl d'Iéna, 16th (01.56.52.53.00/ www.museeguimet.fr). M° Iéna. **Open** 10am-5.45pm Mon, Wed-Sun (last entry 5.15pm). **Admission** €6; free-€4 reductions. **Map** p58 B4 **8**

Founded by industrialist Emile Guimet in 1889 to house his collection of Chinese and Japanese religious art, and later incorporating oriental collections from the Louvre, the museum has 45,000 objects from Neolithic times onwards, in a voyage across Asian religions and civilisations. Lower galleries focus on India and South-east Asia, centred on Hindu and Buddhist Khmer sculpture from Cambodia. Upstairs, Chinese antiquities include mysterious jade discs and a bronze, elephant-shaped Shang dynasty pot.

Palais de la Découverte

Av Franklin-D-Roosevelt, 8th (01.56.43.20.21/www.palais-decouverte.fr). M° Champs-Elysées Clemenceau or Franklin D. Roosevelt. **Open** 9.30am-6pm Tue-Sat; 10am-7pm Sun (last entry 30mins before closing). **Admission** €7; free-€4.50 reductions. *Planetarium* €3.50. **Map** p59 D4 **9**

The city's original science museum houses designs dating from Leonardo da Vinci's time right up to the present day. Models, real apparatus and audio-visual material bring the displays to life, while permanent exhibits cover astrophysics, astronomy, biology, chemistry, physics and earth sciences. The pertinent Planète Terre section highlights the latest developments in meteorology, while one room is dedicated to the sun.

Palais de Tokyo: Site de Création Contemporaine

13 av du Président-Wilson, 16th (01. 47.23.54.01/www.palaisdetokyo.com). M° Alma Marceau or Iéna. **Open** noon-midnight Tue-Sun. **Admission** €6; free-€4.50 reductions. **Map** p58 C4 **10**

When it opened in 2002, many thought the Palais' stripped-back interior with visible air-conditioning and lighting was a design statement. In fact, it was a practical answer to tight finances. The 1937 building has now come into its own as an open-plan space with a skylit central hall, hosting exhibitions, installations, fashion shows and performances. Extended opening hours and a funky café have succeeded in drawing a younger audience.

Parc Monceau

Bd de Courcelles, av Hoche, rue Monceau, 8th. M° Monceau. **Open** *Nov-Mar* 7am-8pm daily. *Apr-Oct* 7am-10pm daily. **Map** p59 D1 **11**

Surrounded by *hôtels particuliers* and elegant Haussmannian apartments, Monceau is a favourite with well-dressed children and their nannies. It was laid out in the 18th century for the Duc de Chartres in the English style, with a lake, lawns and follies: an Egyptian pyramid, Corinthian colonnade, Venetian bridge and sarcophagi.

Eating & drinking

Alain Ducasse au Plaza Athénée

Hôtel Plaza Athénée, 25 av Montaigne, 8th (01.53.67.65.00/www.alain-ducasse.com). M° Alma Marceau.

Pedal power

A sprint finish on the Champs-Elysées.

The country's most famous sporting event, which grips the nation for three weeks each July, has come under considerable pressure in the last few years, riddled as it has been by doping scandals at every turn. But whatever the competitors may have tucked in their panniers, there are still few more amazing sights than watching the peloton flood down the Champs-Elysées on the traditional final leg of the Tour de France (www.letour.fr), after slogging some 3,000km around France.

By the time the riders reach Paris, the competition is usually done and dusted and the ride through the capital is more of a victory procession than a tight finish, with the day traditionally kicking off with a glass of bubbly. But there have been a couple of close run final stages over the years: the closest of all, and a heartbreaker for the locals, came in 1989 when American Greg LeMond beat Frenchman Laurent Fignon by 58 seconds on the final day and so wiped out a 50-second deficit to win the Tour by the slimmest of slim margins – just eight seconds.

The route through the heart of Paris takes the riders up rue de Rivoli, around place de la Concorde and on to the Champs-Elysées, before a few laps between Arc de Triomphe and the Louvre. The overall race winner is presented with the *maillot jaune* (yellow jersey) under the Arc de Triomphe.

Open 7.45-10.15pm Mon-Wed; 12.45-2.15pm, 7.45-10.15pm Thur, Fri. Closed mid July-mid Aug & 2wks Dec. €€€€. **Haute cuisine**. Map p58 C4 ⑫

The sheer glamour factor would be enough to recommend this restaurant, Alain Ducasse's most lofty Paris undertaking. The dining room has a cheerful colour scheme; the ceiling drips with 10,000 crystals. An amuse-bouche of a single langoustine in a lemon cream with a touch of Iranian caviar starts the meal off beautifully, but other dishes can be inconsistent: Breton lobster in an overwhelming sauce of apple, quince and spiced wine. Cheese is predictably delicious, as is the *rum baba comme à Monte-Carlo*.

Les Ambassadeurs

Hôtel de Crillon, 10 pl de la Concorde, 8th (01.44.71.16.17/www.crillon.com). M° *Concorde.* **Open** 7-10.30am Mon; 7-10.30am, 12.30-1.45pm, 7.30-9.45pm Tue-Sat; noon-3pm Sun. Closed 1st wk Jan & Aug. €€€€. **Haute cuisine**. **Map** p59 F3 ⑬

Since the arrival of chef Jean-François Piège, the experience of eating at Les Ambassadeurs has become sublime. At €70 per person it may sound pretty absurd to say that the lunch menu is excellent value, but compared with almost anywhere serving haute cuisine this is value indeed. A succession of bright ideas makes the meal memorable: bite-sized ice-creams arrive straight after the mains, followed by tiny citrus-flavoured *madeleines* and pineapple macaroons.

Le Cou de la Girafe

7 rue Paul-Baudry, 8th (01.56.88. 29.55). M° *St- Philippe-du-Roule.* **Open** 12.30-2.30pm, 7.30-11pm Mon-Fri; 7.30-11pm Sat. Closed Aug & 1wk Dec. €€€. **Haute cuisine**. **Map** p59 D2 ⑭

Though the menu here doesn't make a particularly original read, the food is impeccable. Thin, crunchy slices of red onion and plenty of fresh herbs make herring with potato salad seem a modern dish rather than a bistro classic, while a little black casserole bursts

Parc Monceau p61

with chunks of juicy rabbit and tiny spring vegetables. Prices are lower at lunch, coming in at around €24-€35.

Le Dada

12 av des Ternes, 17th (01.43.80.60.12). Mº Ternes. **Open** 6am-2am Mon-Sat; 6am-10pm Sun. **Bar. Map** p58 B1 ⑮

Perhaps the hippest café on this classy avenue in a stuffy part of town, Le Dada is best known for its well-placed, sunny terrace. Inside, the wood-block carved tables and red walls provide a warm atmosphere for a crowd that tends towards the well heeled, well spoken and, well, loaded. That said, the atmosphere is friendly; if terracing is your thing, you could happily spend a summer's day here.

Granterroirs

30 rue de Miromesnil, 8th (01.47.42. 18.18/www.granterroirs.com). Mº Miromesnil. **Open** 9am-8pm Mon-Fri. *Food served* noon-3pm. Closed 3wks Aug. €€. **Bistro. Map** p59 E2 ⑯

This *épicerie* with a difference is the perfect remedy for anyone for whom the word '*terroir*' conjures up visions of big, indigestible helpings of grease-soaked peasant food. Come in early to ensure that you can choose from the five succulent *plats du jour* on offer

(such as marinated salmon with dill on a bed of warm potatoes). Plonk yourself at one of the communal tables, make your order and soak up the laid-back ambience.

Ladurée

75 av des Champs-Elysées, 8th (01.40.75.08.75/www.laduree.fr). Mº George V or Franklin D. Roosevelt. **Open** 7.30am-midnight daily. €€€. **Café. Map** p58 C3 ⑰

Everything in this elegant tearoom suggests decadence, from the 19th-century style interior and service to the labyrinthine corridors that lead to the toilets. While you bask in the warm glow of bygone wealth, indulge in tea, pastries and, above all, the wonderful hot chocolate. It's a rich, bitter, velvety tar that will leave you in the requisite stupor for any lazy afternoon. The original branch at 16 rue Royale (8th, 01.42.60.21.79) is also known for its divine macaroons.

Maxan

37 rue de Miromesnil, 8th (01.42.65. 78.60/www.rest-maxan.com). Mº Miromesnil. **Open** noon-2.30pm Mon; noon-2.30pm, 7.30-10.30pm Tue-Fri; 7.30-10.30pm Sat. Closed Aug. €€. **Bistro. Map** p59 E2 ⑲

PARIS BY AREA

Le Dada p63

This is a welcome new-wave bistro in an area where eating options tend to veer between fashion haunts, grand tables and tourist traps. Owner chef Laurent Zajac uses quality seasonal ingredients, giving them a personal spin in dishes such as scallops with curry spices and artichoke hearts, classic veal sweetbreads with wild asparagus, and an exotic take on *île flottante*. Popular with ministry of interior types at lunch, quieter by night.

La Table de Lauriston

129 rue de Lauriston, 16th (01.47.27.00.07). M° Trocadéro. **Open** noon-2.30pm, 7-10.30pm Mon-Fri; 7-10.30pm Sat. Closed 3wks Aug & 1wk Dec. €€€. **Haute cuisine. Map** p58 A4 ⑲

Serge Barbey's dining room has a refreshingly feminine touch: stripes of pink, orange and silver paint, with velvety chairs in indigo and gold. In spring, stalks of asparagus from the Landes are served with the simplest *vinaigrette d'herbes*. More extravagant is the *foie gras cuit au torchon*, in which the duck liver is wrapped in a cloth and poached in a bouillon. Skip the crème brûlée, and order a dessert with attitude: the giant *baba au rhum*.

Taillevent

15 rue Lamennais, 8th (01.44.95. 15.01/www.taillevent.com). M° George V. **Open** 12.15-1.30pm, 7.15-9.30pm Mon-Fri. Closed Aug. €€€. **Haute cuisine. Map** p58 C2 ⑳

Taillevent owes much of its ongoing success to the personality of its owner, Jean-Claude Vrinat. *Rémoulade de coquilles St-Jacques* is a technical feat, with slices of raw, marinated scallop wrapped in a tube shape around a diced apple filling, encircled by a *rémoulade* sauce. An earthier and lip-smacking dish is the trademark *épeautre* – an ancient wheat – cooked 'like a risotto' with bone marrow, black truffle, whipped cream and parmesan, and topped with sautéed frogs' legs.

Shopping

Alléosse

13 rue Poncelet, 17th (01.46.22. 50.45/www.fromage-alleosse.com). M° Ternes. **Open** 9am-1pm, 4-7pm Tue-Thur; 9am-1pm, 4.30-7pm Fri, Sat. **Map** p58 B1 ㉑

People cross town for these cheeses – wonderful farmhouse camemberts, delicate st-marcellins, a choice of *chèvres* and several rarities.

Balenciaga

10 av George-V, 8th (01.47.20.21.11/ www.balenciaga.com). M° Alma Marceau or George V. **Open** 10am-7pm Mon-Sat. **Map** p58 C4 ㉒

With Nicolas Ghesquière at the helm, the Spanish fashion house is ahead of Japanese and Belgian designers in the hip stakes. Floating fabrics contrast with dramatic cuts, producing a sophisticated urban style that the fashion *haut monde* can't wait to slip into. Bags and shoes are also available.

Dior

26-30 av Montaigne, 8th (01.40.73. 73.73/www.dior.com). M° Franklin D. Roosevelt. **Open** 10am-7pm Mon-Sat. **Map** p59 D4 ㉓

The whole Dior universe is here on avenue Montaigne, from the main prêt-à-porter store through jewellery, menswear and eyewear to Baby Dior, where impossibly rich babes-in-arms are coochy-cooed by drooling assistants.

Drugstore Publicis

133 av des Champs-Elysées, 8th (01.44.43.79.00/www.publicisdrugstore. com). **Open** 8am-2am Mon-Fri; 10am-2am Sat, Sun. **Map** p58 B2 ㉔

A 1960s legend, Drugstore Publicis has been clad with neon swirls by architect Michele Saee following a renovation in 2004; a glass-and-steel café oozes on to the pavement. On the ground floor there's a newsagent, pharmacy, bookshop and deli full of quality olive oils and elegant biscuits; a video screen reminds you that Publicis is an advertising agency. The basement is a macho take on Colette, keeping design items and lifestyle mags, but replacing high fashion with wines and a cigar cellar.

Fnac

74 av des Champs-Elysées, 8th (01.53.53.64.64/ticket office 08.92.68. 36.22/www.fnac.com). M° George V. **Open** 10am-midnight Mon-Sat; noon-midnight Sun. **Map** p58 C3 ㉕

Fnac is a supermarket of culture: books, DVDs, CDs, audio kit, computers and photographic equipment. Most branches – notably the enormous Forum des Halles one – stock everything; others specialise. All branches operate as a concert box office. This one stays open latest.

Givenchy

NEW *28 rue du Fbg-St-Honoré, 8th (01.42.68.31.00/www.givenchy.com). M° Madeleine or Concorde.* **Open** 10am-7pm Mon-Sat. **Map** p59 F3 ㉖

With Riccardo Tisci at the helm since 2005, Givenchy is on a roll, and in March 2008 opened this new flagship Fbg St-Honoré store for men's and women's prêt-à-porter and accessories. Designed by Jamie Fobert, who has worked at the Tate, it incorporates surreal rooms within rooms – cut-out boxes filled with white, black or mahogany panelling – providing a contemporary art gallery setting for Givenchy's cutting-edge, sculptural and monochrome designs.

LE66

NEW *66 av des Champs-Elysées, 8th (01.53.53.33.80/www.le66.fr). M° George V.* **Open** 11am-8pm daily. **Map** p59 D3 ㉗

Two young entrepreneurs have set up this newcomer to the Champs-Elysées with its totally original, youthful selection of hip designers. It is arranged into three glass-sided showrooms in a kind of shopping mall. The first, triangular one is a book and magazine store run by Black Book; the second has a small selection of clothes and accessories; and the third descends to a large lower-level showroom with the majority of the 130 labels. The new vintage store is there too. There's a party atmosphere on Sundays with musical events.

Louis Vuitton

101 av des Champs-Elysées, 8th (08.10.81.00.10/www.vuitton.com). M° George V. **Open** 10am-8pm Mon-Sat. **Map** p58 C2 ㉘

The 'Promenade' flagship sets the tone for Vuitton's global image, from the 'bag bar', bookstore and new jewellery department to the women's and men's ready-to-wear. Contemporary art, videos by Tim White Sobieski and a pitch-black elevator by Olafur Eliasson complete the picture.

Prada

10 av Montaigne, 8th (01.53.23.99.40/ www.prada.com). M° Alma Marceau. **Open** 11am-7pm Mon; 10am-7pm Tue-Sat. **Map** p58 C4 **㉙**

Fashionistas just can't seem to get enough of Miuccia Prada's elegant designs. Handbags of choice are complemented by a ready-to-wear line.

Sephora

70 av des Champs-Elysées, 8th (01.53.93.22.50/www.sephora.fr). M° Franklin D. Roosevelt. **Open** Sept-June 10am-midnight daily. *July, Aug* 10am-1.30am. **Map** p58 C3 **㉚**

The flagship branch of the cosmetic supermarket chain has 12,000 brands of scent and slap on offer. Sephora Blanc (14 cour St-Emilion, 12th, 01.40.02.97.79) features beauty products in a minimalist interior.

Virgin Megastore

52-60 av des Champs-Elysées, 8th (01.49.53.50.00/www.virginmega.fr). M° Franklin D. Roosevelt. **Open** 10am-midnight Mon-Sat; noon-midnight Sun. **Map** p59 D3 **㉛**

The luxury of perusing CDs and DVDs till midnight makes this a choice spot, and the listening posts let you sample any CD by scanning its barcode. Tickets for concerts and sports events are available here too. This main branch has the best selection of books.

Nightlife

Le Baron

6 av Marceau, 8th (01.47.20.04.01/ www.clublebaron.com). M° Alma Marceau. **Open** times vary. **Admission** free. **Map** p58 C4 **㉜**

Owned by André and Lionel, the brains behind Paris Paris, this small but supremely exclusive hangout for the international jet set used to be an upmarket brothel and has the decor to prove it. It only holds 150, most of whom are regulars you'll need to befriend in order to get past the door. But if you manage to get in, you'll be rubbing shoulders with celebrities.

Le Lido

116bis av des Champs-Elysées, 8th (01.40.76.56.10/www.lido.fr). M° Franklin D. Roosevelt or George V. **Lunch** 1pm. **Matinée** 3pm Tue, Sun (once a mth, dates vary). **Dinner** 7pm. **Shows** 9.30pm, 11.30pm daily. **Admission** *Matinée show* (incl champagne) €85. *Lunch & matinée show* (incl champagne) €125. *9.30pm show* (incl champagne) €100; €20 under-12s. *11.30pm show* (incl champagne) €90; free under-12s. *Dinner & show* €140-€250; €30 under-12s. **Map** p58 C2 **㉝**

This is the largest, priciest cabaret of the lot: high-tech touches (check out the descending balcony and disappearing lamps) optimise visibility, and chef Philippe Lacroix, who trained under Alain Ducasse, provides fabulous gourmet nosh. On stage, 60 Bluebell Girls slink around, shaking their boobs with sequinned panache and donning wild and wacky costumes.

Queen

102 av des Champs-Elysées, 8th (01.53.89.08.90/www.queen.fr). M° George V. **Open** midnight-7am Mon-Thur, Sun; midnight-8am Fri, Sat. **Admission** €15 Mon-Thur, Sun; €20 Fri, Sat. **Map** p58 C2 **㉞**

Once the city's most fêted gay club and the only venue that could hold a torch to the Rex, with a roster of top local DJs holding court, Queen's star faded a little in the early noughties, but is now starting to shine brightly again. Last year, it introduced more themed nights and still packs 'em in every night.

VIP Room

76-78 av des Champs-Elysées, 8th (01.58.36.46.00/www.viproom.fr). M° Franklin D. Roosevelt. **Open** midnight-5am Tue-Sun. **Admission** free. **Map** p58 C3 **㉟**

Suite dreams

Spend a night on top of the Palais de Tokyo.

Hôtel Everland

If luxury is a hotel just for you, then where better than **Hôtel Everland** (13 av du Président Wilson, 16th, €333-€444 per night, www.palaisdetokyo.com/everland) which recently alighted on the roof of the Palais de Tokyo? After Yverdon in Switzerland for Expo 2002 and Leipzig in 2006, the creation of Swiss artist duo Sabina Lang and Daniel Baumann (alias L/B) is in Paris until 31 December 2008, with just one suite and amazing views of Quai Branly and the Eiffel Tower.

It's a cross between luxury hotel, with monogrammed towels and well-stocked minibar courtesy of the hip Hôtel Sezz, and that slightly unnerving dream of being locked up in the museum after closing time: once the exhibitions shut at midnight, you are on your own. Perched in your eyrie, an impression of alien spaceship is heightened by a design that is not so much futuristic as timewarp, with swirly green and blue carpet climbing over walls and ceiling, and Curtis Mayfield, Donna Summer and the Beatles among the vinyl to put on the turntable.

What makes it interesting is the ambiguity: are you privileged client or part of the artwork? Viewer or the viewed? While the stunning vantage point is yours alone, you are also constantly on show – a webcam observes from the opposite rooftop (although guests can pull down the blind over the bed). So hotel or artwork? Or, as Marc-Olivier Wahler, director of the Palais de Tokyo, puts it: 'Hotel and artwork, Everland escapes all attempts at categorisation and offers a night when you can reflect on the impact of contemporary art on our way of thinking.'

This is no doubt where past guests see themselves, in a comments book full of letters, poems and drawings that is beginning to resemble an artwork in itself. As to reservation, that is something of a conceptual game: rooms come vacant on the web 60 days in advance, at a time that varies according to chance. So if you want to be the talk of the town, put your name down now. And if you miss out, there are guided visits at 4.30pm daily except Sunday.

O'Sullivans
IRISH PUBS PARIS

'we don't stop playing because we get old, we get old because we stop playing'
'nous n'arretons pas de jouer parce qu'on vieillit – nous vieillisons parce qu'on arrete de jouer' *George Bernard Shaw*

fish n chips

1 BOULEVARD MONTMARTRE 75002 PARIS
92 BOULEVARD DE CLICHY 75018 PARIS
10 RUE DES LOMBARDS 75004 PARIS

photos courtesy of Byron Keane & Will

The name says it all for this stylish spot – a hit with the crowd that populates places such as Paris Paris. It has sister venues in Cannes and St Tropez.

Arts & leisure

Salle Gaveau

45 rue La Boétie, 8th (01.49.53.05.07/ www.sallegaveau.com). M° Miromesnil. **Box office** 10am-6pm Mon-Fri. **Admission** €10-€75. **Map** p59 E2 ㊱
Many of the smaller underachieving Paris orchestras have found refuge in the Salle Gaveau, but the programming lacks the top-quality chamber music that used to be the hall's core repertoire.

Salle Pleyel

252 rue du Fbg-St-Honoré, 8th (01.42.56.13.13/www.sallepleyel.fr). M° Ternes. **Box office** noon-7pm Mon-Sat. *By phone* 11am-7pm Mon-Sat; 11am-5pm Sun. **Admission** €10-€85. **Map** p59 E2 ㊲
Home to the Orchestre de Paris, the restored concert hall looks splendid, but the improved acoustics are only partially successful. The London Symphony Orchestra visited in June 2008, and the hall has regained its status as the only venue dedicated to large-scale symphonic concerts in the capital, at least until the completion of the city's new concert hall in 2012.

Théâtre des Champs-Elysées

15 av Montaigne, 8th (01.49.52.50.50/ www.theatrechampselysees.fr). M° Alma Marceau. **Box office** 1-7pm Mon-Sat. *By phone* 10am-noon, 2-6pm Mon-Fri. **Admission** €5-€156. **Map** p58 C4 ㊳
This beautiful theatre hosted the scandalous premiere of Stravinsky's *Le Sacre du Printemps* in 1913. It remains the favourite venue for foreign orchestras, including Vienna Philharmonic.

Théâtre Marigny

Av de Marigny, 8th (01.53.96.70.30/ www.theatremarigny.fr). M° Champs Elysées Clemenceau or Franklin D. Roosevelt. **Box office** 11am-6.30pm Mon-Sat; 11am-3pm Sun. **Admission** €37-€72. **Map** p59 E3 ㊴
Théâtre Marigny is one of the most expensive nights out for theatregoers in Paris. But then not many other theatres can boast a location off the Champs-Elysées, a deluxe interior conceived by Charles Garnier of Opéra fame, high-profile casts and an illustrious pedigree stretching back 150 years.

Salle Pleyel

Palais Garnier p86

Opéra to Les Halles

Charles Garnier's wedding-cake **Palais Garnier** is all gilt and grandeur, just as an opera house should be. Behind, in the Jockey Club (now the Hôtel Scribe), the Lumière brothers held the world's first public cinema screening in 1895. To the south-east, Les Halles is the geographic centre of Paris, an ugly nexus of commerce and entertainment, with a massive RER-métro interchange. For centuries, it was the city's wholesale food market, but in 1969 the market moved to the suburb of Rungis, leaving a giant hole. After a long political dispute, it was filled in the early 1980s by the miserably designed **Forum des Halles** underground shopping/transport hub and the unloved Jardin des Halles, though the area is due for a makeover in the coming years.

A short distance west of Les Halles is the **Louvre**, no longer the centre of French power though it still exerts considerable influence: first as a grandiose architectural ensemble, a palace within the city; and, second, as a symbol of the capital's cultural pre-eminence. Across rue de Rivoli from the Louvre stands the elegant **Palais-Royal**, once Cardinal Richelieu's mansion. After a stroll in its quiet gardens, it's hard to believe this was the starting point of the French Revolution. Today, its arcades house a mix of antiques dealers, philatelists and fashion showcases.

Far less frenzied than Wall Street, the city's traditional business district is squeezed between the elegant calm of the Palais-Royal and shopping hub the Grands Boulevards.

Sights & museums

Eglise de la Madeleine

*Pl de la Madeleine, 8th (01.44.51.
69.00/www.eglise-lamadeleine.com).
M° Concorde or Madeleine.* **Open**
9am-7pm daily. **Map** p72 A2 ❶

The building of a church on this site
began in 1764, and in 1806 Napoleon
sent instructions from Poland for
Barthélémy Vignon to design a 'Temple
of Glory' dedicated to his Grand Army.
After the emperor's fall, construction
slowed and the building, by now a
church again, was finally consecrated
in 1845. The exterior is ringed by huge
fluted Corinthian columns, with a frieze
of the Last Judgement just above the
portico. Inside are giant domes, an
organ and pseudo-Grecian side altars in
a sea of multicoloured marble.

Forum des Halles

*1st. M° Les Halles/RER Châtelet
Les Halles.* **Map** p73 E4 ❷

The labyrinthine mall and transport
interchange extends three levels underground and includes the Ciné Cité multiplex cinema, the Forum des Images
and a swimming pool, as well as clothing chains, a branch of Fnac and the
Forum des Créateurs, a section for
young designers. Despite an open central courtyard, a sense of gloom pre-
vails. All should change by 2012, with
a new landscaping of the whole area.

Jardin des Tuileries

*Rue de Rivoli, 1st. M° Concorde or
Tuileries.* **Open** 7.30am-7pm daily.
Map p72 B4 ❸

Between the Louvre and place de la
Concorde, the gravelled alleyways of
these gardens have been a chic promenade ever since they opened to the
public in the 16th century; and the popular mood persists with the funfair
that sets up along the rue de Rivoli
side in summer. André Le Nôtre created the prototypical French garden
with terraces and a central vista running down the *Grand Axe* through
circular and hexagonal ponds. There's
a specialist gardeners' bookshop by
place de la Concorde.

Jeu de Paume

*1 pl de la Concorde, 8th (01.47.03.12.50/
www.jeudepaume.org). M° Concorde.*
Open noon-9pm Tue; noon-7pm Wed-
Fri; 10am-7pm Sat, Sun (last admission
30mins before closing). **Admission** €6;
€3 reductions. **Map** p72 A3 ❹

The city's Centre National de la
Photographie moved into this site in
2005. The building, which once served
as a tennis court, has been divided into
two white, almost hangar-like galleries.
It is not an intimate space, but it works
well for showcase retrospectives. A
video-art and cinema suite in the basement offers new digital installation
work, plus feature-length films made
by artists. There is also a sleek café and
a decent bookshop.

Event highlights Lee Miller retrospec-
tive (14 Oct 2008-4 Jan 2009)

Musée des Arts Décoratifs

*107 rue de Rivoli, 1st (01.44.55.57.50/
www.lesartsdecoratifs.fr). M° Palais
Royal Musée du Louvre or Pyramides.*
Open 11am-6pm Tue, Wed, Fri; 10am-
6pm Sat, Sun. Closed some hols.
Admission (with Musée de la Mode &
Musée de la Publicité) €8; free-€6.50
reductions. **Map** p72 C4 ❺

Taken as a whole along with the Musée
de la Mode et du Textile and Musée de
la Publicité, this is one of the world's
major collections of design and the decorative arts. The venue reopened in
2006 after a decade-long, €35-million
restoration, both of the building and of
6,000 of the 150,000 items donated
mainly by private collectors. The major
focus here is French furniture and
tableware, from extravagant carpets to
delicate crystal and porcelain. Ten
reconstructed period rooms show how
the other (French) half lived from the
late 1400s to the early 20th century.

Musée de la Mode
et du Textile

*107 rue de Rivoli, 1st (01.44.55.57.50/
www.lesartsdecoratifs.fr). M° Palais
Royal Musée du Louvre or Pyramides.*
Open *Exhibitions* 11am-6pm Tue-Fri;
10am-6pm Sat, Sun. **Admission** €8;
free-€6.50 reductions. **Map** p72 C4 ❻

A | **B** Eglise de la Trinité | **C** Musée Gustave Moreau

Gare St Lazare

Saint Lazare Ⓜ

R. D'ATHENES

R. DE LONDRES

RUE DE ROME

RUE SAINT LAZARE

Ⓜ St Augustin

La Pepinière

HAUSSMANN

RUE DE CHATEAUDIN

RUE DE LA VICTOIRE

DE LA

RUE TAITBOUT

RUE DE PROVENCE

RUE LA FAYE

Havre 52 Caumartin Ⓜ

Chaussée d'Antin La Fayette Ⓜ

BOULEVARD 40 HAUSSMANN

R. DES MATHURINS

R. DES MATHURINS

Palais Garnier

Auber RER

RUE AUBER

RUE HALEVY

RUE DE HELDER

RUE LAFFITTE

RUE TRONCHET

RUE VIGNON

R. GODOT DE MAUROY

SCRIBE

Opéra Ⓜ

BD. DES ITALIENS

GRANGE

RUE DE CHOISEUL

RUE DE MARIVAUX 69

41

Eglise de la Madeleine

1

BD. DE LA MADELEINE

57

21

BD. DES CAPUCINES

DES CAPUCINES

PL. DE L'OPERA

16

Quatre Septembre Ⓜ

R. DU QUA

AUGUSTIN

R. DE LOUVOIS CO

RUE CHOISEUL

STE ANNE

Madeleine Ⓜ PL. DE LA MADELEINE

RUE ROYALE

RUE SAINT HONORE

RUE DUPHOT

33

Min. de la Justice

R. VOLNEY

RUE DE LA PAIX

RUE LOUIS

RUE DANIELLE CASANOVA

20

AVENUE

GAILLON

MONSIGNY

ST

Bibliothèqu Nationale Richelieu

RUE DES PE

31

11

PL. VENDOME

PL. DU MARCHE ST-HONORE

DE

L'OPERA

Pyramides Ⓜ

VILLEDO

THERESA

RUE DE RICHELIEU

49

RUE MOLIERE

36 5

51

30

12

RUE DE MONT-

CASTIGLIONE

RUE

THABOR

RUE DU

RUE SAINT ROCH

RUE DE LA SOURDIERE

RUE DES PYRAMIDES

58

Palais Royal

RUE DE RIVOLI

4

26

34

Eglise St-Roch

60

HONORE

9

Jeu de Paume

Tuileries Ⓜ

1

8 Musée de l'Orangerie

Jardin des Tuileries

Musée des Arts Décoratifs

RUE DE RIVOLI

5 6

15 56 55

39

PLACE DU PALAIS ROYAL

Palais Ro Musée du Lou

3

Jardin du Carrousel

PLACE DU CARROUSEL

Pyramide

Musée du Louvre

QUAI FRANÇOIS MITTERRAND

Seine

PASSERELLE SOLFERINO

Musée d'Orsay

PONT ROYAL

QUAI DU LOUVRE

QUAI DU

LOUVRE

RUE DE LILLE

RUE DE VERNEUIL

QUAI VOLTAIRE

Q. MALAQUAIS

Institut Franç

Ministère des Transports

ST-GERMAIN-DES-PRES & ODEON

Ecole des Beaux Arts

PONT DES ARTS

ts & museums
ng & drinking
ping
tlife
& leisure

Musée du Louvre

This municipal fashion museum holds Elsa Schiaparelli's entire archive and hosts exciting themed exhibitions. Dramatic black-walled rooms make a fine background to the clothes, while video screens and a small cinema space shows how the clothes move, as well as interviews with the creators.

✱Musée du Louvre

Rue de Rivoli, 1st (01.40.20.50.50/ www.louvre.fr). M° Palais Royal Musée du Louvre. **Open** 9am-6pm Mon, Thur, Sat, Sun; 9am-10pm Wed, Fri. **Admission** €9; free-€6 reductions. **Map** p72 C5 ❼

Some 35,000 works of art and artefacts are on show, divided into eight departments and housed in three wings: Denon, Sully and Richelieu. Treasures from the Egyptians, Etruscans, Greeks and Romans each have their own galleries in the Denon and Sully wings, as do Middle Eastern and Islamic works of art. The first floor of Richelieu is taken up with European decorative arts from the Middle Ages up to the 19th century.

The main draw, though, is the painting and sculpture. Two glass-roofed sculpture courts contain the famous Marly horses on the ground floor of Richelieu, with French sculpture below and Italian Renaissance pieces in the Denon wing. The Grand Galerie and Salle de la Joconde (home to the *Mona Lisa*) run the length of Denon's first floor with French Romantic painting alongside. Dutch and French painting occupies the second floor of Richelieu and Sully. Mitterrand's Grand Louvre project expanded the museum twofold, but the organisation and restoration of the Louvre are still very much a work in progress: check the website or lists in the Carrousel du Louvre to see which galleries are closed on certain days to avoid missing what you really want to see. Laminated panels found throughout provide a lively commentary, and the superb website is a technological feat unsurpassed by that of any of the world's major museums.

Musée de l'Orangerie

Jardin des Tuileries, 1st (01.44.77. 80.07/www.musee-orangerie.fr). M° Concorde. **Open** 12.30-7pm Mon, Wed, Thur, Sat, Sun; 12.30-9pm Fri. **Admission** €6.50; free-€4.50 reductions. **Map** p72 A4 ❽

The long-delayed reopening of this Monet showcase finally took place in 2006, and the Orangerie is now firmly back on the tourist radar: beware long queues. Stylistically, the new look is utilitarian and fuss-free, with the museum's eight, tapestry-sized *Nymphéas* (water lilies) paintings housed in two oval rooms. They provide a simple backdrop for the astonishing, ethereal romanticism of Monet's works, painted late in his life. Downstairs, the Jean Walter and Paul Guillaume collection is a mixed bag of sweet-toothed Cézanne and Renoir portraits, along with works by Modigliani, Rousseau, Matisse, Picasso and Derain.

Palais-Royal

Pl du Palais-Royal, 1st. Mº Palais Royal Musée du Louvre. **Open** Gardens 7.30am-8.30pm daily. **Admission** free. **Map** p72 C4 ❾

Cardinal Richelieu left this building to Louis XIII, whose widow Anne d'Autriche rechristened it when she moved in with her son, the young Louis XIV. In the 1780s, the Duc d'Orléans, Louis XVI's brother, enclosed the gardens in a three-storey peristyle and filled it with cafés, shops, theatres, sideshows and accommodation to raise money for rebuilding the burned-down opera. Daniel Buren's modern installation of black-and-white striped columns graces the main courtyard.

Place de la Concorde

1st/8th. Mº Concorde. **Map** p72 A3 ❿

This is the city's largest square, its grand east-west perspectives stretching from the Louvre to the Arc de Triomphe, and north-south from the Madeleine to the Assemblée Nationale across the Seine. Royal architect Gabriel designed it in the 1750s, along with the two colonnaded mansions astride rue Royale. In 1792, the centre statue of Louis XV was replaced with the guillotine for Louis XVI, Marie-Antoinette and many more. The square was embellished in the 19th century with sturdy lampposts, the Luxor obelisk and ornate fountains.

Place Vendôme

1st. Mº Opéra or Tuileries. **Map** p72 B3 ⓫

This eight-sided square houses sparkling jewellers and top fashion houses, as well as the Justice Ministry and the Hôtel Ritz, from where Diana and Dodi Al-Fayed set off on their last journey. At No.12, you can visit the

In the Lab

Where art meets science.

Viruses, pollution, food and the activity of the brain itself are all potential subjects fermenting in Paris's latest public art space, **Le Laboratoire** (p86). But in fact art is just one pole of this initiative dedicated to the brave new world of 'artscience'.

So what does this mean in practice? For its opening shows, on a broad theme of intelligence, artist Fabrice Hyber developed a series of paintings 'Food for Thought' from his meeting with MIT biotechnology professor Robert Langer, showing the artist's visualisation of stem cell transformations.

The collaboration between David Edwards and hot young designer Mathias Lehanneur showed more concrete potential with Lehanneur's striking Bel-Air project, a prototype living air filter system. Adapting Nasa research on air pollution in space capsules to household pollution from everyday furniture and carpets, Lehanneur designed a ventilation system by which air is wafted through glass globes containing pollution-absorbing plants to clean air in domestic interiors.

Other recent projects have included chef Thierry Marx exploring the future of food with physicist Jérôme Bibette of the ESPCI (Ecole Supérieure de Physique et de Chimie Industrielles), and Indian artist Shilpa Gupta in dialogue with neuroscientist Dean Mobbs on the effect of media indoctrination on the brain: brainstorming guaranteed.

PARIS BY AREA

Grand Salon where Chopin died in 1849; its fabulous allegorical decoration dates from 1777 and has been restored as part of the new museum above jewellers Chaumet.

Eating & drinking

L'Ardoise

28 rue du Mont-Thabor, 1st (01.42.96.28.18). Mº Concorde or Tuileries. **Open** noon-2.30pm, 6.30-11pm Tue-Sat; 6.30-11pm Sun. Closed 1st 3wks Aug. €. **Bistro**. Map p72 B3 ⑫
One of the city's outstanding modern bistros, L'Ardoise is also one of the few to open its doors on Sundays. The room is soon packed out with gourmets eager to sample Pierre Jay's delicious cooking. A wise choice might be six oysters with warm chipolatas and a pungent shallot dressing, an unusual combination from Bordeaux. A lightly chilled Chinon, from a wine list sensibly arranged by price, provides a perfect complement.

Aux Lyonnais

32 rue St-Marc, 2nd (01.42.96.65.04). Mº Bourse or Richelieu Drouot. **Open** noon-1.45pm, 7.30-10.45pm Tue-Fri; 7.30-10.45pm Sat. Closed Aug & 1wk Dec. €€. **Bistro**. Map p72 C2 ⑬

This Ducasse-run bistro has perfectly preserved the *bouchon* style and the pretty c1900 decor. As is the wont of today's new-look, rustic-chic *terroir* cooking, most things here arrive in cast-iron casseroles or glass preserving jars, such as poached egg in a frothy sauce of morels and crayfish. Veal Marengo – named after a Napoleonic battle – proves to be a hefty veal shank braised in wine with confit tomatoes, whole cloves of garlic and tiny potatoes.

La Bourse ou la Vie

12 rue Vivienne, 2nd (01.42.60.08.83). Mº Bourse. **Open** noon-10pm Mon-Fri. Closed 1wk Aug & 1wk Dec. €€. **Bistro**. Map p73 D3 ⑭
The owner of La Bourse ou la Vie has a mission in life: to revive the dying art of the perfect *steak-frites*. The only decision you'll need to make is which cut of beef to order with your chips, unless you pick the cod. Rich, creamy pepper sauce is the speciality here, but the real surprise is the chips, which gain a distinctly animal flavour from the suet in which they are cooked.

Café Marly

93 rue de Rivoli, cour Napoléon du Louvre, 1st (01.49.26.06.60). Mº Palais Royal Musée du Louvre. **Open** 8am-2am daily. €€. **Café**. Map p72 C4 ⑮

PARIS BY AREA

A class act, this, as you might expect of a Costes café whose lofty arcaded terrace overlooks the Louvre's glass pyramid. Accessed through the passage Richelieu, the prime location comes at a price: it's €6 for a Heineken – so you might as well splash out €12 on a Shark of vodka, lemonade and grenadine. Brasserie fare and sandwiches are on offer too.

Café de la Paix
12 bd des Capucines, 9th (01.40.07. 36.36). Mº Opéra. **Open** 7am-midnight daily. **€€**. **Café**. Map p72 B2 ⑯
The sumptuous terrace café-restaurant of the InterContinental Paris Le Grand exudes history. Your table, beneath the ornate, stucco ceiling or overlooking Garnier's opera house, may have been patronised by Oscar Wilde, Josephine Baker or Emile Zola. You'll be treated as one of their equals by the immaculate staff, and presented with little bowls of crisps, nuts and olives to accompany your €10 kir or €8 glass of draught Grimbergen. Lap it up – this is once-in-a-holiday stuff.

De la Ville Café
34 bd Bonne-Nouvelle, 10th (01.48.24. 48.09). Mº Bonne Nouvelle. **Open** 11am-2am daily. **Bar**. Map p73 E2 ⑰
Opened by the Café Charbon crew and other Ménilmontant movers, De la Ville has brought good news to Bonne-Nouvelle. Inside, the distressed walls and hippie feel remain, but the curvy club section at the back has become über-cool. A grand staircase leads up to a first-floor lounge and exhibition space. Having elevated the 11th to bar legend, can the crew transform the 10th, and bring a café boom back to the boulevards?

Drouant
18 rue Gaillon, 2nd (01.42.65.15.16/ www.drouant.com). Mº Quatre Septembre or Pyramides. **Open** noon-2.30pm, 7pm-midnight daily. **€€€**. **Brasserie**. Map p72 C3 ⑱
Alsatian chef Antoine Westermann has whisked this landmark 1880 brasserie into the 21st century with bronze-coloured banquettes and armchairs, a pale parquet floor and butter-yellow paint and fabrics. The restaurant is dedicated to the art of the hors d'oeuvre, served in themed sets of four ranging from the global (a Thai beef salad with vegetables, coriander, and a sweet and spicy sauce) to the nostalgic (silky leeks in vinaigrette). The bite-sized surprises continue with the main course accompaniments and multiple mini-desserts.

Le Fumoir
6 rue de l'Amiral-de-Coligny, 1st (01.42.92.00.24/www.lefumoir.fr). Mº Louvre Rivoli. **Open** 11am-2am daily. Closed 2wks Aug. **Bar**. Map p73 D5 ⑲
This elegant bar facing the Louvre has become a local institution: neo-colonial fans whirr lazily, oil paintings adorn the walls and even the bar staff seem to have sprung from the interior decorator's sketches. A sleek crowd sips Martinis or reads papers at the long mahogany bar, giving way to young professionals in the restaurant and pretty things in the library.

Harry's New York Bar
5 rue Daunou, 2nd (01.42.61.71.14/ www.harrys-bar.fr). Mº Opéra. **Open** 10.30am-4am daily. **Bar**. Map p72 B2 ⑳
The city's quintessential American bar is still an institution beloved of expats, visitors and hard-drinking Parisians. The white-coated bartenders mix some of the most lethal cocktails in town, from the trademark Bloody Mary (invented here, so they say) to the Pétrifiant, an aptly named elixir of half a dozen spirits splashed into a beer mug.

Hemingway Bar at the Ritz
Hôtel Ritz, 15 pl Vendôme, 1st (01.43.16.33.65/www.ritzparis.com). Mº Concorde or Opéra. **Open** 6.30pm-2am daily. **Bar**. Map p72 B3 ㉑
This is a wonderfully civilised place in which to get smashed. The bartender dispenses fabulous cocktails, plus compliments and flowers for the ladies, all in a gloriously suave manner.

Un Jour à Peyrassol

*13 rue Vivienne, 2nd (01.42.60.12.92/
www.peyrassol.com). M° Bourse.* **Open**
12.30-2pm, 7.30-10pm Mon-Fri. Closed
Aug & 1wk Dec. **€€. Brasserie.**
Map p72 C3 ㉒

As anyone who has travelled around
Provence will know, come winter the
restaurants there go truffle-crazy. This
chic little offshoot of the Commanderie
de Peyrassol, a wine-producing castle
in the Var, keeps up the game with its
blackboard menu full of truffle treats.
They can be eaten on toast, atop a
baked potato, in scrambled eggs or in
a rich, creamy sauce enveloping fluffy
gnocchi. The natural complement is
the Commanderie's wine – white, red
and rosé AOC Côtes de Provence.

Kai

*18 rue du Louvre, 1st (01.40.15.01.99).
M° Louvre Rivoli.* **Open** noon-2pm,
7-10.30pm Tue-Sat; 7-10.30pm Sun.
Closed 1wk Apr & 3wks Aug. **€€.**
Japanese. Map p73 D4 ㉓

This Japanese restaurant has rapidly
developed a following among fashionable diners with discriminating tastes.
The 'Kai-style' sushi is a modern and
zesty take on a classic: marinated and
lightly grilled yellowtail is pressed on
to a roll of *shiso*-scented rice. Seared
tuna with avocado, miso and roasted
pine nuts also delights. Thoroughly
French desserts come courtesy of
celebrity pastry chef Pierre Hermé.

Kong

*1 rue du Pont-Neuf, 1st (01.40.39.
09.00). M° Pont Neuf.* **Open** noon-
2am Mon-Thur, Sun; noon-3am Fri,
Sat. **Bar.** Map p73 D5 ㉔

Set on the top two floors of the Kenzo
building overlooking the Pont Neuf,
this Philippe Starck-designed bar is
one of the city's hottest places for cocktails. The bright, mishmash interior is
manga-inspired, with lots of neon and
Hello Kitty knick-knacks. The best bet
is to perch yourself at the long bar and
order an excellent Vodkatini or three.
After dark, you can make a music sug-
gestion with each order; at weekends,
they carve out a tiny dancing space.

Liza

*14 rue de la Banque, 2nd (01.55.35.
00.66). M° Bourse.* **Open** 12.30-2pm,
8-10.30pm Mon-Thur; 12.30-2pm,
8-11pm Fri, Sat; noon-4pm Sun. **€€.**
Lebanese. Map p73 D3 ㉕

Liza Soughayar's eaterie showcases
the superb food of contemporary
Beirut. Lentil, fried onion and orange
salad is delicious, as are the *kebbe*
(minced seasoned raw lamb) and
grilled halloumi cheese with home-
made apricot preserve. Main courses
such as minced lamb with coriander-
spiced spinach and rice are light,
flavoursome and well presented. Try
one of the excellent Lebanese wines,
and finish up with the halva ice-cream
with carob molasses.

Le Meurice

*Hôtel Meurice, 228 rue de Rivoli, 1st
(01.44.58.10.10/www.meuricehotel.
com). M° Tuileries.* **Open** 12.30-2pm,
7.30-10pm Mon-Fri. Closed 2wks
Feb & Aug. **€€€. Haute cuisine.**
Map p72 B3 ㉖

Yannick Alléno, chef here since 2003,
has really hit his stride and is doing
some glorious, if rather understated,
contemporary French luxury cooking.
Turbot is sealed in clay before cooking
and then sauced with celery cream and
a coulis of flat parsley, while Bresse
chicken stuffed with foie gras and
served with truffled *sarladais* potatoes
is breathtakingly good. A fine cheese
tray comes from Quatrehomme, and
the pastry chef amazes with his signature millefeuille.

Senderens

*9 pl de la Madeleine, 8th (01.42.65.
22.90/www.senderens.fr). M° Madeleine.*
Open noon-3pm, 7.30-11.30pm daily.
Closed 3wks Aug. **€€€€. Haute
cuisine.** Map p72 A3 ㉗

Long live Alain Senderens. The veteran
chef has reinvented his art nouveau
institution (formerly Lucas Carton) with
a *Star Trek* interior and fusion menu:
roast duck foie gras with a warm salad
of black figs and liquorice powder, or
monkfish steak with Spanish mussels
and green curry sauce. Each dish comes

Jazz lives on at the Duc

Au Duc des Lombards

In 2007, it looked like the legendary **Au Duc des Lombards** (p84) would close for ever, and take with it a 23-year-long chapter in the history of Paris's jazz scene.

Since 1984, the Duc has seen many of the world's greatest jazz stars swing, sweat and jam on its stage. Like its rue des Lombards neighbours – Le Baiser Salé, La Chapelle des Lombards (now in Bastille), and Le Sunset/Sunside (p85) – the Duc attracted home-grown names like Henri Texier, Daniel Humair and Eric Le Lann alongside top US jazz musicians like Joe Lovano and Kirk Lightsey, giving it a reputation as one of the best places to watch international talents play impromptu jam sessions. But a few years ago, the club hit hard times and was set to be sold as a brasserie – an event that would have irreparably changed the face of rue des Lombards and jazz in Paris.

So imagine everyone's surprise when Gérard Brémond, the CEO of France's leading holiday rental company Pierre & Vacances, saved the day and bought the club with his own money. And what's

more, he's proved himself to be a dab hand at jazz club management. Thanks to a makeover, overseen by designer Elliot Barnes, the interior has swapped its nicotine yellow walls and faded posters for a decor decidedly more modern with the walls and furniture all kitted out in sleek blacks, beiges and browns (the colours of Duke Ellington's first symphony played at the Carnegie hall in 1943).

Chef Alain Alexanian feeds hungry punters throughout the day with fresh, seasonal dishes, and at night (until 3am on Friday and Saturday) with a Croq 'n' Jazz menu accompanied by wine, whisky or champagne.

And the line-up of artists is excellent with a mix of big-name stars such as Kenny Burrell, Johnny Griffin, James Moody, Herbie Hancock and Wayne Shorter, and new talents like pianist Alexandre Saada and saxophonists Geraldine Laurent and Olivier Temime.

It seems jazz here is well and truly back on track and Brémond's Duc is king of rue des Lombards.

PARIS BY AREA

Forum des Images

After three years of taking its eclectic film programming *hors les murs*, the hyperactive **Forum des Images** (p86) resumes activities in the Forum des Halles at the beginning of 2009. A major facelift has given this cinephile's paradise a new, more open layout that makes it easier to move between the different spaces: five cinemas, bar, library and research centre.

Opened in 1988, the Forum was conceived as an archive centre for films, documentaries, adverts and newsreels featuring Paris. Today, the collection numbers over 6,500 films, from Lumière brother shorts to *Superman II*, and the entire backlog has been painstakingly digitised in time for the Forum's grand reopening. Researchers will thus have quicker, easier access to the centre's extensive database and film archives.

The most exciting new addition is the Bibliothèque du Cinéma François-Truffaut, a public library where cinema buffs can consult and borrow film-related books, magazines, DVDs and music CDs. Furthermore, the Forum's new glass-fronted entrance hall promises to give it more visibility on rue du Cinéma, the new name given to the walkway in the Forum des Halles that houses both the Forum des Images and the UGC multiscreen complex. Visitors will thus be able to choose between blockbusters at the UGC and the Forum's programme of thought-provoking film cycles and wacky festivals.

with a suggested wine, whisky, sherry or punch. Sole tempura was not as crisp as it might be, but even a faintly flawed meal here is an event.

Le Tambour

41 rue Montmartre, 2nd (01.42.33. 06.90). M° Sentier. **Open** 6pm-6am daily. **Bar**. **Map** p73 D3 ㉓
The Tambour is a classic nighthawks' bar, decked out with vintage transport chic, its slatted wooden banquettes and bus-stop-sign bar stools occupied by chatty regulars. Neither tatty nor threatening, there's a long dining room memorable for its métro map from Stalingrad station.

Shopping

Agnès b

2, 3, 6 & 19 rue du Jour, 1st (men 01.42.33.04.13/women 01.45.08.56.56/ www.agnesb.com). M° Les Halles. **Open** *Oct-Apr* 10am-7pm Mon-Sat. *May-Sept* 10am-7.30pm Mon-Sat. **Map** p73 D4 ㉙
Agnès b rarely wavers from her design vision: pure lines in fine quality cotton, merino wool and silk. Best buys are shirts, pullovers and cardigans that keep their shape for years. Her mini-empire of men's, women's, children's, travel and sportswear shops is compact; see the website for details.

Alice Cadolle

4 rue Cambon, 1st (01.42.60.94.22/ www.cadolle.com). M° Concorde or Madeleine. **Open** 10am-1pm, 2-7pm Mon-Sat. Closed Aug. **Map** p72 B3 ㉚
Five generations of lingerie-makers are behind this boutique, founded by Hermine Cadolle, who claims to be the inventor of the bra. Great-great-grand-daughter Poupie Cadolle continues the tradition in a cosy space devoted to a luxury ready-to-wear line of bras, panties and corsets. Cadolle Couture, by appointment only, is at 255 rue St-Honoré, 1st (01.42.60.94.94).

Boucheron

26 pl Vendôme, 1st (01.42.61.58.16/ www.boucheron.com). M° Opéra. **Open** 10.30am-7pm Mon-Sat. **Map** p72 B3 ㉛

Boucheron was the first to set up on place Vendôme, eager for celebrity custom from the nearby Ritz hotel. Owned by Gucci, the grand jeweller still manages to produce stunning pieces, using traditional motifs with new accents: witness, for example, its fabulous chocolate-coloured gold watch.

Boutique M Dia

5-7 rue des Innocents, 1st (01.40.26. 03.31/www.mdiawear.com). M° Châtelet/RER Châtelet Les Halles. **Open** 1-8pm Mon; 11am-8pm Tue-Sat. **Map** p73 E4 ㉜

Mohammed Dia, a rebel from the Sarcelles *banlieue*, went to America and came back with an idea to get him out of the ghetto: fashion design. Some €20 million later, he has his own line of men's and women's urban sports clothes, plus shoe line Tariq, worn by the NBA's Dallas Mavericks. His first boutique is a shrine to his vision, offering all from the Dia range.

Chanel

31 rue Cambon, 1st (01.42.86.28.00/ www.chanel.com). M° Concorde or Madeleine. **Open** 10am-7pm Mon-Sat. **Map** p72 B3 ㉝

Fashion legend Chanel has managed to stay relevant today, thanks to Karl Lagerfeld. Coco opened her first boutique in this street, at No.21, in 1910, and the tradition continues in this elegant space. Lagerfeld has been designing for Chanel since 1983 and keeps on rehashing the classics, like the little black dress and the Chanel suit, with great success.

Colette

213 rue St-Honoré, 1st (01.55.35. 33.90/www.colette.fr). M° Pyramides or Tuileries. **Open** 11am-7pm Mon-Sat. **Map** p72 B3 ㉞

Renowned and much-imitated one-stop concept and lifestyle store Colette is still influential. This shrine to the limited edition displays must-have accessories in clinical glass cases. Books, media, shiny new gadgets, and the hair and beauty brands själ, Kiehl's and uslu airlines are scattered amid the magazines and photo albums on the ground floor and mezzanine. Upstairs has a selection of 'in' clothes and accessories. Lunch, with a global selection of mineral water, can be nibbled in the chic basement Water Bar.

Comme des Garçons

54 rue du Fbg-St-Honoré, 8th (01.53.30.27.27). M° Concorde or Madeleine. **Open** 11am-7pm Mon-Sat. **Map** p72 A2 ㉟

Rei Kawakubo's design ideas and revolutionary mix of materials have influenced fashions of the past two decades, and are showcased in this fire engine-red, fibreglass store. Exclusive perfume lines get a futuristic setting at Comme des Garçons Parfums (23 pl du Marché-St-Honoré, 1st, 01.47.03.15.03).

Didier Ludot

20-24 galerie de Montpensier, 1st (01.42.96.06.56/www.didierludot.com). M° Palais Royal Musée du Louvre. **Open** 11am-7pm Mon-Sat. **Map** p72 C3 ㊱

Didier Ludot's temples to vintage haute couture today appear in Printemps, London's Harrods and New York's Barneys, stocking his own line of little black dresses – also available at aptly named La Petite Robe Noire (125 galerie de Valois, 1st, 01.40.15.01.04). The prices are steep, but the pieces are stunning: Dior, Molyneux, Balenciaga, Pucci, Féraud and, of course, Chanel, from the 1920s onwards.

Ekivok

39 bd de Sébastopol, 1st (01.42.21. 98.71/www.ekivok.com). M° Les Halles/ RER Châtelet Les Halles. **Open** 11am-7.30pm Mon-Sat. **Map** p73 E4 ㊲

In Ekivok's graffiti-covered boutique you'll find major brands Bullrot, Carhartt, Hardcore Session and Juicy Jazz for men, and Golddigga, Punky Fish, Skunk Funk, Emilie the Strange and Hardcore Session for women, plus Eastpak accessories.

Erès

2 rue Tronchet, 8th (01.47.42.28.82/ www.eres.fr). M° Madeleine. **Open** 10am-7pm Mon-Sat. **Map** p72 B2 ㊳

Kabuki Femme

Erès' beautifully cut swimwear has embraced a sexy '60s look complete with buttons on the low-cut briefs. One advantage for the natural woman is that the top and bottom can be purchased in different sizes, or you can buy just one piece of a bikini.

La Galerie du Carrousel du Louvre

99 rue de Rivoli, 1st (01.43.16.47.10/ www.lecarrouseldulouvre.com). M° Palais Royal Musée du Louvre. **Open** 10am-8pm daily. **Map** p72 C4 ③

This massive underground centre – open every day of the year – is home to more than 35 shops, mostly big-name chains vying for your attention and cash. The Petit Prince boutique and Réunion des Musées Nationaux shops are great for last-minute gifts.

Galeries Lafayette

40 bd Haussmann, 9th (01.42.82. 34.56/fashion shows 01.42.82.30.25/ fashion advice 01.42.82.35.50/www. galerieslafayette.com). M° Chaussée d'Antin/RER Auber. **Open** 9.30am-7.30pm Mon-Wed, Fri, Sat; 9.30am-9pm Thur. **Map** p72 C2 ④

There are more than 90 designers represented on the first and second floors, including Cavalli, Lacroix and Givenchy. There are five fashion and beauty consultants to guide you through the sartorial maze, and the men's fashion space on the third floor, Lafayette Homme, has natty designer corners and a 'Club' area with internet access. On the first floor, Lafayette Gourmet has exotic foods galore, and a vast wine cellar. The domed ceiling is eminently photogenic, and there's a rooftop café. Over the road, Lafayette Maison (www.lafayettemaison.com) offers five floors of design for the home.

Hédiard

21 pl de la Madeleine, 8th (01.43.12. 88.88/www.hediard.fr). M° Madeleine. **Open** 8.30am-9pm Mon-Sat. **Map** p72 A2 ④

The first to introduce exotic foods to Paris, Hédiard specialises in rare teas and coffees, spices, jams and candied fruits. The original shop, dating from 1880, has a posh tearoom upstairs.

Hermès

24 rue du Fbg-St-Honoré, 8th (01.40.17.46.00/www.hermes.com). M° Concorde or Madeleine. **Open** 10.30am-6.30pm Mon-Sat. **Map** p72 A3 ④

The fifth generation of the family directs the Hermès empire from this venerable 1930s building. Originally – and still – a saddler, it is no also-ran in the fashion stakes with Jean-Paul Gaultier at the reins. Most of its clients, however, are wealthy tourists.

Jean-Paul Gaultier

*6 rue Vivienne, 2nd (01.42.86.05.05/
www.jeanpaulgaultier.com). M° Bourse.*
Open 10.30am-7pm Mon-Fri; 11am-
7pm Sat. **Map** p73 D3 ❸

Having celebrated his 30th year in the
fashion business, Gaultier is still going
strong. His boudoir boutique with its
peach taffeta walls stocks men's and
women's ready-to-wear and the reasonably priced JPG Jeans lines, with the
haute couture department upstairs
(01.42.97.48.12, by appointment only).

Kabuki Femme

*25 rue Etienne-Marcel, 1st
(01.42.33.55.65/www.babarabui.com).
M° Etienne Marcel.* **Open** 10.30am-
7.30pm Mon-Sat. Closed 29 July-22
Aug. **Map** p73 E4 ❹

On the ground floor there's footwear
and bags by Costume National, Miu
Miu and Prada, plus Fendi's cult creations; Burberry belts and Miu Miu
sunglasses are also stocked. Upstairs
are outfits by Véronique Leroy, Prada
and Costume National.

Kiliwatch

*64 rue Tiquetonne, 2nd (01.42.21.
17.37/www.kiliwatch). M° Etienne
Marcel.* **Open** 2-7pm Mon; 11am-
7.30pm Tue-Sat. **Map** p73 E3 ❺

The trailblazer of the rue Etienne-
Marcel revival is filled with hoodies,
casual shirts and washed-out jeans.
Brands such as Gas, Edwin and Pepe
Jeans accompany pricy, good-condition
second-hand garb.

Kokon to Zai

*48 rue Tiquetonne, 2nd (01.42.36.
92.41/www.kokontozai.co.uk). M°
Etienne Marcel.* **Open** 11.30am-7.30pm
Mon-Sat. **Map** p73 E4 ❻

Always a spot-on spotter of the latest
creations, this tiny style emporium is
sister to the Kokon to Zai in London.
The neon club feel of the mirrored interior matches the dark glamour of the
designs. Unique pieces straight off the
catwalk share space with creations by
Marjan Pejoski, Noki, Raf Simons,
Two Tom, Ziad Ghanem and new
Norwegian designers.

Lanvin

`NEW` *22 rue du Fbg-St-Honoré, 8th
(01.44.71.31.73; www.lanvin.com).
M° Concorde or Madeleine.* **Open**
10am-7pm Mon-Sat. **Map** p72 A3 ❼

The couture house that began in the
1920s with Jeanne Lanvin has been
reinvented by the indefatigable Albert
Elbaz. In October 2007, he unveiled
this, the revamped showroom that set
new standards for luxury fashion
retailing. Original art deco furniture
from the Lanvin archive has been
restored, while Armand Albert Rateau
has designed new metal pieces, such as
the kimono-influenced display stands.
All this would be nothing, of course, if
the clothes themselves were not exquisite with their Grecian draping and
tactile appeal, including the chic and
informal wedding collection.

Legrand Filles et Fils

*1 rue de la Banque, 2nd (01.42.60.
07.12). M° Bourse.* **Open** 11am-7pm
Mon-Sat. Closed Mon in July & Aug.
Map p73 D3 ❽

Fine wines and brandies, teas and
bonbons, plus a showroom for regular
wine tastings.

Marc Jacobs

*34 galerie de Montpensier, 1st
(01.55.35.02.60/www.marcjacobs.
com). M° Palais Royal Musée du
Louvre.* **Open** 11am-8pm Mon-Sat.
Map p72 C3 ❾

By choosing the Palais-Royal for his
first signature boutique in Europe,
Marc Jacobs brought new life, and an
influx of fashionistas, to these elegant
cloisters. Stocking womenswear,
menswear, accessories and shoes, it's
already become a place of pilgrimage
for the designer's legion of admirers,
who are snapping up his downtown
New York style.

Marithé et
François Girbaud

*38 rue Etienne-Marcel, 2nd
(01.53.40.74.20/www.girbaud.com).
M° Etienne Marcel.* **Open** 11.30am-
7.30pm Mon; 10.30am-7.30pm Tue-Sat.
Map p73 D3 ❺⓿

The pioneering *soixante-huitard* Girbaud pair came up with streetwear in high-tech fabrics using laser cutting and welding. This flagship store has four floors and a garden.

Martin Margiela

23 & 25bis rue de Montpensier, 1st (01.40.15.07.55/www.maisonmartin margiela.com). M° Palais Royal Musée du Louvre. **Open** 11am-7pm Mon-Sat. **Map** p72 C4 ⑤

The first Paris outlet for the JD Salinger of fashion is a pristine, white, unlabelled space. His collection for women (Line 1) has a blank label but is recognisable by the external white stitching. You'll find Line 6 (women's basics) and Line 10 (menswear), plus accessories for men and women and shoes.

Printemps

64 bd Haussmann, 9th (01.42.82.50.00/www.printemps.com). M° Havre Caumartin/RER Auber. **Open** 9.35am-7pm Mon-Wed, Fri, Sat; 9.35am-10pm Thur. **Map** p72 B1 ⑤

Printemps is the home of superlatives: its shoe department (on the fifth floor of Printemps de la Mode) and beauty department are the largest in the world, the latter stocking some 200 brands. The lingerie department is the stuff of fantasy, with gorgeous smalls from Erès, Gaultier, Pucci and the like. On the second floor of Printemps de la Mode, French designers APC and Zadig et Voltaire sit side by side with Moschino and Dolce & Gabbana. Along with furnishings, Printemps de la Maison contains the 'function floor', with saucepans and coffee machines neatly organised on steel shelving. The ninth-floor terrace restaurant sports an art nouveau cupola. The building is also a classified historic monument.

Salons du Palais-Royal Shiseido

Jardins du Palais-Royal, 142 galerie de Valois, 1st (01.49.27.09.09/ www.salons-shiseido.com). M° Palais Royal Musée du Louvre. **Open** 10am-7pm Mon-Sat. **Map** p72 C3 ⑤

Under the arcades of the Palais-Royal, Shiseido's perfumer Serge Lutens practises his aromatic arts. A former photographer at Paris *Vogue* and artistic director of make-up at Christian Dior, Lutens is a maestro of rare taste. Look out for Fleurs d'Oranger, which the great man defines as the smell of happiness. Many of the perfumes are exclusive to the Salons; prices start at around €100.

Le Vestibule

3 pl Ste-Opportune, 1st (01.42.33.21.89). M° Châtelet. **Open** 10.30am-8pm Mon-Sat. **Map** p73 E5 ⑤

No longer doing vintage street and clubwear, Le Vestibule still has a juicy selection of insider labels and footwear.

Nightlife

Au Duc des Lombards

42 rue des Lombards, 1st (01.42.33.22.88/www.ducdeslombards.com). M° Châtelet. **Open** times vary. **Admission** €19-€25. **Map** p73 E5 ⑤

See box p79.

Le Cab

2 pl du Palais-Royal, 1st (01.58.62.56.25/www.cabaret.fr). M° Palais Royal Musée du Louvre. **Open** 11.30pm-6am Wed-Sat. **Admission** free Tue-Thur; €20 Fri, Sat. **Map** p72 C4 ⑤

The Cabaret, now 'Le Cab', is owned by the management behind Club Mix and Queen, and has had an interior facelift by Franco-Japanese designer Ora Ito. R&B and commercial house dominate.

Olympia

28 bd des Capucines, 9th (08.92.68.33.68/www.olympiahall.com). M° Opéra. **Open** times vary. **Map** p72 B2 ⑤

The Beatles, Sinatra, Hendrix and, of course, Piaf all performed here. Now it's mainly a nostalgia shop, but Coco Rosie and Rachid Taha brought some more contemporary sounds in 2007.

Paris Paris

5 av de l'Opéra, 1st (01.42.60.64.45/ www.leparisparis.com). M° Pyramides. **Open** 11pm-5am Tue-Sat. **Admission** free. **Map** p72 C3 ⑤

Still the hottest spot in Paris, Paris Paris has the city's club glitterati regularly passing through its doors, either to DJ or to enjoy the party – or both. Getting in isn't easy, but once inside you'll find a bustling basement where the focus is on having fun, with an on-the-button music policy.

Rex

5 bd Poissonnière, 2nd (01.42.36. 10.96/www.rexclub.com). M° Bonne Nouvelle. **Open** 11.30pm-6am Wed-Sat. **Admission** free-€10. **Map** p73 E2 ❺❾
The Rex's new sound system, with over 40 different sound configurations at the DJ's fingertips, has proved to be a magnet for top turntable stars. Once associated with iconic techno pioneer Laurent Garnier, the Rex has remained at the top of the Paris techno scene and occupies an unassailable position as the city's serious club music venue.

La Scala

186bis rue de Rivoli, 1st (01.42.60. 45.64/www.lascalaparis.com). M° Palais Royal Musée du Louvre. **Open** 11pm-6am Tue-Sun. **Admission** free-€15. **Map** p72 C4 ❻⓪
A huge central club with three floors and a commercial music policy that embraces house, techno, R&B, hip hop, Caribbean music and salsa.

Le Slow Club

130 rue de Rivoli, 1st (01.42.33.84.30). M° Châtelet. **Open** *Concerts* 10pm Fri, Sat. **Admission** €9-€13. **Map** p73 D5 ❻❶
This medieval cellar may be tiny but compensates with boogie-woogie big bands and dance-friendly R&B. One of the most famous jazz joints in Europe.

Le Sunset/Le Sunside

60 rue des Lombards, 1st (Sunside 01.40.26.21.25/Sunset 01.40.26. 46.60/www.sunset-sunside.com). M° Châtelet. **Open** *Concerts* 9pm, 10pm daily. **Admission** €8-€25. **Map** p73 E5 ❻❷
Split-personality venue, with Sunset dealing in electric groups and Sunside catering for acoustic performances. The reputation of both pulls in big names from both sides of the Atlantic, making this an essential port of call for any jazz pilgrimage to Paris.

Théâtre du Châtelet

1 pl du Châtelet (information 01.40. 28.28.00/booking 01.40.28.28.40/ www.chatelet-theatre.com). M° Châtelet. **Admission** €16-€69. **Map** p73 E5 ❻❸
This venerable theatre and classic music hall has another life as a jazz and chanson venue.

Châtelet p86

Le Triptyque

*142 rue Montmartre, 2nd (01.40.28.
05.55/www.letriptyque.com). M° Bourse
or Grands Boulevards.* **Open** 11.30pm-
3am Wed; 11pm-6am Thur-Sat.
Admission free-€12. **Map** p73 D3 **64**
Hip rock venue Le Triptyque has been
among the top five clubs in Paris since
it opened, largely thanks to its varied,
spot-on music programming.

Arts & leisure

Châtelet – Théâtre Musical de Paris

*1 pl du Châtelet, 1st (01.40.28.28.40/
www.chatelet-theatre.com). M° Châtelet.*
Box office 11am-7pm daily. *By phone*
10am-7pm Mon-Sat. Closed July, Aug.
Admission €10-€125. **Map** p73 E5 **65**
New director Jean-Luc Choplin is
attempting to create a more popular
cultural experience than that provided
by the esoteric programming at the
Opéra National. The concert program-
ming is more traditional.
Event highlights Australian Ballet's
Swan Lake (2-4 Oct); Martha Graham
Dance Company (14-18 Apr 2009).

Forum des Images

NEW *2 Grande Galerie, Porte St-
Eustache, Forum des Halles, 1st
(01.44.76.63.00/www.forumdesimages.
net). M° Les Halles.* **Open** 1-9pm Tue-
Sun. Closed 2wks Aug. **Admission**
€4.50-€5.50. **Map** p73 D4 **66**
See box p80.

Le Grand Rex

*1 bd Poissonnière, 2nd (01.45.08.
93.58/reservations 08.92.68.05.96/
www.legrandrex.com). M° Bonne
Nouvelle.* **Tour** *Les Étoiles du Rex*
every 5mins 10am-7pm Wed-Sun;
daily during school hols. **Admission**
€7-€8; tour & film €12. **Map** p73 E2 **67**
Opened in 1932, this huge art deco cinema was designed by Auguste Bluysen
with fantasy interiors. Go behind the
scenes in the crazy 50-minute guided
tour, which includes a presentation
about the construction of the auditorium and a visit to the production room,
complete with Sensurround effects.

Le Laboratoire

NEW *4 rue du Bouloi, 1st (01 78 09 49
50, www.lelaboratoire.org). M° Palais-
Royal.* **Open** noon-7pm Mon, Fri-Sun.
Admission €6; free-€4.50 reductions.
Map p73 D4 **68**
See box p75.

Opéra Comique

*Pl Boieldieu, 2nd (01.42.44.45.40/
www.opera-comique.com). M° Richelieu
Drouot.* **Box office** 9am-9pm Mon-
Sat. *By phone* 11am-6pm Mon-Sat.
Admission €7-€100. **Map** p72 C2 **69**
Jérôme Deschamps' first season at this
previously underachieving theatre featured a repertoire ranging from Lully
to the contemporary work of Pascal
Dusapin, and the public look set to welcome this jewel box of a theatre back to
the centre of the Parisian music scene.

Palais Garnier

*1 pl de l'Opéra, 9th (08.92.89.90.90/
www.operadeparis.fr). M° Opéra.* **Open**
10am-5pm daily. Guided tours in
English (01.40.01.22.63) 11.30am &
2.30pm daily July-Aug; Wed, Sat &
Sun Sep-June. **Admission** €8; €4
reductions. Guided tours €12; €6-€10
reductions. **Map** p72 B2 **70**
Brimming with gilt and red velvet, the
Opera House designed by Garnier is a
monument to Second Empire high society. The auditorium seats more than
2,000 people – and the exterior is just
as opulent. The Grand Foyer, its mirrors and parquet, coloured marble,
moulded stucco, sculptures and allegorical paintings by Baudry have all
been magnificently restored.

Théâtre de la Ville

*2 pl du Châtelet, 4th (01.42.74.22.77/
www.theatredelaville-paris.com).
M° Châtelet.* **Box office** 11am-7pm
Mon-Sat. **Admission** €12-€30.
Map p73 E5 **71**
Programming in this vertiginous con-
crete amphitheatre features hip cham-
ber music outfits such as the Kronos
Quartet, along with soloists such as
pianist Alexandre Tharaud. The sea-
son spills over to performances at Les
Abbesses (31 rue des Abbesses, 18th).

Sacré-Coeur p88

Montmartre & Pigalle

Montmartre is the highest point in Paris, its tightly packed houses spiralling round the mound below the oversized, sugary-white dome of **Sacré-Coeur**. Despite the thronging tourists, it is easy to fall under the spell of this, the most unabashedly romantic district of Paris. Climb quiet stairways, peer down narrow alleys and into ivy-covered houses and deserted squares, and explore streets such as rue des Abbesses, rue des Trois-Frères and rue des Martyrs, with their cafés, quirky boutiques and bohemian residents.

Pigalle is Paris's centre of sleaze. Despite a police crackdown, which sought to eliminate tourist rip-offs and rough-ups, passers-by may still be hassled by barkers and hawkers trying to corral them into some peep show or other.

Sights & museums

Cimetière de Montmartre

20 av Rachel, access by staircase from rue Caulaincourt, 18th (01.53.42.36.30). M° Blanche or Place de Clichy. **Open** *6 Nov-15 Mar* 8am-5.30pm Mon-Sat; 9am-5.30pm Sun & public hols. *16 Mar-5 Nov* 8am-6pm Mon-Sat; 9am-6pm Sun & public hols. **Admission** free. **Map** p89 A1 ❶
Truffaut, Nijinsky, Berlioz, Degas, Offenbach, German poet Heine and Surrealist painter Victor Brauner are all buried here. So too are La Goulue, the first great cancan star and model

e-Lautrec, celebrated local
e Récamier, and the
eroine Alphonsine Plessis,
for Dumas' *La Dame aux
Camélias* and Verdi's *La Traviata*.
Flowers are still left for pop diva and
gay icon Dalida (see box p91), who
used to live on nearby rue d'Orchampt.

Musée de l'Erotisme

*72 bd de Clichy, 18th (01.42.58.28.73/
www.musee-erotisme.com). M° Blanche.*
Open 10am-2am daily. **Admission**
€8; €6 reductions. **Map** p89 A2 ❷
Seven floors of erotic art and artefacts
amassed by collectors Alain Plumey
and Joseph Khalif. The first three run
from first-century Peruvian phallic pot-
tery through Etruscan fertility symbols to Yoni sculptures from Nepal; the
fourth gives a history of Paris brothels;
and the recently refurbished top floors
host exhibitions of modern erotic art.
In the basement you'll find titillations
such as a vagina dinner plate.

Musée d'Art Halle
St-Pierre

*2 rue Ronsard, 18th (01.42.58.72.89/
www.hallesaintpierre.org). M° Anvers.*
Open *Jan-July, Sept-Dec* 10am-6pm
daily. *Aug* noon-6pm Mon-Fri.
Admission €7; free-€5.50 reductions.
Map p89 C2 ❸
The former covered market in the
shadow of Sacré-Coeur specialises in
art brut, *art outsider* and *art singulier*
from its own and other collections.
Event highlights Fred Deux & Cécile
Reims (15 Sept 2008-8 Mar 2009)

Musée Gustave Moreau

*14 rue de La Rochefoucauld, 9th
(01.48.74.38.50/www.musee-
moreau.fr). M° Trinité.* **Open** 10am-
12.45pm, 2-5.15pm Mon, Wed-Sun.
Admission €5; free-€3 reductions.
Map p89 A4 ❹
This wonderful museum combines the
small private apartment of Symbolist
painter Gustave Moreau (1825-98) with
the vast two-floor gallery he built to
display his work. Downstairs shows
his obsessive collector's nature with
family portraits, Grand Tour souvenirs

and a boudoir devoted to the object
of his unrequited love, Alexandrine
Durem. Upstairs is Moreau's fantasy
realm, which plunders Greek mytho-
logy and biblical scenes for canvases
filled with writhing maidens, trance-
like visages, mystical beasts and
strange plants.

Musée de Montmartre

*12 rue Cortot, 18th (01.49.25.
89.37/www.museedemontmartre.fr).
M° Abbesses or Lamarck-Caulaincourt.*
Open 11am-6pm Wed-Sun.
Admission €7; free-€5.50 reductions.
Map p89 B1 ❺
At the back of a garden, this 17th-
century manor displays the history of
the hilltop, with rooms devoted to
composer Gustave Charpentier and a
tribute to the Lapin Agile cabaret,
with some original Toulouse-Lautrec
posters. There are paintings by
Suzanne Valadon, who had a studio
above the entrance pavilion, as did
Renoir, Raoul Dufy and Valadon's
son Maurice Utrillo.

Musée de la Vie
Romantique

*Hôtel Scheffer-Renan, 16 rue
Chaptal, 9th (01.55.31.95.67/www.
vie-romantique.paris.fr). M° Blanche
or St-Georges.* **Open** 10am-6pm Tue-
Sun. **Admission** free. *Exhibitions* €7;
free-€3.50 reductions. **Map** p89 A3 ❻
When Dutch artist Ary Scheffer lived
in this small villa, the area thronged
with composers, writers and artists.
George Sand was a guest at Scheffer's
soirées, and many other great names
crossed the threshold. The museum is
devoted to Sand, although the water-
colours, lockets, jewels and plastercast
of her right arm that she left behind
reveal little of her ideas or affairs.
There's a pretty rose garden and a con-
servatory that serves as a café.

✖Sacré-Coeur

*35 rue du Chevalier-de-la-Barre, 18th
(01.53.41.89.00/www.sacre-coeur-
montmartre.com). M° Abbesses
or Anvers.* **Open** *Basilica* 6am-
10.30pm daily. *Crypt & dome* Winter

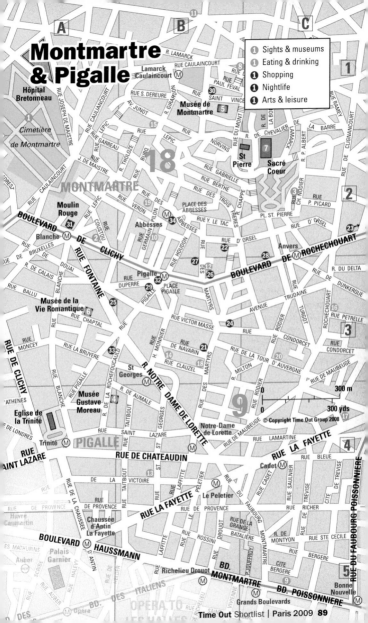

Montmartre & Pigalle

Legend:
- Sights & museums
- Eating & drinking
- Shopping
- Nightlife
- Arts & leisure

Hôpital Bretonneau

Cimetière de Montmartre

Lamarck Caulaincourt

Musée de Montmartre

MONTMARTRE

Moulin Rouge

Blanche

Musée de la Vie Romantique

Abbesses

Pigalle

St Pierre

Sacré Coeur

PL. ST. PIERRE

Anvers

BOULEVARD DE ROCHECHOUART

BOULEVARD DE CLICHY

RUE FONTAINE

RUE CAULAINCOURT

St Georges

Musée Gustave Moreau

Eglise de la Trinité

Trinité

PIGALLE

R. NOTRE DAME DE LORETTE

Notre-Dame de Lorette

RUE DE CHATEAUDIN

RUE LA FAYETTE

Cadet

Le Peletier

RUE DE PROVENCE

Chaussée d'Antin La Fayette

Palais Garnier

BOULEVARD HAUSSMANN

Opéra

Richelieu Drouot

BD. MONTMARTRE

BD. POISSONNIERE

Bonne Nouvelle

Grands Boulevards

© Copyright Time Out Group 2008

300 m

300 yds

18

9

10am-5.45pm daily. Summer 9am-6.45pm daily. **Admission** free. *Crypt & dome* €5. **Map** p89 C2 ➐

Work on this enormous mock Romano-Byzantine edifice began in 1877. It was commissioned after the nation's defeat by Prussia in 1870, voted for by the Assemblée Nationale and built from public subscription. Finally completed in 1914, it was consecrated in 1919 – by which time a jumble of architects had succeeded Paul Abadie, winner of the original competition. The interior boasts lavish mosaics, and there's a fine view from the dome.

Eating & drinking

A. Beauvilliers

52 rue Lamarck, 18th (01.42.55. 05.42). M° Lamarck-Caulaincourt. **Open** 12.15-2.30pm, 8-10.30pm Tue-Sat. Closed 2wks Aug & 1wk Dec. **€€. Bistro. Map** p89 B1 ➑

Named after Marie-Antoinette's cook, this chandelier-bedecked restaurant is run by young chef Yohan Paran. Its provincial air contrasts pleasantly with the inventive French cooking. For a romantic experience – aim for the terrace, weather permitting – it's worth splurging on the €63 tasting menu, which makes abundant use of luxury ingredients such as foie gras, scallops, farm-raised pigeon, truffles and rare argania oil from Morocco.

Le Brébant

32 bd Poissonnière, 9th (01.47.70. 01.02). M° Grands Boulevards. **Open** 7.30am-6am daily. **Bar. Map** p89 C5 ➒

If anything points to a new broom sweeping the Grands Boulevards, it's this prominent, round-the-clock bar-bistro. Prices are steep, even by Paris standards, so push the boat out and opt for an expertly made fruit daiquiri, or a Bonne Nouvelle of Bombay Sapphire gin and Pisang Ambon. A board advertises a decent range of proper eats: steak tartare (€14) and so on.

Chez Toinette

20 rue Germain-Pilon, 18th (01.42.54. 44.36). M° Abbesses or Pigalle. **Open**

7.30-11.30pm Mon-Sat. Closed last 3wks Aug. **€€. Bistro. Map** p89 B2 ➓

This stalwart purveyor of bistro fare has steadily upped its prices in line with its burgeoning success. However, the blackboard menu is still good value. Of the starters, try the wild boar terrine, the gloriously creamy *chèvre chaud* or the soufflé-like asparagus quiche. Carnivorous mains include *mignon de porc*, spring lamb and assorted steaks. Round it all off with Armagnac-steeped prunes.

La Divette de Montmartre

136 rue Marcadet, 18th (01.46.06. 19.64). M° Lamarck-Caulaincourt. **Open** 5pm-1am Mon-Sat; 5-11pm Sun. **Bar. Map** p89 B1 ⓫

Tucked away among Montmartre's hilly backstreets, this cavern of colourful nostalgia is run by Serge and serves as his *Recherche du temps perdu*. Beatles albums line up over the bar, Rolling Stones under it and an Elvis clock ticks in between; this decorative trinity is interrupted by yé-yé pop tat, St-Etienne football iconography and an old red phone box. On tap are Wieckse Witte, Afflighem and Pelforth.

La Fourmi

74 rue des Martyrs, 18th (01.42.64. 70.35). M° Pigalle. **Open** 8.30am-2am Mon-Thur; 8.30am-4am Fri, Sat; 10am-2am Sun. **Bar. Map** p89 B3 ⓬

La Fourmi is retro-industrial at its best: an old bistro that has been converted for today's tastes, with picture windows giving light and visual bustle to the spacious, roughshod, sand-coloured main interior. The classic zinc bar counter is crowned by industrial lights, and an excellent music policy and cool clientele ensure a pile of flyers. As good a place as any to find out what's happening in town.

Georgette

29 rue St-Georges, 9th (01.42.80. 39.13). M° Notre-Dame-de-Lorette. **Open** noon-2.45pm, 7.30-11pm Tue-Fri. Closed 1wk Apr, Aug & 1wk Nov. **€. Bistro. Map** p89 B4 ⓭

A mix of 1950s Formica tables (with matching bar) and ancient wooden beams provides the external charm, but what has won Georgette a loyal following since it opened three years ago is the chef's loving use of seasonal ingredients. Hearty meat dishes satisfy the local business crowd, while lighter options might include sea bream with provençal vegetables. The creamy fontainebleau cheese with raspberry coulis is divine.

Kastoori

4 pl Gustave-Toudouze, 9th (01.44.53. 06.10). M° St-Georges. **Open** 11.30am-2.30pm, 7-11.30pm daily. **€€**. **Indian**. Map p89 B3 ⓮
This friendly, family-run Indian restaurant is one of the few good-value eateries in the area. Amid dangling lanterns, Indian fabrics and (perhaps too much) incense inside, or under hot lamps outside, choose from tangy *raita* and *kaleji* as starters, followed by a choice of tandoori chicken, chicken curry, *saag paneer* or the dish of the day. You can bring your own wine and there's no corkage fee.

Le Moulin de la Galette

83 rue Lepic, 18th (01.46.06.84.77). M° Notre-Dame-de-Lorette. **Open** noon-2.45pm, 7.30-11pm Tue-Fri. Closed Aug. **€€€**. **Haute cuisine**. Map p89 B1 ⓯
The butte Montmartre was once dotted with windmills, and this one survives, housing a chic restaurant with a few romantic tables in the cobbled courtyard outside. It's hard to imagine a more picturesque setting, but the kitchen makes an effort nonetheless with updated dishes such as foie gras with melting beetroot cooked in lemon balm and juniper or suckling pig alongside potato purée.

Pétrelle

34 rue Pétrelle, 9th (01.42.82.11.02). M° Anvers. **Open** 8-9.30pm Tue-Sat. Closed 4wks July/Aug & 1wk Dec. **€€**. **Haute cuisine**. Map p89 C3 ⓰
Jean-Luc André is as inspired a decorator as he is a cook, and the quirky

Queen of the hill

Singers are a revered breed in France and Egyptian-born Dalida is a bona fide legend. During her 30-year career she recorded more than 1,000 songs, scoring 45 gold records and two platinum albums. However, her professional success was paralleled by extreme personal lows. Three of her lovers committed suicide, and Dalida ended her life in the late 1980s.

Her success in the anglophone world was limited. But in Paris, her adopted town, it feels as if Dalida's every step has been sanctified, and 20 years after her suicide, a cult dedicated to the singer continues to evolve.

Much of the Dalida myth is rooted in Montmartre where she lived in the 'Castle of Sleeping Beauty', a four-storey house on rue d'Orchampt. Geographic consecration is an honour usually reserved for generals, cardinals and artists, but Dalida had one of the most picturesque squares in the neighbourhood dedicated to her. Place Dalida is graced by a bronze bust of the idol. Her graveyard in the Montmartre cemetery is another place of pilgrimage.

Paris's latest ode to the singer came in the form of an exhibition at the Hôtel de Ville in September 2007. Everything from mythical dresses to family photographs and personal letters went on display.

Dalida's presence lives on as Paris refuses to let the memory of one of its most flamboyant residents fade.

La Fourmi

charm of his dining room has made it popular with fashion designers and film stars alike. The €29 no-choice menu is huge value for money (on our last visit, marinated sardines with tomato relish, rosemary-scented rabbit with roasted vegetables, deep purple poached figs); or you can splash out with dishes such as tournedos Rossini.

Poussette Café

NEW *6 rue Pierre Sémard, 9th (01.78. 10.49.00/www.lepoussettecafe.com). Mº Poissonnière or Cadet.* **Open** 10.30am-6.30pm Tue-Sat. **€**. **Café**. **Map** p89 C4 ⑰

Fed up with the impracticalities of pushing her pram (*poussette*) into the local café, mother-of-two Laurence Constant designed her own parent-friendly establishment. This upmarket *salon de thé* caters for the harassed parent (herbal teas, smoothies, quiches and salads) and demanding baby (purées, solids and cuddly toys). Sign up for magic shows and parenting workshops via the café's website.

Rose Bakery

46 rue des Martyrs, 9th (01.42.82. 12.80). Mº Notre-Dame-de-Lorette. **Open** 9am-7pm Tue-Fri; 10am-5pm Sat, Sun. Closed 2wks Aug & 1wk Dec. **€**. **Café**. **Map** p89 B3 ⑱

This English-themed café run by a Franco-British couple stands out for the quality of its ingredients – organic or from small producers – as well as the too-good-to-be-true puddings: carrot cake, sticky toffee pudding and, in winter, a chocolate-chestnut tart. The DIY salad plate is crunchily satisfying, but the thin-crusted *pizzettes*, daily soups and occasional risottos are equally good choices.

Le Sancerre

35 rue des Abbesses, 18th (01.42.58. 08.20). Mº Abbesses. **Open** 7am-2am Mon-Thur; 7am-4am Fri, Sat; 9am-2am Sun. **Bar**. **Map** p89 B2 ⑲

Of the many choices on rue des Abbesses this is the most popular, its large, dark-wood interior an attractive mix of cool and cosy. Taps of Paulaner, Grimbergen and Record accompany bottled Belgians Kriek and Mort Subite; standard cocktails (€5.50 on Mondays) are presented with the same care as the couple of *plats du jour* and there's a pretty good range of mains and salads. However, the service can be teeth-grindingly slow.

Spring

*28 rue de la Tour d'Auvergne,
9th (01.45.96.05.72). M° Anvers
or Cadet.* **Open** 8.30pm Tue, Wed;
1pm & 8.30pm Thur, Fri. Closed
Aug & 1wk Dec. **€€**. **Bistro.**
Map p89 C3 ㉑

Where do Michelin inspectors tend to
go on their day off? To Spring, where
30-year-old American chef Daniel Rose
has wowed the critics since opening
this sleek 16-seat bistro in 2006. He
keeps things simple by serving a no-
choice four-course menu that changes
every day according to what he finds
at the place des Fêtes market. On a late
spring day this might result in a velvety cauliflower soup, chunky octopus
salad with potatoes, radishes and
herbs, poached guinea hen with root
vegetables, and baked apple with
French toast.

Shopping

Arnaud Delmontel

*39 rue des Martyrs, 9th (01.48.78.
29.33/www.arnaud-delmontel.com).
M° St-Georges.* **Open** 7am-8.30pm
Mon, Wed-Sun. No credit cards.
Map p89 B3 ㉑

With its crisp crust and chewy crumb
shot through with irregular holes,
Delmontel's Renaissance bread is one
of the finest in Paris. He puts the same
skill into his unsurpassable almond
croissants and *tarte au citron à l'anci-
enne*, available in individual portions.

Base One

*47bis rue d'Orsel, 18th (01.53.28.
04.52/www.baseoneshop.com). M°
Anvers.* **Open** 12.30-8pm Tue-Sat;
3.30-8pm Sun. Closed 2wks Aug.
Map p89 B2 ㉒

The dynamic clubland duo Princesse
Léa and Jean-Louis Faverole squeeze
items from little known local and international designers (Shai Wear, Li-Lei,
Drolaic, 0K47), plus a selection of small,
established brands (Fenchurch, Motel,
Consortium) into their sitting-room
style boutique. Calling it an underground Colette would be somewhere
near the mark.

Tati

*4 bd de Rochechouart, 18th (01.55.
29.52.50/www.tati.fr). M° Barbès
Rochechouart.* **Open** 10am-7pm
Mon-Sat. **Map** p89 C2 ㉓

Expect to find anything from T-shirts
to wedding dresses, as well as bargain
children's clothes and household goods
at this discount heaven. It's unbeatably
cheap, but don't expect high quality.

Wochdom

*72 rue Condorcet, 9th (01.53.21.
09.72). M° Anvers or Pigalle.* **Open**
noon-8pm Mon-Sat. **Map** p89 B3 ㉔

This temple to vintage stocks a mainly
female collection, inclined towards the
spotty and stripy 1980s.

Nightlife

Le Bus Palladium

*6 rue Fontaine, 9th (01.45.26.80.35/
01.42.23.18.62/www.lebuspalladium.
com). M° Pigalle or St-Georges.* **Open**
8.30pm-dawn Wed-Sat; 3pm-dawn Sun.
Admission varies. No credit cards.
Map p89 A3 ㉕

This mythical 1960s venue has managed to re-establish itself in recent
years as a vital locale, attracting rock
acts along with electro and hip hop.

La Cigale/La Boule Noire

*120 bd de Rochechouart, 18th (01.49.
25.81.75/www.lacigale.fr). M° Anvers
or Pigalle.* **Open** times vary.
Admission varies. **Map** p89 B3 ㉖

One of the city's finest venues, the
handsome, horseshoe-shaped Cigale is
linked to the more intimate Boule Noire,
good for catching cult visiting acts.

Le Divan du Monde

*75 rue des Martyrs, 18th (01.42.52.
02.46/www.divandumonde.com).
M° Abbesses or Pigalle.* **Open** 8pm-
2am Tue-Thur; 8pm-5am Fri, Sat.
Admission €6-€30. **Map** p89 B3 ㉗

Used for one-off parties and regular
events, the upstairs specialises in VJ
events, while downstairs holds dub,
reggae, funk and world music club
nights. It's also where the Spoutnik
crew holds its rock and electro parties.

Elysée Montmartre

72 bd de Rochechouart, 18th (01.44. 92.45.38/www.elyseemontmartre. com). Mº Anvers. **Open** midnight-6am Fri, Sat. **Admission** €10-€15. **Map** p89 C2 ㉘

Both a gig venue and a club, Elysée hosts big nights by outside promoters, such as Open House, Panik and Nightfever, for young clubbers.

Folies Pigalle

11 pl Pigalle, 9th (01.48.78.55.25/ www.folies-pigalle.com). Mº Pigalle. **Open** midnight-dawn Mon-Thur; midnight-noon Fri, Sat; 6pm-midnight Sun. **Admission** €20 (incl 1 drink); €7 Sun eve. **Map** p89 B3 ㉙

The Folies Pigalle's programme includes everything from dancehall and hip hop to techno and electro, fashion shows, go go dancers and striptease shows, plus a gay tea dance on Sunday evenings.

Au Lapin Agile

22 rue des Saules, 18th (01.46.06. 85.87/www.au-lapin-agile.com). Mº Lamarck-Caulaincourt. **Shows** 9pm-2am Tue-Sun. **Admission** *Show* (incl 1 drink) €24; €17 reductions (except Sat & public hols). No credit cards. **Map** p89 B1 ㉚

The prices have gone up and they sell their own compilation CDs, but that's all that seems to have changed since this quaint, pink bar first opened in 1860. Tourists now outnumber the locals, but the Lapin harbours an echo of old Montmartre.

Moulin Rouge

82 bd de Clichy, 18th (01.53.09.82.82/ www.moulin-rouge.com). Mº Blanche. **Dinner** 7pm. **Shows** 9pm, 11pm daily. **Admission** *9pm show* (incl champagne) €99. *11pm show* €89 (incl champagne). *Dinner & show* €145-€175. **Map** p89 A2 ㉛

Toulouse-Lautrec posters, glittery lampposts and fake trees lend a certain tacky charm to this most traditional of glamour revues, while 60 dancers cavort with faultless synchronisation. Costumes are flamboyant, the entr'acte acts funny and the sets seamlessly change before your eyes. The downer is space. But if you can bear intimacy with international businessmen, the Moulin Rouge won't disappoint.

Nouvelle Athènes

NEW *9 pl Pigalle, 9th (01.49.70.03.99/ www.myspace.com/lanouvelleathenes). Mº Pigalle.* **Open** 10am-2am Mon-Sat. *Concerts* 10.30pm Tue-Sat. **Admission** varies. **Map** p89 B3 ㉜

La Nouvelle Athènes has a weight of history behind it. It was the café pictured in Degas' *L'Absinthe*, a striptease frequented by the Nazis and Liberation troops, then rock venue the New Moon, before burning down in 2004. The place has been resurrected to form Pigalle's first jazz venue for decades. Though dining is not obligatory, we recommend it, for Gilles Rivard's cuisine is fabulous, and is followed by classic jazz in an intimate atmosphere that may finish, as on the night we visited, with a top quality jam session.

Project 101

44 rue de La Rochefoucauld, 9th (01.49.95.95.85/www.project-101.com). Mº Pigalle. **Open** 10pm-2am Fri. **Admission** free-€5. **Map** p89 A3 ㉝

While others in Paris have moved on to big times, this tiny basement venue has kept the bijou vibe. Connected to an Anglo-French owned shop, it offers occasional Friday nights featuring experimental electronic live acts and DJs. Check the website for details before venturing down.

Arts & leisure

Théâtre de la Ville – Les Abbesses

2 pl du Châtelet, 4th (01.42.74.22.77/ www.theatredelaville-paris.com). Mº Châtelet. **Open** *Box office* 11am-8pm Mon-Sat. *Telephone bookings* 11am-7pm Mon-Sat. Closed July, Aug. **Admission** €12-€23. **Map** p89 B2 ㉞

This leading contemporary dance venue has nurtured long-standing collaborations with international choreographers. Book early – most shows sell out well before opening night.

Parc des Buttes-Chaumont p96

North-east Paris

The other side of place de la République from the aristocratic Marais lies the more proletarian north-east. Here, charming *quartiers* stand cheek by jowl with grotty ones, and modern housing developments rub shoulders with relics from the old villages of Belleville, La Villette, Ménilmontant and Charonne.

Romantic Canal St-Martin begins at the Seine at Pont Morland, disappears underground at Bastille, then emerges east of place de la République. The first stretch of the canal, lined with shady trees and crossed by iron footbridges and locks, has the most appeal. The quays are traffic-free on Sundays. Many canalside warehouses have been snapped up by artists and designers or turned into loft apartments.

The area also encompasses one of the city's most beautiful parks, **Buttes-Chaumont**, and a centre of counter-culture, Belleville. Legend has it that Edith Piaf was born on the pavement outside 72 rue de Belleville, marked by a plaque.

Sights & museums

Canauxrama
13 quai de la Loire, 19th (01.42. 39.15.00/01.42.39.11.24/www. canauxrama.fr). **Departs** Port de l'Arsenal (50 bd de la Bastille, 12th, M° Bastille) 9.45am, 2.30pm daily. *Apr-Sept* Bassin de la Villette (13 quai de la Loire, 19th, M° Jaurès) 9.45am, 2.45pm daily. **Admission** €14; free-€11 reductions. **Map** p97 C1 ❶
If the Seine palls, take a trip up the city's second waterway, the Canal St-Martin. The tree-lined canal is a pretty and characterful sight, and the

150-minute trip even goes underground for a stretch, where the tunnel walls are enlivened by a light show.

Gare du Nord

Rue de Dunkerque, 10th (08.91.36.20. 20). M° Gare du Nord. **Map** p97 A2 ❷
The grandest of the great 19th-century train stations (and Eurostar terminal since 1994) was designed by Hittorff between 1861 and 1864. A stone façade, with Ionic capitals and statues representing towns served by the station, hides a vast iron-and-glass vault. The airy refurbishment of the suburban section by rue du Fbg-St-Denis makes the Eurostar's digs look a little drab.

Parc des Buttes-Chaumont

Rue Botzaris, rue Manin, rue de Crimée, 19th. M° Buttes Chaumont. **Open** *Oct-Apr* 7am-8.15pm daily. *May, mid Aug-Sept* 7am-9.15pm daily. *June-mid Aug* 7am-10.15pm daily. **Map** p97 E2 ❸
With its meandering paths and vertical cliffs, this lovely park – a former gypsum quarry, tip and public gibbet – was designed by Adolphe Alphand for Haussmann in the 1860s. Waterfalls now cascade out of a man-made cave. A bridge (cheerfully named the Pont des Suicides) crosses the lake to an island crowned by a mini-temple.

Eating & drinking

L'Atmosphère

49 rue Lucien-Sampaix, 10th (01.40.38.09.21). M° Gare de l'Est or Jacques Bonsergent. **Open** 9.30am-1.45am Mon-Sat; 9.30am-midnight Sun. No credit cards. **Bar**. **Map** p97 B3 ❹
L'Atmosphère remains at the centre of the Canal St-Martin renaissance and sums up the spirit of the area. Parisians of all kinds chat, read and gaze from the waterside terrace; within, the simple, tasteful interior, animated conversation and cheapish drinks provide entertainment enough. It's always packed out, but brave the crowds on Sundays for early-evening world and experimental music slots.

Bar Ourcq

68 quai de la Loire, 19th (01.42.40. 12.26). M° Laumière. **Open** *Winter* 5pm-midnight Wed, Thur, Sun; 3pm-2am Fri, Sat. *Summer* 5-9.30pm Wed-Fri, Sun; 3pm-2am Sat. **Bar**. **Map** p97 D1 ❺
The Ourcq is set along a canal embankment broad enough to accommodate *pétanque* games (ask at the bar) and a cluster of deckchairs. It's a completely different scene from the crowded bustle along Canal St-Martin: more discerning and less self-satisfied. The cabin-like interior has a cosy raised area at the back. Drinks are listed in a hit parade of prices, starting with €2 for a *demi* or glass of red wine, €3 for a Pelforth or Kir, and €4 for a lively Mojito. Pastas at €7, exhibitions and a regular DJ spot keep the clientele sated. Closed on rainy weekdays in summer.

A la Bière

104 av Simon-Bolivar, 19th (01.42.39. 83.25). M° Colonel Fabien. **Open** noon-3pm, 7pm-1.30am daily. **€**. **Brasserie**. **Map** p97 D2 ❻
A la Bière looks like one of those nondescript corner brasseries with noisy pop music, but what makes it stand out is an amazingly good-value €13.40 prix fixe full of fine bistro favourites. Starters of thinly sliced pig's cheek with a nice French dressing on the salad, and a home-made rabbit terrine exceed expectations. The mains live up to what's served before: charcoal-grilled entrecôte with hand-cut chips, and juicy Lyonnais sausages with potatoes drenched in olive oil, garlic and parsley. The staff know their wine and never hurry the diners; there's usually jolly banter going on at the bar. This is one of the few bargains left in Paris – let's hope it stays that way.

Chez Jeanette

NEW *47 rue du Fbg-St Denis, 10th (01.47.70.30.89). M° Strasbourg St-Denis or Château d'Eau.* **Open** 8am-2am daily. **€**. **Café**. **Map** p97 A3 ❼
When she sold her café in March 2007 Jeanette chose the young team from Chez Justine because they promised

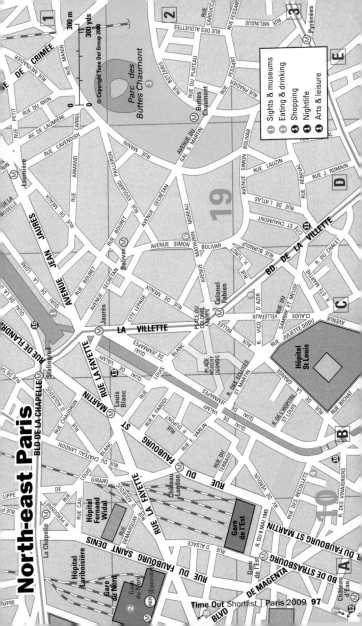

North-east Paris

Parc des Buttes Chaumont

Legend:
- Sights & museums
- Eating & drinking
- Shopping
- Nightlife
- Arts & leisure

© Copyright Time Out Group 2008

300 m
300 yds

Gare du Nord

Gare de l'Est

Hôpital St Louis

Hôpital Lariboisière

Hôpital Fernand Widal

Chez Michel

not to change a thing. Now the monstrous 1940s lights, tobacco-stained wallpaper depicting the Moulin Rouge and PVC-covered banquettes have been rewarded with a Fooding prize for decor and the café is quickly becoming one of Paris's hippest spots for an aperitif. There's a *plat du jour* at lunch and *assiettes* of cheese and charcuterie at night. At 8pm, the fluorescent lights go off and candlelight takes over, to a cheer.

Chez Michel

10 rue de Belzunce, 10th (01.44.53. 06.20). Mº Gare du Nord. **Open** 6.45pm-midnight Mon; noon-2pm, 7pm-midnight Tue-Fri. Closed 2wks Aug. **€€. Brasserie. Map** p97 A2 ⑧

Thierry Breton is from Brittany, and so proud of his origins that he sports the Breton flag on his chef's whites. His menu is stacked with hearty offerings from said hearty region. Marinated salmon with purple potatoes served in a preserving jar, pickled herring-style, is succulently tender. Blackboard specials, which carry a €5-€25 supplement, follow the seasons: game-lovers are spoilt in the cooler months with wood pigeon, wild boar and venison.

L'Ile Enchantée

65 bd de la Villette, 10th (01.42.01. 67.99). Mº Colonel Fabien. **Open** 8am-2am Mon-Fri; 5pm-2am Sat. **Bar. Map** p97 C3 ⑨

The latest DJ bar on the burgeoning scene north-west of Belleville, the Enchanted Island's minimal house/ electro sounds allow the focus to stay firmly on conversation. The high ceilings and French windows let in acres of Belleville skyline, and the studded banquettes add to the chic but retro vibe. The wine list is formidable and sturdy cocktails come in at €6.50 a hit.

Shopping

Antoine et Lili

95 quai de Valmy, 10th (01.40.37. 41.55/www.antoineetlili.com). Mº Jacques Bonsergent. **Open** 11am-7pm Mon, Sun; 11am-8pm Tue-Fri; 10am-8pm Sat. **Map** p97 B3 ⑩

Antoine et Lili's fuchsia-pink, custard-yellow and apple-green shopfronts, reflected in the waters of the Canal St-Martin, are a colour therapist's dream. The bobo designer's clothes, often in wraparound styles, adapt to all sizes and shapes. The Canal St-Martin

One of the best for the latest cutting-edge jazz exponents, but with a broad policy embracing *chanson*, blues, world and sophisticated pop.

Point Ephémère

200 quai de Valmy, 10th (01.40.34. 02.48/www.pointephemere.org). M° Jaurès or Louis Blanc. **Open** 10am-2am daily. **Admission** varies. **Map** p97 C2 ⑬

Generally thought of as a bit of Berlin relocated to Paris, Point Ephémère is one of the coolest arrivals on the scene in the last few years. An uncompromising programming policy delivers some of the best electronic music to be had in town. There's also a restaurant and bar with decks and a gallery, and terrace space by the canal in summer.

Arts & leisure

Hammam Med Centre

43-45 rue Petit, 19th (01.42.02. 31.05/www.hammammed.com). M° Ourcq. **Open** Women 11am-10pm Mon-Fri; 9am-7pm Sun. Mixed 10am-9pm Sat. **Map** p97 E1 ⑭

This hammam is hard to beat – spotless mosaic-tiled surroundings, flowered sarongs and a relaxing pool. The exotic 'Forfait florale' option (€139) will have you enveloped in rose petals and massaged with *huile d'Argan* from Morocco, while the more simple hammam and *gommage* followed by mint tea and pastries is €39. Plan to spend a few hours here as the soft-voiced staff take things at their own pace.

MK2

14 quai de la Seine, 19th (08.92.69. 84.84/www.mk2.fr). M° Stalingrad. **Open** times vary. **Admission** €9.40; €5.30-€6.80 reductions. **Map** p97 C1 ⑮

MK2's mini multiplex on the quai de la Loire was seen as a key factor in the social rise of what had previously been a scuzzy part of town. Now the chain has opened another multiplex across the water – with a boat taking punters from one to the other. Programming is as innovative and international as at other MK2s in the city.

'village' comprises womenswear, a kitsch home decoration boutique and childrenswear, which has replaced the former Antoine et Lili café.

Nightlife

Café Chéri(e)

44 bd de la Villette, 19th (01.42.02. 02.05). M° Belleville. **Open** 8am-2am daily. **Map** p97 D3 ⑪

This splendid DJ bar has expanded its brief and its opening hours to become an all-day café – without watering down any of the funky chic that keeps it well ahead of the pack after dark. Large jars on the bar pack all kinds of punches, such as the €5 Chéri(e) of dark rum; fruit vodkas are another speciality. DJ nights are conceived with equal craft. There's a front terrace if you need some conversational respite from the BPM.

New Morning

7-9 rue des Petites-Ecuries, 10th (01.45.23.51.41/www.newmorning. com). M° Château d'Eau. **Open** Box office 4-7.30pm Mon-Fri. Concerts 9pm daily. **Admission** €15-€21. **Map** p97 A3 ⑫

Centre Pompidou

The Marais & Eastern Paris

Between boulevard Sébastopol and the Bastille are Beaubourg – site, since 1977, of the **Centre Pompidou** – and the Marais, largely built between the 16th and 18th centuries and now jam-packed with boutiques, museums and bars.

The narrow streets of the Marais contain aristocratic *hôtels particuliers*, art galleries, boutiques and stylish cafés, with beautiful carved doorways and early street signs carved into the stone. The area is a favourite spot for a Sunday stroll, as many of the shops are open – though if you come during the week you have more chance of wandering into some of the elegant courtyards.

A little further east is the edgy Oberkampf district, home to some of the city's best bars and a nightlife hub for the last decade.

Sights & museums

Atelier Brancusi

Piazza Beaubourg, 4th (01.44.78. 12.33/www.centrepompidou.fr). M° Hôtel de Ville or Rambuteau. **Open** 2-6pm Mon, Wed-Sun. **Admission** free. **Map** p102 A2 ❶
When Constantin Brancusi died in 1957, he left his studio and its contents to the state. Brancusi's studio has been faithfully reconstructed by the Centre Pompidou. His fragile works in wood and plaster, the endless columns and streamlined bird forms, show how Brancusi revolutionised sculpture.

Centre Pompidou (Musée National d'Art Moderne)

Rue St-Martin, 4th (01.44.78.12.33/ www.centrepompidou.fr). M° Hôtel de Ville or Rambuteau. **Open** 11am-9pm (last entry 8pm) Mon, Wed-Sun (until 11pm some exhibitions); 11am-11pm Thur. **Admission** *Museum & exhibitions* €10; free-€8 reductions. **Map** p102 A2 ②

The primary colours, exposed pipes and air ducts make this one of the best-known sights in Paris. The Centre Pompidou (or 'Beaubourg') holds the largest collection of modern art in Europe, rivalled only in its breadth and quality by MoMA in New York.

For the main collection, buy tickets on the ground floor and take the escalators up to level four for post-1960s art. Level five spans 1905 to 1960. Masterful ensembles let you see the span of Matisse's career on canvas and in bronze, the variety of Picasso's invention, and the development of cubic orphism by Sonia and Robert Delaunay. Others on the hits list include Braque, Duchamp, Mondrian, Malevich, Kandinsky, Dali, Giacometti, Ernst, Miró, Calder, Magritte, Rothko and Pollock.

Level four's thematic rooms concentrate on the career of one artist or focus on movements such as Anti-form or *arte povera*. Recent acquisitions line the central corridor, while at the far end you can find architecture and design.

Cimetière du Père-Lachaise

Bd de Ménilmontant, 20th (01.55.25. 82.10). M° Père-Lachaise. **Open** *6 Nov-15 Mar* 8am-5.30pm Mon-Fri; 8.30am-5.30pm Sat; 9am-5.30pm Sun. *16 Mar-5 Nov* 8am-6pm Mon-Fri; 8.30am-6pm Sat; 9am-6pm Sun & hols. **Map** p103 F2 ③

Père-Lachaise has as starry a line-up of illustrious corpses as anywhere in the world – it's the celebrity cemetery. Here lie Delacroix, Proust, Bizet – in fact, almost anyone French, talented and dead that you care to mention. Not even French, for that matter. Creed and nationality have never prevented entry: you just had to have lived or died in Paris or have an allotted space in a family tomb. Finding a particular grave can be tricky. Buy a map from the hawkers at the Père Lachaise métro entrance or from shops nearby.

Hôtel de Sully

62 rue St-Antoine, 4th (01.42.74. 47.75). M° St-Paul. **Open** noon-6.30pm Tue-Fri; 10am-6.30pm Sat, Sun. **Admission** €5; €2.50 reductions. **Map** p102 C4 ④

Along with the Jeu de Paume, the former Patrimoine Photographique forms part of the two-site home for the Centre National de la Photographie.

Hôtel de Ville

29 rue de Rivoli, 4th (01.42.76.43.43/ www.paris.fr). M° Hôtel de Ville. **Open** 10am-7pm Mon-Sat. **Map** p102 A3 ⑤

The palatial, multi-purpose Hôtel de Ville is both the heart of the city administration and a place to entertain visiting dignitaries. Free exhibitions are held in the Salon d'Accueil (open 10am-6pm Mon-Fri); the rest of the building, accessible only by weekly guided tours (book in advance), features parquet floors, marble statues, crystal chandeliers and painted ceilings.

Maison Européenne de la Photographie

5-7 rue de Fourcy, 4th (01.44.78.75.00/ www.mep-fr.org). M° St-Paul. **Open** 11am-7.30pm Wed-Sun. **Admission** €6; free-€3 reductions. **Map** p102 B4 ⑥

Probably the capital's best photographic centre, hosting retrospectives by Larry Clark and Martine Barrat, along with work by emerging photographers. The building, an airy mansion with a modern extension, contains a huge permanent collection. The venue organises the biennial Mois de la Photo and the Art Outsiders festival of new media web art in September.

Maison de Victor Hugo

Hôtel de Rohan-Guéménée, 6 pl des Vosges, 4th (01.42.72.10.16/www. paris.fr/musees). M° Bastille or

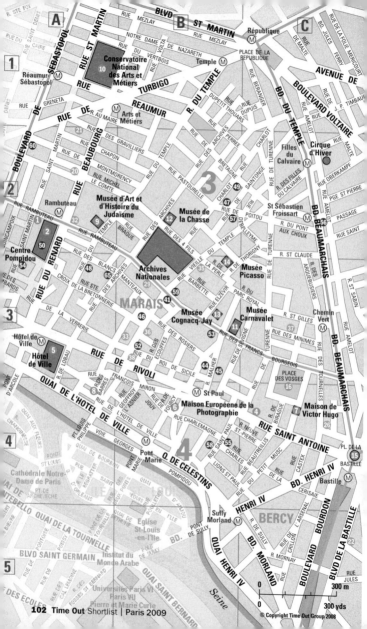

The Marais & Eastern Paris

St-Paul. **Open** 10am-6pm Tue-Sun.
Admission free. *Exhibitions* prices
vary. **Map** p102 C4 **7**

Victor Hugo lived here from 1833-48,
and today the house is a museum
devoted to the life and work of France's
favourite son. On display are his first
editions, nearly 500 drawings and,
more bizarrely, the great man's home-
made furniture.

Le Mémorial de la Shoah

*17 rue Geoffroy-l'Asnier, 4th
(01.42.77.44.72/www.memorialdela
shoah.org). M° St-Paul or Pont Neuf.*
Open 10am-6pm Mon-Wed, Fri-Sun;
10am-10pm Thur. *Research centre*
10am-5.30pm Mon-Wed, Fri, Sun;
10am-7.30pm Thur. **Admission** free.
Map p102 A4 **8**

Airport-style security checks mean
queues, but don't let that put you off.
The Mémorial du Martyr Juif Inconnu
is an impressively presented and mov-
ing memorial to the Holocaust. Enter
via the Wall of Names, where limestone
slabs are engraved with the first and
last names of each of the 76,000 Jews
deported from France from 1942 to
1944. The excoriation continues in
the basement-level permanent exhibition, which documents the plight of
French and European Jews through
photographs, written texts, films
and individual stories.

Musée d'Art et d'Histoire
du Judaïsme

*Hôtel de St-Aignan, 71 rue du
Temple, 3rd (01.53.01.86.60/www.
mahj.org). M° Rambuteau.* **Open**
11am-6pm Mon-Fri; 10am-6pm
Sun. Closed Jewish hols. **Admission**
€6.80; free-€4.50 reductions.
Map p102 A2 **9**

Set in a Marais mansion, this museum
sprang from the collection of a private
association formed in 1948 to safe-
guard Jewish heritage after the
Holocaust. Displays illustrate cere-
monies, rites and learning, and show
how styles were adapted across the
globe through examples of Jewish decorative arts. The Holocaust is marked
by Boris Taslitzky's sketches from

Buchenwald and Christian Boltanski's
courtyard memorial to the Jews who
lived in the building in 1939, 13 of
whom died in the camps.

Musée des Arts
et Métiers

*60 rue Réaumur, 3rd (01.53.01.
82.00/www.arts-et-metiers.net).
M° Arts et Métiers.* **Open** 10am-6pm
Tue, Wed, Fri-Sun; 10am-9.30pm
Thur. **Admission** €6.50; free-€4.50
reductions. **Map** p102 A1 **10**

After the monks of St-Martin-des-
Champs lost their heads in the
Revolution, Abbé Henri Grégoire kept
his by thinking up a new use for the
building – as a repository of technological marvels. The collection has since
expanded to fill three floors of a neighbouring modern building with glass
cases of beautifully crafted scientific
instruments, from astrolabes to steam
engines, plus reconstructions of
famous inventors' workshops. The
restored church houses an original
Foucault's Pendulum, Blériot's biplane,
a model of Bartholdi's Statue of Liberty
and Alain Prost's Formula 1 Renault.
Event highlights Destination Pôle Air:
50 ans d'observation de l'atmosphère
et du climat à partir des régions
polaires (21 Oct 2008-30 Apr 2009).

Musée Carnavalet

*23 rue de Sévigné, 3rd (01.44.59.
58.58/www.paris.fr/musees). M°
St-Paul.* **Open** 10am-6pm Tue-Sun.
Admission free. *Exhibitions* €7; free-
€5.50 reductions. **Map** p102 B3 **11**

Here, 140 rooms depict the history of
Paris, from pre-Roman Gaul to the 20th
century. Original 16th-century rooms
house Renaissance collections, the first
floor covers the period up to 1789,
and neighbouring Hôtel Le Peletier de
St-Fargeau covers the period from
1789 onwards. Displays relating to
1789 detail that year's convoluted
politics and bloodshed, with prints and
memorabilia, including a chunk of
the Bastille prison. There are items
belonging to Napoleon, plus a cradle
given by the city to Napoleon III and
Proust's bedroom.

Musée de la Chasse et de la Nature

Hôtel Guénégaud, 62 rue des Archives, 3rd (01.53.01.92.40/www.chasse nature.org). Mº Rambuteau. **Open** 11am-6pm Tue-Sun. **Admission** €6; free-€4.50 reductions. **Map** p102 B2 ⑫

Housed in a 17th-century mansion, this museum reopened in 2007 after a two-year overhaul. It's a store of everything from ornate hunting weapons to studies by Alexandre-François Desportes, including his portrait of Louis XIV's hunting dogs.

Musée Cognacq-Jay

Hôtel Donon, 8 rue Elzévir, 3rd (01.40.27.07.21/www.paris.fr/musees). Mº St-Paul. **Open** 10am-6pm Tue-Sun. **Admission** free. **Map** p102 B3 ⑬

This cosy museum houses a collection put together in the early 1900s by La Samaritaine founder Ernest Cognacq and his wife Marie-Louise Jay. They stuck mainly to 18th-century French works, focusing on rococo artists such as Watteau, Fragonard and Greuze, though some English artists (Reynolds, Romney, Lawrence) and Dutch and Flemish names (an early Rembrandt, Ruysdael, Rubens), plus Canalettos and Guardis, have managed to slip in.

✳Musée National Picasso

Hôtel Salé, 5 rue de Thorigny, 3rd (01.42.71.25.21/www.musee-picasso.fr). Mº Chemin Vert or St-Paul. **Open** *Oct-Mar* 9.30am-5.30pm Mon, Wed-Sun. *Apr-Sept* 9.30am-6pm Mon, Wed-Sun. **Admission** €6.50; free-€4.50 reductions. *Exhibitions* prices vary. **Map** p102 B3 ⑭

Picasso's paintings, sculptures, collages, drawings and ceramics are shown off in style in this stately Marais mansion. Many of the 'greatest hits' hang in other state-owned Paris museums, but to get a feeling for Picasso's artistic development this is the best resource in the city. A small covered sculpture garden displays pieces that sat around Picasso's studio until his death, and there is a summer café.

Place de la Bastille

4th/11th/12th. Mº Bastille. **Map** p102 C4 ⑮

Nothing remains of the prison that, on 14 July 1789, was stormed by revolutionary forces. Parts of the foundations can be seen in the métro. The Colonne de Juillet, topped by a gilded génie of Liberty, is a monument to Parisians who fell during the revolutions of July 1830 and 1848.

Musée de la Chasse et de la Nature

PARIS BY AREA

Place des Vosges

4th. Mº St-Paul. **Map** p102 C4 ⑯

Paris's first planned square was commissioned in 1605 by Henri IV and inaugurated by his son Louis XIII in 1612. It was called place Royale prior to the Napoleonic Wars, when the Vosges was the first region of France to pay its war taxes. Mme de Sévigné, salon hostess and letter-writer, was born at No.1bis in 1626. At that time, the garden hosted duels and trysts; now it attracts children from the nearby nursery school.

La Promenade Plantée

Av Daumesnil, 12th. Mº Gare de Lyon or Ledru-Rollin. **Map** p103 D5 ⑰

The railway tracks atop the Viaduc des Arts were replaced in the late 1980s by a promenade planted with roses, shrubs and rosemary. It continues at ground level through the Jardin de Reuilly and the Jardin Charles Péguy on to the Bois de Vincennes.

Le Viaduc des Arts

15-121 av Daumesnil, 12th (www. viaduc-des-arts.com). Mº Gare de Lyon or Ledru-Rollin. **Map** p103 D5 ⑱

Glass-fronted workshops in the arches beneath the Promenade Plantée provide a handsome showroom for furniture and fashion designers, picture-frame gilders, tapestry restorers, porcelain decorators, and chandelier, violin and flute makers. Design industry body VIA holds exhibitions of work at Nos.29-35.

Eating & drinking

L'Alimentation Générale

64 rue Jean-Pierre-Timbaud, 11th (01.43.55.42.50). Mº Parmentier. **Open** 5pm-2am Mon-Sat. **Bar**. **Map** p103 D1 ⑲

The 'Grocery Store' is a big old space filled with junk. Cupboards of kitsch china or plastic peppers face the long bar counter, while elsewhere lampshades made from kitchen sponges are a particularly inspired touch. The beer is equally well chosen

– Flag, Sagres, Picon and Orval. Expect a €5 cover price for big names or live bands.

L'Ambassade d'Auvergne

22 rue du Grenier-St-Lazare, 3rd (01.42.72.31.22/www.ambassade-auvergne.com). Mº Arts et Métiers. **Open** noon-2pm, 7.30-10pm daily. **€. Bistro**. **Map** p102 A2 ⑳

This rustic *auberge* is a fitting embassy for the hearty fare of central France. The salad bowl is chock-full of green lentils cooked in goose fat, studded with bacon and shallots. *Rôti d'agneau* arrives as a pot of melting chunks of lamb in a rich sauce with a helping of tender white beans. Dishes arrive with the flagship *aligot*, a creamy mash-and-cheese concoction.

Andy Whaloo

69 rue des Gravilliers, 3rd (01.42. 71.20.38). Mº Arts et Métiers. **Open** 4pm-2am Mon-Sat. **Bar**. **Map** p102 A2 ㉑

Andy Whaloo – created by the people behind its neighbour 404 and London's Momo and Sketch – is Arabic for 'I have nothing'. Bijou? The place brings new meaning to the word. A formidably fashionable set crowds in here and fights for a coveted place on an upturned paint can; from head to toe, it's a beautifully designed venue, crammed with Moroccan artefacts and a spice-rack of colours.

L'Antenne Bastille

32ter bd de la Bastille, 12th (01.43.43. 34.92). Mº Bastille. **Open** 8am-2am Mon-Fri; noon-2am Sat; 2-9pm Sun. **Bar**. **Map** p102 C5 ㉒

A great little retro bar just minutes from the Bastille opera, L'Antenne has a terrace overlooking the Port de l'Arsenal marina and a simple interior. You can get a humble *jambon-beurre* sandwich for under €3 or a Toblerone from the rows arranged in sweet-shop fashion under the Maurice Chevalier posters. There's more substantial (and equally cheap) food too: a *plat du jour* at €8.50 and an €11.50 daily *formule*.

Au P'tit Garage

63 rue Jean-Pierre-Timbaud, 11th (01.48.07.08.12). M° Parmentier. **Open** 6pm-2am daily. **Bar**. **Map** p103 D1 ㉓

This quite marvellous rock 'n' roll bar is the pick of the bunch on rue J-P-T. Not that the owners have fitted it with Americana or waitresses on roller-skates; the L'il Garage is as basic as the real car-fit business a few doors down the road. Regulars cluster around the twin decks at the bar, while music-savvy Frenchettes gossip at the back.

Le Baron Rouge

1 rue Théophile-Roussel, 12th (01.43.43.14.32). M° Ledru-Rollin. **Open** 10am-3pm, 5-10pm Tue-Thur; 10am-10pm Fri, Sat; 10am-3pm Sun. **Bar**. **Map** p103 E5 ㉔

Calling this simply a wine bar might give the wrong impression. It sells wine, certainly, piled high and sold at very reasonable prices by the glass. But there are draught beers too, St-Omer and far rarer Jenlain and Corsican Pietra. But overall, the Red Baron is best described as a chat room. Regulars congregate to yak while they sip, perhaps with a plate of sausages.

Le Bistrot Paul Bert

18 rue Paul-Bert, 11th (01.43.72.24.01). M° Charonne. **Open** noon-2pm, 7.30-11pm Tue-Thur; noon-2pm, 7.30-11.30pm Fri, Sat. Closed Aug. **€€**. **Bistro**. **Map** p103 F4 ㉕

This heart-warming bistro gets it right almost down to the last crumb. Pared-down cooking is its forte: expect high-quality seasonal produce, very simply prepared. A roast shoulder of suckling pig and a thick steak with a raft of golden, home-made, thick-cut *frites* look inviting indeed. Desserts are superb too, including what may be the best *île flottante* in Paris. The lunch prix fixe menu is remarkable value.

Bofinger

5-7 rue de la Bastille, 4th (01.42.72.87.82/www.bofingerparis.com). M° Bastille. **Open** noon-3pm, 6.30pm-12.30am Mon-Fri; noon-12.30am Sat, Sun. **€€**. **Brasserie**. **Map** p102 C4 ㉖

Opposite the Bastille opera house, Bofinger is a post-show haunt that draws big crowds at other times for its authentic art nouveau setting and brasserie atmosphere. Downstairs is the prettiest place to eat, but upstairs is air-conditioned. Go for the foolproof brasserie meal of oysters and fillet steak, followed by a rabidly pungent plate of munster cheese and bowl of cumin, washed down by fine Gigondas.

Café Charbon

109 rue Oberkampf, 11th (01.43.57.55.13/www.nouveaucasino.net). M° Parmentier or Ménilmontant. **Open** 9am-2am Mon-Thur, Sun; 9am-4am Fri, Sat. **Bar**. **Map** p103 E1 ㉗

This beautifully restored belle époque building sparked the Oberkampf nightlife boom. Its booths, mirrors, chandeliers and adventurous music policy put trendy locals at ease. After 15 years or more, the formula still works, copied by scores of nearby bars. The management opened the equally popular Nouveau Casino nightclub next door and has continued the empire-building with the groovified De la Ville Café in the 10th.

Le Chateaubriand

129 av Parmentier, 11th (01.43.57.45.95). M° Goncourt. **Open** noon-2pm, 8-11pm Tue-Fri; 8-11pm Sat. Closed 3wks Aug, 1wk Dec. **€€€**. **Bistro**. **Map** p103 D1 ㉘

After a hit debut at La Famille in Montmartre, self-taught Basque chef Iñaki Aizpitarte has taken over this very stylish bistro. His menu displays the same gastronomic daring that made La Famille a hit. You'll understand if you try starters such as chunky steak tartare garnished with a quail's egg or asparagus with tahini foam and little splinters of sesame-seed brittle. Book a few days ahead.

Le Dôme du Marais

53bis rue des Francs-Bourgeois, 4th (01.42.74.54.17). M° Rambuteau. **Open** noon-2.30pm, 7-10.30pm Tue-Sat. Closed 1wk Jan & 3wks Aug. **€€**. **Bistro**. **Map** p102 B3 ㉙

Lying somewhere between casual and formal, bistro and haute cuisine, Le Dôme du Marais seems to have got it just about right. The staff won't turn a hair if you show up in jeans, but should you feel the urge to mark the occasion with finery, the octagonal, domed dining room would provide a fitting backdrop. Owner-chef Pierre Lecoutre loves to work with seasonal produce, serving, say, *filet de courbine*, a white fish available only for three weeks of the year, in a chorizo cream sauce.

L'Encrier

55 rue Traversière, 12th (01.44.68.08.16). Mº Ledru-Rollin or Gare de Lyon. **Open** noon-2.15pm, 7.30-11pm Mon-Fri; 7.30-11pm Sat. Closed Aug & Christmas wk. €. **Bistro**. **Map** p103 D5 ⑳

Through the door and past the velvet curtain, you find yourself face to face with the kitchen and a crowd of locals. Start with fried rabbit kidneys on a bed of salad dressed with raspberry vinegar, and follow with goose *magret* with honey – a welcome change from the usual duck version and served with crunchy, thinly sliced sautéed potatoes. To end, share a chocolate cake, or try the popular profiteroles.

Le Fanfaron

6 rue de la Main-d'Or, 11th (01.49.23.41.14). Mº Ledru-Rollin. **Open** 6pm-2am Mon-Sat. Closed 2wks Aug. **Bar**. **Map** p103 E4 ㉛

On a small backstreet, Le Fanfaron (named after Dino Risi's 1962 cult movie) is the favoured haunt for musically inclined retro dudes. Owner Xavier's enviable collection of rare film soundtracks, the cheap beer and sound of needle against crackly vinyl pack them in. The decor is kitsch-cool, with Stones and Iggy memorabilia, secondhand furniture and '60s movie posters.

Le Hangar

12 impasse Berthaud, 3rd (01.42.74.55.44). Mº Rambuteau. **Open** noon-2.30pm, 7.30-11pm Tue-Sat. Closed Aug. €. **Bistro**. No credit cards. **Map** p102 A2 ㉜

It's worth making the effort to find this bistro tucked away by the Centre Pompidou. A bowl of tapenade and toast is supplied to keep you going while choosing from the comprehensive *carte*. It yields, for starters, tasty and grease-free *rillettes de lapereau* (rabbit) alongside pumpkin and chestnut soup. Main courses include a well-seasoned steak tartare, served with a crisp salad and *pommes dauphines*. Puddings such as chocolate soufflé and warm white-wine tart with cinnamon are also tempting.

Lizard Lounge

18 rue du Bourg-Tibourg, 4th (01.42.72.08.11/www.cheapblonde.com). Mº Hôtel de Ville. **Open** noon-2am daily. **Bar**. **Map** p102 B3 ㉝

An anglophile favourite deep in the Marais, this loud and lively pick-up joint provides lager in pints, strong, well-mixed cocktails and a viewing platform from which the beer-goggled can ogle their prey. Bargain boozing kicks off at 5pm; at 8pm another happy hour begins down in the sweaty cellar bar, ending at 10pm. Mercifully, given the five straight hours of cheap drinks, the dancefloor is minuscule.

Le Bistrot Paul Bert p107

La Mercerie

*98 rue Oberkampf, 11th (01.43.38.
81.30). M° Parmentier.* **Open** 7pm-
2am daily. **Bar**. **Map** p103 E1 ㉞
Opposite the landmark Charbon and
infinitely more grungy, the Mercerie
features bare walls – bare everything,
in fact – allowing room for the usual
Oberkampf shenanigans of death-wish
drinking against a loud musical backdrop. Happy hour stretches to 9pm, so
you can cane the house vodkas (apricot, mango, honey) and have enough
euros to finish the job after dusk.

La Perle

*78 rue Vieille-du-Temple, 3rd (01.42.
72.69.93). M° Chemin Vert or St-Paul.*
Open 6am-2am Mon-Fri; 8am-2am Sat,
Sun. **Bar**. **Map** p102 B3 ㉟
This recent Marais hit is commendably
simple. Cool little touches – arty dab-
blings on the walls, the old locomotive
over the bar – meet sleek rows of grey
chairs outside and patterned banquettes within. The Pearl's real triumph is its all-day and late-night
hetero/homo mix: it feels like a neighbourhood bar, with labourers and cra-
vatted screenwriters rubbing elbows at
the counter. Expect a DJ later on.

Le Petit Fer à Cheval

*30 rue Vieille-du-Temple, 4th
(01.42.72.47.47). M° St-Paul.* **Open**
9am-2am daily. **Bar**. **Map** p102 B3 ㊱
If Glasgow's Horseshoe boasts the
UK's longest bar counter, its Paris
near-namesake must contain one of
France's smallest. It may be tiny, but
it's charming: a marble ring surrounded by old film and promotional posters
and headed by a vintage clock and an
ornate mirror backdrop. Behind the
glassy façade hides a friendly dining
room lined with old métro benches.

Le Petit Marché

*9 rue de Béarn, 3rd (01.42.72.06.67).
M° Chemin Vert.* **Open** noon-3pm,
7.30pm-midnight Mon-Fri; noon-4pm
Sat, Sun. **€€**. **Bistro**. **Map** p102 C3 ㊲
Just a step away from place des
Vosges, Petit Marché attracts a fash-
ion-conscious crowd. The menu is
short and modern with Asian touches.
Raw tuna is flash-fried in sesame seeds
and served with a Thai sauce; pan-fried
scallops with lime are precision-cooked
to avoid any hint of rubberiness, and
accompanied by a good purée and
more beans. There's a short wine list;
the house red is unusually good.

Stolly's

16 rue Cloche-Perce, 4th (01.42.76. 06.76/www.cheapblonde.com). M° Hôtel de Ville or St-Paul. **Open** 4.30pm-2am daily. **Bar**. **Map** p102 B3 ❸❽

This seen-it-all drinking den has been serving a mainly anglophone crowd expert vodka tonics and old Velvets tunes for nights immemorial. The staff make the place what it is, smoothing the passage from arriving sober to sinking them relentlessly until you're rotten. A summer terrace eases libation, as do long happy hours, but don't expect anyone to faff about with food. There's football on TV and a plastic shark to compensate.

Le Temps au Temps

13 rue Paul-Bert, 11th (01.43.79. 63.40). M° Faidherbe Chaligny. **Open** noon-2.30pm, 8-10.30pm Tue-Sat. Closed Aug & 1wk Dec. **€€**. **Bistro**. **Map** p103 F4 ❸❾

This bistro's friendly new owners have retained its original name, but replaced the former riot of broken timepieces with just two or three clocks. The €27 menu might begin with a home-made *fromage de tête*, worth the three days it took in the making. The quality of the main courses doesn't flag, with, for instance, a fillet of verbena-steamed John Dory on a bed of cauliflower 'couscous'. Ice-creams are home-made.

Le Train Bleu

Gare de Lyon, pl Louis-Armand, 12th (01.43.43.09.06/www.le-train-bleu.com). M° Gare de Lyon. **Open** 11.30am-3pm, 7-11pm daily. **€€**. **Brasserie**. **Map** p103 D5 ❹❶

This listed dining room – with vintage frescoes of the alluring destinations of the Paris-Lyon-Marseille railway and big oak benches with shiny brass coat racks – exudes a pleasant air of expectation. Expect fine renderings of French classics. Lobster on walnut oil-dressed salad leaves is a generous, beautifully prepared starter. Mains of veal chop topped with a cap of cheese, and *sandre* (pike-perch) with a 'risotto' of *crozettes* are also pleasant. A few reasonably priced wines would be a welcome addition.

Shopping

A-poc

47 rue des Francs-Bourgeois, 4th (01.44.54.07.05). M° Rambuteau or St-Paul. **Open** 11am-7pm Mon-Sat. Closed 3wks Aug. **Map** p102 B3 ❹❶

La Perle p109

The unusual name is an acronym for 'A Piece of Cloth', and Issey Miyake's lab-style boutique takes a conceptual approach to fashion. Alongside ready-to-wear cotton Lycra clothes are rolls of wool jersey cut *sur mesure*; Miyake's assistants will be happy to advise. His original shop (3 pl des Vosges, 4th, 01.48.87.01.86) today houses the creations of Naoki Takizawa, protégé to the old master.

L'Autre Boulange

43 rue de Montreuil, 11th (01.43.72. 86.04). Mº Faidherbe Chaligny or Nation. **Open** 7.30am-1.30pm, 3.30-7.30pm Tue-Sat. Closed Aug. **Map** p103 F5 ㊷
Michel Cousin bakes up to 23 kinds of organic loaves in his wood-fired oven – types like the *flutiot* (rye bread with raisins, walnuts and hazelnuts), the *sarment de Bourgogne* (sourdough and a little rye) and a spiced cornmeal bread ideal with foie gras.

Come On Eline

16-18 rue des Taillandiers, 11th (01.43.38.12.11). Mº Ledru-Rollin. **Open** *Sept-July* 11.30am-8.30pm Mon-Thur; 11.30am-7.30pm Fri; 4-8pm Sun. *Aug* 2-8pm Mon-Fri. **Map** p103 D4 ㊸
The owners of this three-floor vintage wonderland have an eye for what's funky, from cowboy gear to 1960s debutantes frocks. They can afford to charge high prices (Hermès scarves cost around €100), but the stock is well sourced and in good condition.

L'Eclaireur

3ter rue des Rosiers, 4th (01.48. 87.10.22/www.leclaireur.com). Mº St-Paul. **Open** 11am-7pm Mon-Sat. **Map** p102 B3 ㊹
Housed in a dandified warehouse, L'Eclaireur stocks designs by Comme des Garçons, Martin Margiela, Dries van Noten, Carpe Diem and Junya Watanabe. Among its exclusive finds, check out smocks by Finnish designer Jasmin Santanen. At the secretive rue Hérold branch you have to ring the doorbell to enter. A new space in rue

Robot city

In this boutique on car-clogged boulevard Beaumarchais, a technological revolution is afoot. R2D2 has become a video projector, small humanoids dance to the sound of techno, Manga-style white rabbits broadcast podcasts and wireless vacuum cleaners move around as if by magic.

Robopolis (p113) is the only store in France entirely devoted to robots – a meeting point for robotics aficionados from all walks of life and a place where the differences between man and machine are increasingly difficult to distinguish.

Models such as Roboreptile, a grumpy futuristic dinosaur who walks freely around the house and growls until you feed him, and Meccano's 'build-your-own' Speed Play Interactive Robot, whose sounds and movements can be downloaded from the internet, sit at the top of boys' birthday wish lists.

Other popular models include the Roomba 560, a discreet, circular vacuum cleaner that detects dirt and cleans the floor without human intervention; the Hitec Robonova-I, a funky orange and black 'Robosapian' that can be taught to dance thanks to 16 movement-generating motors; and Nabaztag – a cute, little white rabbit that reads emails and podcasts, plays and sings music, obeys vocal commands and even reads books.

No vacuuming, no story-telling – artificial intelligence might not be such a frightening prospect after all.

A-poc p110

Boissy d'Anglas, near Concorde, sells chic fashions for men and women.

L'Eclaireur Homme

12 rue Malher, 4th (01.44.54.22.11/ www.leclaireur.com). M° St-Paul. **Open** 11am-7pm Mon-Sat. **Map** p102 B3 ❹❺
Amid the exposed ducts of this old printworks you'll find items by Prada, Comme des Garçons, Dries van Noten and Martin Margiela. The star is Italian Stone Island, whose radical clothing features parkas with a steel shell to counteract pollution.

Free 'P' Star

8 rue Ste-Croix-de-la-Bretonnerie, 4th (01.42.76.03.72). M° St-Paul. **Open** noon-11pm Mon-Sat; 2-10pm Sun. **Map** p102 B3 ❹❻
Late-night shopping is fun at this Aladdin's cave of retro glitz, ex-army wear and glad rags that provides many a cross-dresser with partywear.

L'Habilleur

44 rue de Poitou, 3rd (01.48.87.77.12). M° St-Sébastien Froissart. **Open** noon-8pm Mon-Sat. **Map** p102 B2 ❹❼
L'Habilleur, in the newly christened 'haut Marais', has an ever-changing selection of *dégriffés* (designer wear with the label cut out). Urbanites use this slick store for its menswear and womenswear by the likes of Roberto Collina, Paul & Joe and Stefano Mortari, at up to 60 per cent off original prices.

I Love My Blender

NEW *36 rue du Temple, 4th (01.42.77. 50.32/www.ilovemyblender.fr). M° Rambuteau.* **Open** 10am-7.30pm Tue-Sun. **Map** p102 A3 ❹❽
Anglo literature is the theme of this off-beat bookshop. Original editions sit opposite their French translations, and range from best-selling American novels to more obscure Indian and South African works. Why the strange name? Because, on top of the books, owner Christophe Persouyre sells a mix of his favourite things: cool mugs, tea, funky stationery, candles, incense and children's games.

Julien, Caviste

50 rue Charlot, 3rd (01.42.72.00.94). M° Filles du Calvaire. **Open** 9am-1.30pm, 3.30-7.30pm Tue-Sat; 10.30am-1.30pm Sun. Closed 3rd wk Aug. **Map** p102 B2 ❹❾
Julien promotes the small producers he has discovered, and often holds wine tastings on Saturdays.

Librairie Flammarion

Centre Pompidou, 19 rue Beaubourg, 4th (01.44.78.43.22/www.flammarion centre.com). M° Rambuteau. **Open** 11am-10pm Mon, Wed-Sun. Closed 2wks Sept. **Map** p102 A2 ⑤⓪

A pleasant place in which to peruse first-rate art, design, photography and cinema titles, this shop also stocks children's books and arty magazines.

Moisan

5 pl d'Aligre, 12th (01.43.45.46.60). M° Ledru-Rollin. **Open** 7am-8pm Tue-Sat; 7am-2pm Sun. No credit cards. **Map** p103 E5 ⑤①

Moisan's organic bread, *viennoiseries* and rustic tarts are outstanding. At this branch, by the market, there's always a queue snaking out the door.

Nodus

22 rue Vieille-du-Temple, 4th (01.42. 77.07.96/www.nodus-boutique.fr). M° Hôtel de Ville or St-Paul. **Open** 10.45am-2pm, 3-7.30pm Mon-Sat; 1-7.30pm Sun. **Map** p102 B3 ⑤②

Under the wooden beams of this men's shirt specialist are neat rows of striped, checked and plain dress shirts, stylish silk ties with subtle graphic designs, and silver-plated crystal cufflinks.

Paris-Musées

29bis rue des Francs-Bourgeois, 4th (01.42.74.13.02). M° St-Paul. **Open** 2-7pm Mon; 11am-1pm, 2-7pm Tue-Fri; 11am-7pm Sat; noon-7.30pm Sun. **Map** p102 B3 ⑤③

Run by the museum federation, this shop sells lamps and ceramics from local museums.

Rag

83-85 rue St-Martin, 4th (01.48.87. 34.64). M° Rambuteau. **Open** 10am-8pm Mon-Sat; noon-8pm Sun. No credit cards. **Map** p102 A3 ⑤④

One half of Rag focuses on pilots' navy jumpers and 1970s shirts at €15, colourful puffer jackets and '70s heels; the other may yield a vintage Hermès scarf or Gucci accessory.

Red Wheelbarrow

22 rue St-Paul, 4th (01.48.04.75.08/ www.theredwheelbarrow.com). M° St Paul. **Open** 10am-6pm Mon; 10am-7pm Tue-Sat; 2-6pm Sun. **Map** p102 B4 ⑤⑤

Canadian Penelope Fletcher Le Masson and American Abigail Altman run this friendly literary bookshop, which also has an excellent children's section.

Robopolis

NEW *107 bd Beaumarchais, 3rd (01.44.78.01.18/www.robopolis.com). M° Filles du Calvaire.* **Open** 11am-1pm, 2-7pm Tue-Sat. **Map** p102 C2 ⑤⑥

See box p111.

Shine

15 rue de Poitou, 3rd (01.48.05.80.10). M° Filles du Calvaire. **Open** 11am-7.30pm Mon-Sat. **Map** p102 B2 ⑤⑦

For funky clothes, Vinci d'Helia has what you need: sexy T-shirts with unusual detailing, Luella's knits, and Earl Jeans trousers and jackets.

Le Village St-Paul

Rue St-Paul, rue Charlemagne & quai des Célestins, 4th. M° St-Paul. **Open** 10am-7pm Mon-Sat. No credit cards. **Map** p102 B4 ⑤⑧

This colony of antiques sellers, spread across small linking courtyards, is a source of retro furniture, kitchenware and wine gadgets.

Mixing it at the Métallos

Maison des Métallos

After serving over a century as a focal point for working-class activities, the Maison des Métallos has recently reopened as a cutting-edge cultural showcase for contemporary artists. The new-look venue offers up an ambitious multi-cultural programme of concerts, dance, film screenings, exhibitions, and popular debates.

The building first saw life as a musical instrument factory in 1881 and provided a headquarters for resistance movements during the Spanish Civil War, World War II and wars in Algeria and Vietnam. It was bought by City Hall in 2001, and for the building's most recent makeover architect Vincent Brossy has preserved the industrial charm of the original structure, while simultaneously injecting a dynamism and modernity that deftly reflect its new role.

Back in its industrial heyday, the Maison des Métallos served as a meeting point and social venue for metalworkers and their families, and this spirit of openness and exchange remains firmly intact thanks to the expansive, renovated entry hall, a luminous glass roof, and a large mezzanine (which houses a café). Brossy's design also creates transparency between the different performance and exhibition areas, while the main auditorium can easily be transformed to accommodate different shows.

Its programming reaches across cultures and generations – recent highlights have included Malian singer Mah Damba in concert with local musicians, a Chinese *Alice in Wonderland* for children, and two days of debate with philosopher and Résistant Edgar Morin. On the high-tech side, the Bruits de Fond series makes the most of the Métallos' formidable sound system for avant-garde electronic music concerts.

Many of the events are free and €13 is the maximum ticket price. Far from Left Bank ivory tower intellectualism, the Maison des Métallos really seems to be achieving its goals of cross-cultural fertilisation and social awareness in an accessible and enjoyable atmosphere.

Zadig & Voltaire

*42 rue des Francs-Bourgeois, 3rd (01.
44.54.00.60/www.zadig-et-voltaire.com).
Mº Hôtel de Ville or St-Paul.* **Open**
1.30-7.30pm Mon, Sun; 10.30am-7.30pm
Tue-Sat. **Map** p102 B3 ❻❾

Z&V's relaxed, urban collection is a
winner. Popular separates include
cotton tops, shirts and faded jeans; its
winter range of cashmere jumpers is
superb. The more upmarket Zadig &
Voltaire De Luxe is at 18 rue François
1er (01.40.70.97.89).

Nightlife

Les Bains Douches

*7 rue du Bourg-l'Abbé, 3rd
(01.48.87.01.80/www.lesbainsdouches.
net). Mº Etienne Marcel.* **Open**
midnight-6am Wed-Sun. **Admission**
€10-€20. **Map** p102 A2 ❻⓪

Once a global leader, Les Bains lost its
way in the 1990s, relying on its reputation to pull in tourists. This all changed
recently, and now local star DJs like
Busy P and international names such
as Erol Alkan grace its decks. It's also
home to 6am, one of the city's hottest
after-parties, which ends in time for
lunch. The clientele is increasingly, but
not yet exclusively, gay.

Le Bataclan

*50 bd Voltaire, 11th (01.43.14.00.30/
www.le-bataclan.com). Mº Oberkampf.*
Open times vary. No credit cards.
Map p103 D2 ❻❶

Established in 1864, this highly distinctive venue is still standing after the odd
facelift and remains discerning in its
booking of major rock, world, jazz and
hip hop acts.

Café de la Danse

*5 passage Louis-Phillipe, 11th (01.47.
00.57.59/www.chez.com/cafedela
danse). Mº Bastille.* **Open** times vary.
Closed July, Aug. No credit cards.
Map p103 D4 ❻❷

Pristine sound and a rarefied ideal of
pop and rock perfection typify this former dancehall. It's mostly seated, but
there's room to shake a tailfeather
down at the front.

Maison des Métallos

NEW *94 rue Jean-Pierre Timbaud,
11th (01.48.05.88.27/www.maisondes
metallos.org). Mº Parmentier or
Couronnes.* **Map** p103 E1 ❻❸

See box p112.

Nouveau Casino

*109 rue Oberkampf, 11th (01.43.
57.57.40/www.nouveaucasino.net).
Mº Parmentier or St-Maur.* **Open**
Concerts times vary. **Map** p103 E1 ❻❹

Loveable if rather commercial venue
run by the adjacent Café Charbon, with
great acoustics, gigs and club nights
featuring rock, dub and garage, plus
reasonable drinks prices.

Arts & leisure

Les Bains du Marais

*31-33 rue des Blancs-Manteaux,
4th(01.44.61.02.02/www.lesbains
dumarais.com). Mº St-Paul.* **Open**
Men 11am-11pm Thur; 10am-8pm
Fri. *Women* 11am-8pm Mon;
11am-11pm Tue; 10am-7pm Wed.
Mixed 7-11pm Wed; 10am-8pm
Sat; 11am-11pm Sun. Closed Aug.
Map p102 A3 ❻❺

This hammam and spa mixes the modern and traditional (lounging beds and
mint tea). Facials, waxing and essential oil massages (€60) are also available. The hammam is €30.

Opéra Bastille

*Pl de la Bastille, 12th (08.36.69.78.68/
www.operadeparis.fr). Mº Bastille.* **Box
office** (130 rue de Lyon, 12th) 10.30am-
6.30pm Mon-Sat. *By phone* 9am-6pm
Mon-Fri; 9am-1pm Sat. **Admission**
€5-€300. **Map** p103 D4 ❻❻

The modern building everyone (except
the skateboarders outside) loves to
hate: even the exterior of the house is
decaying, with netting protecting
passers-by from falling fascia tiles.
Director Gerard Mortier has introduced
cutting-edge dramatic values, but dis-
appointed those who enjoy spectacular
singing and lavish period costume.
Event highlights Carlos Alvarez plays
the title role in Verdi's *Macbeth* (4 Apr-
8 May 2009).

Cathédrale Notre-Dame de Paris p119

The Seine & Islands

➤ The Seine

The Seine is more than just a transport route and tourist attraction; it also splits the city in two, a division that is as much psychological as it is physical. The Right Bank is perceived as briskly mercantile, whereas the image remains of the Left Bank as chic and intellectual. The Seine is still used to transport building materials by barge, and as the wealth of boat tours attests, it's a must-see feature for any visitor.

In 1990, UNESCO added 12 kilometres (7.5 miles) of Paris riverbank to its World Heritage register. Parc Tino-Rossi was created on the Left Bank, where waterside tango became a regular event. Then the floating venues – Batofar and its ilk – became super-trendy; and in the last ten years, it's been one Seine-side cultural attraction after another. Stretches of riverside roads are closed on Sundays to give cyclists and rollerskaters free rein, port de Javel becomes an open-air dancehall in the summer, and there's the summer riverside jamboree of Paris-Plage, Mayor Delanoë's inspired attempt to bring a bit of the south of France to the city – sand, palm trees, loungers, beach huts and all.

Sights & museums

Vedettes du Pont-Neuf

Square du Vert-Galant, 1st (01.46.33.98.38/01.43.29.86.19/ www.vedettesdupontneuf.com). M° Pont Neuf. **Departs** *Mar-Oct* every 30-45mins 10.30am-10.30pm daily. *Nov-Feb* every 45mins

The Seine & Islands

Legend:

- **1** Sights & museums
- **1** Eating & drinking
- **1** Shopping
- **1** Nightlife
- **1** Arts & leisure

Map labels:

- Cathédrale Notre-Dame de Paris — **2**
- Église St-Louis-en-l'Île — **8**
- Conciergerie — **3**
- Sainte Chapelle — **6**
- ÎLE DE LA CITÉ
- ÎLE ST-LOUIS
- PONT NEUF
- LATIN QUARTER
- 300 m / 300 yds

© Copyright Time Out Group 2008

La Conciergerie

10.30am-10pm Mon-Thur; 10.30am-10.30pm Fri-Sun. **Admission** €11; free-€6 reductions. Map p117 B1 ❶

You can sit inside just a foot or two above water level or outside on the top deck – where you may get drenched by pranksters throwing water from bridges as you pass underneath.

The bridges

From the honey-coloured arches of the ancient Pont Neuf to the swooping lines of the Passerelle Simone-de-Beauvoir, the city's 37 bridges are among the most seductive reasons to visit the city, offering some of the best vistas of the cityscape.

Over the years the city's *ponts* have been bombed, bashed by buses, boats and barges, weather-beaten and even trampled to destruction: in 1634, the Pont St-Louis collapsed under the weight of a religious procession.

The 19th century saw a boom in bridge-building – 21 were built in all, including the city's first steel, iron and suspension bridges. Pont de la Concorde used up what was left of the Bastille after the storming of 1789; the romantic Pont des Arts was the capital's first solely pedestrian crossing (built in 1803 and rebuilt in the 1980s). The most glitteringly exuberant bridge is Pont Alexandre III, with its finely wrought lamps, garlanding and gilded embellishments. More stolidly practical is Pont de l'Alma, with its Zouave statue. This has long been a popular flood-level measure: when the statue's toes get wet, the state raises the flood alert and starts to close the quayside roads; when he's up to his ankles in Seine, it's no longer possible to navigate the river by boat. This offers some indication of how devastating the great 1910 flood must have been, when the plucky Zouave disappeared up to his neck – as did large areas of central Paris.

The city's newest crossing, the Passerelle Simone-de-Beauvoir, is a walkway linking the Bibliothèque Nationale to the Parc de Bercy in the 12th arrondissement.

Ile de la Cité

The Ile de la Cité is where Paris was born around 250 BC, when the Parisii, a tribe of Celtic Gauls, founded a settlement on this convenient bridging point of the Seine). Romans, Merovingians and Capetians followed, in what became a centre of political and religious power into the Middle Ages: royal authority at one end, around the Capetian palace; the Church at the other, by **Notre-Dame**.

Perhaps the most charming spot on the island is the western tip, where Pont Neuf spans the Seine. The bridge's arches are lined with grimacing faces, said to be modelled on some of the courtiers of Henri III. Down the steps is a leafy triangular garden, square du Vert-Galant. In the centre of the bridge is an equestrian statue of Henri IV; the original went up in 1635, was melted down to make cannons during the Revolution, and replaced in 1818.

Sights & museums

✪ Cathédrale Notre-Dame de Paris

Pl du Parvis-Notre-Dame, 4th (01.42. 34.56.10/www.cathedraledeparis.com). M° *Cité/RER St-Michel Notre-Dame.* **Open** 8am-6.45pm daily. *Towers* Apr-Sept 10am-6.45pm daily. Oct-Mar 10am-5.30pm daily. **Admission** free. *Towers* €7.10; free-€5.10 reductions. **Map** p117 C2 ❷

A masterpiece of Gothic architecture, Notre-Dame was commissioned in 1160 by Bishop Maurice de Sully, who wanted to rival the smart new abbey that had just gone up in St-Denis. Notre-Dame was constructed between 1163 and 1334, and the amount of time and money spent on it reflected the city's growing prestige. The cathedral was plundered during the French Revolution, and by the 19th century was looking pretty shabby.

Gothic revivalist Viollet-le-Duc restored Notre-Dame to her former glory in the mid 19th century, although work has been going on ever since, with the replacement and cleaning of damaged and eroded finials and sculptures. In 1430, Henry VI of England was crowned here; Napoleon made himself Emperor here in 1804; and in 1909, it hosted the beatification of Joan of Arc.

To properly appreciate the masonry, climb up the towers (only a limited number can ascend at one time). The route runs up the north tower and back down the south, and from the top you can see pretty much every monument in Paris.

La Conciergerie

2 bd du Palais, 1st (01.53.40.60.97). M° *Cité/RER St-Michel Notre-Dame.* **Open** *Mar-Oct* 9.30am-6pm daily. *Nov-Feb* 9am-5pm daily. **Admission** €6.50; free-€4.50 reductions. *With Sainte-Chapelle* €10; €8 reductions. **Map** p117 B1 ❸

Marie-Antoinette was imprisoned here during the Revolution, as were Danton and Robespierre before their executions. The Conciergerie looks every inch the forbidding medieval fortress, yet much of the pseudo-medieval façade was added in the 1850s. The visit takes you through the Salle des Gardes, the medieval kitchens with their four huge chimneys, and the Salle des Gens d'Armes, an impressive vaulted Gothic hall built between 1301 and 1315. After the royals moved to the Louvre, the fortress became a prison under the watch of the Concierge. The wealthy had private cells with their own furniture, which they paid for; others crowded together on beds of straw. In Marie-Antoinette's cell, the Chapelle des Girondins, are her crucifix, some portraits and a guillotine blade.

La Crypte Archéologique

Pl Jean-Paul II, 4th (01.55.42.50.10). M° *Cité/RER St-Michel Notre-Dame.* **Open** 10am-6pm Tue-Sun. **Admission** €3.30; free-€2.20 reductions. **Map** p117 C2 ❹

Hidden under the forecourt in front of the cathedral is a large void that reveals bits and pieces of Roman quaysides, ramparts and hypocausts, medieval cellars, shops and pavements, the foundations of the Eglise Ste-Geneviève-des-Ardens (the church where Geneviève's remains were stored during the Norman invasions), an 18th-century foundling hospital and a 19th-century sewer, all excavated since the 1960s.

Mémorial des Martyrs de la Déportation

Sq de l'Ile de France, 4th (01.46.33.87.56). M° Cité/RER Châtelet or St-Michel Notre-Dame. **Open** *Winter* 10am-noon, 2-5pm daily. *Summer* 10am-noon, 2-7pm daily. **Admission** free. **Map** p117 C2 ❺

This sober tribute to the 200,000 Jews, Communists, homosexuals and *Résistants* deported to concentration camps from France in World War II stands on the eastern tip of the island. A blind staircase descends to river level, where simple chambers are lined with tiny lights and the walls are inscribed with verse. A barred window looks on to the Seine.

Sainte-Chapelle

6 bd du Palais, 1st (01.53.40.60.97). M° Cité/RER St-Michel Notre-Dame. **Open** *Mar-Oct* 9.30am-6pm daily. *Nov-Feb* 9am-4.30pm daily. **Admission** €7.50; free-€4.80 reductions. *With Conciergerie* €10; €8 reductions. **Map** p117 B2 ❻

Devout King Louis IX (St Louis, 1226-70) had a hobby of accumulating holy relics (and children: he fathered no fewer than 11 during his life). In the 1240s, he bought what was advertised as the Crown of Thorns, and ordered Pierre de Montreuil to design a suitable shrine. The result was the exquisite Flamboyant Gothic Sainte-Chapelle. With 15m (49ft) windows, the upper level appears to consist almost entirely of stained glass. The windows depict hundreds of scenes from the Old and New Testaments, culminating with the Apocalypse in the rose window.

Eating & drinking

Quai Quai

NEW *74 quai des Orfèvres, 1st (01.46.33.69.75). M° Pont Neuf.* **Open** noon-2.30pm, 7.30-11pm Tue-Sat. €. **Bistro**. **Map** p117 B1 ❼

The arrival in 2007 of this laidback bistro has brought a whiff of boho chic to Ile de la Cité. Two dining rooms, one opening on to place Dauphine, set the scene for fashionably old-fashioned fare – a salad of crunchy vegetables, classic egg mayonnaise, fresh cod with spinach: not dishes that are going to shake up Paris's culinary elite, but this is an agreeable destination in what is otherwise a foodie desert.

Ile St-Louis

The Ile St-Louis is one of the most exclusive residential addresses in the city. Delightfully unspoiled, it offers fine architecture, narrow streets and pretty views from the tree-lined quays, and still retains the air of a tranquil backwater, curiously removed from city life.

Rue St-Louis-en-l'Ile – lined with fine historic buildings that now house quirky gift shops and gourmet food stores (many open on Sunday), quaint tearooms, stone-walled bars, restaurants and hotels – runs the length of the island. A footbridge crosses from here to the Ile de la Cité.

Sights & museums

Eglise St-Louis-en-l'Ile

19bis rue St-Louis-en-l'Ile, 4th (01.46.34.11.60). M° Pont Marie. **Open** 9am-noon, 3-7pm Tue-Sun. **Map** p117 D3 ❽

The island's church was built between 1664 and 1765, following plans by Louis Le Vau and later completed by Gabriel Le Duc. The Baroque interior boasts Corinthian columns and a sunburst over the altar, and sometimes hosts classical music concerts.

Brasserie de l'Ile St-Louis

Eating & drinking

Brasserie de l'Ile St-Louis

55 quai de Bourbon, 4th (01.43.54.
02.59). M° Pont Marie. **Open** noon-
midnight Mon, Tue, Thur-Sun. Closed
Aug. **€**. **Brasserie**. **Map** p117 D2 ⑨
Happily, this old-fashioned brasserie
soldiers on while exotic juice bars and
fancy tea shops on the Ile St-Louis
come and go. The terrace has one of the
best summer views in Paris and is
invariably packed; the dining room
exudes shabby chic. Nicotined walls
make for an agreeably authentic Paris
mood, though nothing is gastronomi-
cally gripping: a well-dressed *frisée*
aux lardons, a slab of fairly ordinary
terrine, a greasy slice of *foie de veau*
prepared *à l'anglaise* with a rasher of
bacon, and a pan of warming tripes.

Mon Vieil Ami

69 rue St-Louis-en-l'Ile, 4th
(01.40.46.01.35). M° Pont Marie.
Open noon-2.30pm, 7-11.30pm Wed-
Sun. Closed 3wks Jan & 1st 3wks
Aug. **€**. **Bistro**. **Map** p117 D2 ⑩
Antoine Westermann has created a
true foodie destination here. He may be
one of Alsace's greatest chefs, but his
modernised bistro cooking draws on
all the regions of France. Typical of the
mains is a cast-iron casserole of roast
duck with caramelised turnips and
couscous, or an updated bouillabaisse
with red mullet fillets and artichoke.
Desserts revisit bistro favourites – rum
baba, chocolate tart or a light variation
on the *café liègeois* in a cocktail glass.

Shopping

Arche de Noé

70 rue St-Louis-en-l'Ile, 4th (01.46.34.
61.60). M° Pont Marie. **Open** 10.30am-
7pm daily. **Map** p117 D2 ⑪
'Noah's Ark' is a great place for
Christmas shopping, with traditional
wooden toys from eastern Europe,
games, jigsaws and finger puppets.

L'Occitane

55 rue St-Louis-en-l'Ile, 4th (01.40.46.
81.71/www.loccitane.com). M° Pont
Marie. **Open** 11am-7pm Mon; 10am-
7pm Tue; 10am-7.30pm Wed-Fri; 10am-
8pm Sat, Sun. **Map** p117 D2 ⑫
The many branches of this popular
provençal chain offer natural beauty
products in neat packaging. Soap rules,
along with essential oils and perfumes.

PARIS BY AREA

Les Invalides p124

The 7th & Western Paris

Townhouses spread west from St-Germain into the buttoned-up 7th arrondissement, with streetlife and café culture giving way to tranquil residential blocks and government offices. The 7th divides into the intimate Faubourg St-Germain, with its historic mansions and fine shops, and **Les Invalides**, with its wide windswept avenues. South-west of Les Invalides is the massive Ecole Militaire, the military academy built by Louis XV to educate the children of penniless officers. It's still used by the army and closed to the public.

From the north-western side of the Ecole Militaire begins the vast Champ de Mars, a market garden converted into a military drilling ground in the 18th century. It has long been home to the most celebrated Paris monument of all, the **Eiffel Tower**.

Sights & museums

Les Egouts de Paris

Opposite 93 quai d'Orsay, by Pont de l'Alma, 7th (01.53.68.27.81). M° Alma Marceau/RER Pont de l'Alma. **Open** 11am-4pm (until 5pm May-Sept) Wed-Sat. Closed 3wks Jan. **Admission** €3.80; free-€3.05 reductions. No credit cards. **Map** p123 B1 ❶

For centuries, the main source of drinking water in Paris was the Seine, which was also the main sewer. Construction of an underground sewerage system began at the time of Napoleon. Today, the Egouts de Paris constitute a smelly

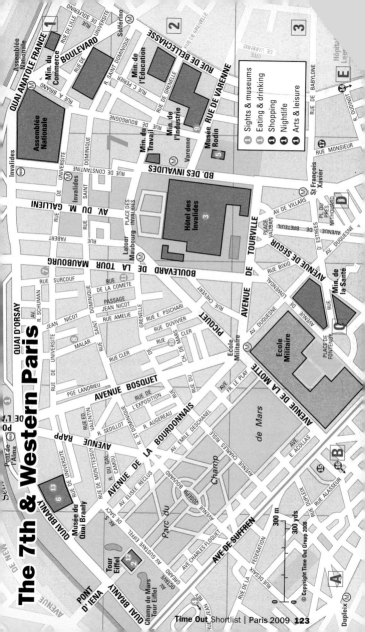

The 7th & Western Paris

...eum; each sewer in the 2,100km (1,305-mile) system is marked with a replica of the street sign above.

🖊 Eiffel Tower

Champ de Mars, 7th (01.44.11.23.45/ recorded information 01.44.11.23.23/ www.tour-eiffel.fr). M° Bir-Hakeim/ RER Champ de Mars Tour Eiffel. **Open** *15 June-9 Sept* 9am-12.45am daily. *10 Sept-14 June* 9.30am-11.45pm daily. **Admission** *By stairs* (1st & 2nd levels, 9am-12.30am) €4; €3.10 reductions. *By lift* (1st level) €4.50; €2.30 reductions; (2nd level) €7.80; €4.30 reductions; (3rd level) €11.50; free-€6.30 reductions. **Map** p123 A2 ❷
No building better symbolises Paris than the Tour Eiffel. The radical cast-iron tower was built for the 1889 World Fair and the centenary of the 1789 Revolution by engineer Gustave Eiffel. Construction took more than two years and used some 18,000 pieces of metal and 2,500,000 rivets. The 300m (984ft) tower stands on four massive concrete piles; it was the tallest structure in the world until overtaken by New York's Empire State Building in the 1930s. Vintage double-decker lifts ply their way up and down; you can walk as far as the second level. At the top (third level), there's Eiffel's cosy salon and a viewing platform with panels pointing out what to see in every direction. Views can reach over 65km (40 miles) on a good day. At night, for ten minutes on the hour, 20,000 flashbulbs attached to the tower provide a beautiful shimmering effect.

Les Invalides & Musée de l'Armée

Esplanade des Invalides, 7th (01.44. 42.40.69/www.invalides.org). M° La Tour-Maubourg or Les Invalides. **Open** *Apr-Sept* 10am-6pm daily. *Oct-Mar* 10am-5pm daily. Closed 1st Mon of mth. **Admission** *Musée de l'Armée & Eglise du Dôme* €7.50; free-€5.50 reductions. **Map** p123 D2 ❸
Its imposing gilded dome is misleading: the Hôtel des Invalides was (and in part still is) a hospital. Commissioned by Louis XIV for wounded soldiers, it once housed as many as 6,000 invalids. Behind lines of topiaried yews and cannons, the main (northern) façade has a relief of Louis XIV and the Sun King's sunburst. Wander through the main courtyard and you'll see grandiose two-storey arcades, sundials on three sides and a statue of Napoleon glaring out. The complex contains two churches: the Eglise St-Louis was for the soldiers, the Eglise du Dôme for the king. You'll find an opening behind the altar that connects the two. Since 1840, the Eglise du Dôme has been solely dedicated to the worship of Napoleon. Included in the entry price is the impressive Musée de l'Armée. See also box p125.

Maison de la Culture du Japon

101bis quai Branly, 15th (01.44.37. 95.00/www.mcjp.asso.fr). M° Bir-Hakeim/RER Champ de Mars Tour Eiffel. **Open** noon-7pm Tue, Wed, Fri, Sat; noon-8pm Thur. Closed Aug. **Admission** free. **Map** p123 A2 ❹

Eiffel Tower

De Gaulle on display

Musée de l'Armée

Where would the mighty Gaul be without the mighty de Gaulle (1890-1970)? Charles André Joseph Pierre-Marie de Gaulle's list of notable achievements are almost as long as his name: he headed the Resistance in World War II, granted women the right to vote in 1944, founded the Fifth Republic in 1958, gave independence back to Algeria in 1962 and contributed to French history in a way that few politicians could ever hope to achieve.

With such sparkling credentials but nowhere to show them off in, the **Musée de l'Armée** at the Hôtel des Invalides (see p124) and the Charles de Gaulle Foundation (www.charles-de-gaulle.org) got together to create L'Historial Charles de Gaulle – a state-of-the-art, audiovisual monument that deals with the whole of de Gaulle's life, particularly his role in World War II, the war in the Pacific and in Algeria.

Sunk several metres below the Invalides' Cour de Valeur wing, it is split into three sections: a 200-seater cinema showing a 25-minute film on de Gaulle (in five languages); a circular walkway of eight light, sound and video installations covering French history from the Belle Epoque to man's first walk on the moon; and a series of interactive alcoves that allow you to pick out as many snippets of de Gaulle's history as you can digest.

The building itself is also a feat of modern technology: it lies below the water table and is designed to withstand flooding from the Seine. Construction had to be carried out by hand so as not to endanger the Invalides' surrounding buildings, which were erected without foundations (although ironically, builders discovered a World War II bunker that had to be destroyed).

While there, use your ticket to see Napoleon's tomb inside the Dôme church (Libéral Bruand and Jules Hardouin-Mansart's golden-domed masterpiece); the Musée de l'Armée, which contains the third largest collection of armoury in the world; the Musée de l'Ordre de la Libération; and the Musée des Plans Reliefs.

Haute, haute cuisine

Jules Verne

You have to have courage to take on an icon like the Eiffel Tower, but superchef and entrepreneur Alain Ducasse has done just that in taking over the **Jules Verne** restaurant (p128), perched in its spectacular eyrie 123 metres above the city. He's transformed the cuisine and brought in his favourite designer, Patrick Jouin, also responsible for Alain Ducasse at the Dorchester and the Plaza Athénée and Mix in Las Vegas.

Jouin's strength is his combination of sophisticated comfort and respect for the setting, and here what at first sight is a low-key restyling is all cleverly thought out, leaving the view untouched to work its spell.

But it's the food that counts, in the hands of Ducasse protégé Pascal Féraud, who updates French classics, combining all the grand ingredients you'd expect with light modern textures and sauces. Try dishes like scallops with tiny florets of different coloured cauliflowers, roundels

of lobster and truffle on crunchy diced vegetables, lamb with artichokes, turbot with champagne zabaglione, and a fabulously airy ruby grapefruit soufflé.

It still feels pretty strange arriving here in smart clothes while everyone else mills around in shorts slurping ice creams, but the Eiffel Tower does at last have a restaurant to match up to the magic of the setting, while Lanvin-clad waiters, who achieve a seemingly effortless blend of casualness and being there just at the right time, ensure that this is a relaxed experience, not the serious, rather awesome affair grand dining can be. There aren't even too many references to the Eiffel Tower – although there is a dessert mysteriously called 'the chocolate tower bolt'.

Reserve well ahead (the waiting list is currently about two months) or ring at the last moment for a cancellation, and come for lunch if you want to make the most of the views.

Constructed in 1996, this glass-fronted Japanese cultural centre screens films and puts on exhibitions and plays. It also contains a library, an authentic Japanese tea pavilion on the roof, and a well-stocked book and gift shop.

Musée National Rodin

Hôtel Biron, 79 rue de Varenne, 7th (01.44.18.61.10/www.musee-rodin.fr). Mº Varenne. **Open** *Apr-Sept* 9.30am-5.45pm Tue-Sun (gardens until 6.45pm). *Oct-Mar* 9.30am-4.45pm (gardens until 5pm) Tue-Sun. **Admission** €6; free-€4 reductions. *Exhibitions* €7; €5 reductions. *Gardens* €1. **Map** p123 D2 ❺

The Rodin museum occupies the *hôtel particulier* where the sculptor lived in the final years of his life. The *Kiss*, the *Cathedral*, the *Walking Man*, portrait busts and early terracottas are exhibited indoors. Rodin's works are accompanied by pieces by his mistress and pupil, Camille Claudel. The walls are hung with paintings by Van Gogh, Monet, Renoir, Carrière and Rodin himself. The gardens are spotted with treasures: look out for the *Burghers of Calais*, the elaborate *Gates of Hell* and the *Thinker*.

Musée du Quai Branly

37-55 quai Branly, 7th (01.56.61.70. 00/www.quaibranly.fr). RER Pont de l'Alma. **Open** 11am-7pm Tue, Wed, Sun; 11am-9pm Thur-Sat. **Admission** €8.50; free-€6 reductions. **Map** p123 B1 ❻

This four-building collection of art and artefacts relating to non-European cultures opened in autumn 2006. An auditorium stages regular concerts – recent performances have included folk music from Rajasthan.

Event highlights Planète Métisse: to mix or not to mix (18 Mar 2008-19 July 2009).

Eating & drinking

Le 144 Petrossian

18 bd de La Tour-Maubourg, 7th (01.44.11.32.32/www.petrossian.fr). Mº La Tour Maubourg. **Open** noon-2.30pm, 7.30-10.30pm Tue-Sat. €€. **Russian**. **Map** p123 C1 ❼

Young Senegalese-French chef Rougui Dia directs the kitchen with intriguing results. You'll find Russian specialities such as blinis, salmon and caviar (at €39 an ounce) from the Petrossian boutique downstairs, but Dia has added preparations and spices from all over the world. You might start with a divine risotto made with carnaroli rice, codfish caviar and crisp parmesan. In a similar Med-meets-Russia vein is a main course of lamb 'cooked for 11 hours' on a raisin-filled blini.

L'Ami Jean

27 rue Malar, 7th (01.47.05.86.89). Mº Ecole Militaire. **Open** noon-2pm, 7pm-midnight Tue-Sat. Closed Aug. €. **Brasserie**. **Map** p123 C1 ❽

This Basque address has become a hit since the arrival of chef Stéphane Jégo. Excellent bread from Poujauran is a perfect nibble when slathered with a tangy *fromage blanc* – as are starters of sautéed baby squid on a bed of ratatouille; tender veal shank comes deboned with a side of baby onions and broad beans with tiny cubes of ham.

L'Arpège

84 rue de Varenne, 7th (01.45.51. 47.33/www.alain-passard.com). Mº Varenne. **Open** noon-2.30pm, 8-10.30pm Mon-Fri. €€€€. **Haute cuisine**. **Map** p123 E2 ❾

Assuming you can swallow the bill and forsake the normal full-dress drill of an haute cuisine meal, the chances are you'll have a spectacular time at chef Alain Passard's Left Bank establishment. His attempt to plane down the haute experience seems a bit of a misstep; but then something edible comes to the table, such as tiny smoked potatoes served with horseradish mousseline. A main course of sautéed free-range chicken with roasted shallot, an onion, potato *mousseline* and pan juices is the apotheosis of comfort food.

Le Café du Marché

38 rue Cler, 7th (01.47.05.51.27). Mº Ecole Militaire. **Open** 7am-midnight Mon-Sat; 7am-5pm Sun. **Café**. **Map** p123 C2 ❿

This well-loved address is frequented by trendy locals, shoppers hunting down a particular type of cheese and tourists who've managed to make it this far from the Eiffel Tower. Its *pichets* of decent house plonk go down a treat, and mention must be made of the food – such as the huge house salad featuring lashings of foie gras and parma ham.

Chez les Anges

54 bd de La Tour-Maubourg, 7th (01.47.05.89.86/www.chezlesanges. com). M° La Tour-Maubourg. **Open** noon-3pm, 7.30-11pm Mon-Fri. **€€**. **Brasserie**. Map p123 C2 ⑪

Jacques Lacipière of the bistro Au Bon Accueil is behind the revival of this restaurant, which was well known for its superb Burgundian cooking during the 1960s and '70s. You can order à la carte or pick the good-value 'Menu Surprise'. This takes a tapas-style approach, with each course arriving in sets of two or three tiny portions. These might include delicate creations such as cauliflower *bavarois* and little frogs' legs fritters.

Jules Verne

NEW *Pilier Sud, Eiffel Tower, 7th (01.45.55.61.44/www.lejulesverne-paris.com).* M° Bir-Hakeim or RER Tour Eiffel. **Open** 12.15-1.30pm, 7-9.30pm daily. **€€€€**. **Haute cuisine**. Map p123 A2 ⑫
See box p126.

Les Ombres

27 quai Branly, 7th (01.47.53.68.00). M° Alma-Marceau. **Open** noon-2.30pm, 7-10.30pm daily. **€€**. **Bistro**. Map p123 B1 ⑬

The full-on view of the glittering Eiffel Tower at night would be reason enough to come to this glass-and-iron restaurant on the top floor of the Musée du Quai Branly, but young chef Arnaud Busquet's food also demands that you sit up and take notice. The influence of Joël Robuchon – a mentor to Busquet's mentor – shows in dishes such as thin green asparagus curved into a nest with tiny lardons and

topped with a breaded poached egg, ribbons of parmesan and meat *jus*.

Shopping

Fromagerie Quatrehomme

62 rue de Sèvres, 7th (01.47.34.33.45). M° Duroc or Vaneau. **Open** 8.45am-1pm, 4-7.45pm Tue-Thur; 8.45am-7.45pm Fri, Sat. Map p123 E3 ⑭

Marie Quatrehomme runs this inviting *fromagerie*. Justly famous for her comté fruité, beaufort and squishy st-marcellin, she also sells specialities such as goat's cheese with pesto.

Marie-Anne Cantin

12 rue du Champ-de-Mars, 7th (01.45.50.43.94/www.cantin.fr). M° Ecole Militaire or Latour Maubourg. **Open** 8.30am-7.30pm Mon-Sat. Map p123 B3 ⑮

Cantin, a defender of unpasteurised cheese and supplier to many posh Paris restaurants, offers aged *chèvres* and amazing morbier, mont d'or and comté.

Village Suisse

38-78 av de Suffren or 54 av de La Motte-Picquet, 15th (www.village suisseparis.com). M° La Motte Picquet Grenelle. **Open** 10.30am-7pm Mon, Thur-Sun. Map p123 B3 ⑯

The mountains and waterfalls created for the Swiss Village at the 1900 Exposition Universelle are long gone, but the village lives on, rebuilt as blocks of flats. The street level has been colonised by some 150 boutiques offering antiques and collectibles.

Arts & leisure

La Pagode

57bis rue de Babylone, 7th (01.45.55.48.48). M° St-François-Xavier. **Admission** €8; €6.50 Mon, Wed, students, under-21s. No credit cards. Map p123 D3 ⑰

This glorious edifice is not, as local legend might have it, a block-by-block import, but instead is a 19th-century replica of a pagoda by a French architect. Renovated in the 1990s, this is one of the loveliest cinemas in the world.

Musée d'Orsay p133

St-Germain-des-Prés & Odéon

For years, the lore of Paris café society and intellectual life was amply fed by the tales that leaked out of St-Germain-des-Prés. Verlaine and Rimbaud drank here; later, Sartre, Camus and de Beauvoir all scribbled and squabbled, and musicians congregated around Boris Vian in the post-war jazz boom.

Earnest types still pose with weighty tomes, and the literati continue to assemble on café terraces – to give interviews. But with the local price hikes, the only writers living here these days are well-established ones.

In the 1990s, a merry band of intellectuals founded 'SOS St-Germain' to battle against the tide of commercialism sweeping through the area. The association's honorary president was Bohemian singer Juliette Gréco, who performed in the local clubs in the 1950s, when she was living in a poky hotel room on rue de Seine.

The campaigners' efforts have been largely in vain: St-Germain almost rivals avenue Montaigne for designer boutiques. Armani, Louis Vuitton, Dior, Cartier and Céline have all set up shop here, and Karl Lagerfeld opened his photography gallery on rue de Seine. The old jazz clubs and musicians, meanwhile, have mostly moved away.

City life is sweet

The annual Fête du Miel.

The **Jardin du Luxembourg** (p132) is one of Paris's most popular parks and a great place to escape the urban chaos for a couple of hours, but its charms stretch well beyond the manicured flower beds and perfectly maintained grass.

One of the most offbeat features is the oldest city beehive in France and the several thousand bees that call it home. The Jardin's resident bees benefit from a huge variety of flora and fauna. Pollen from some 6,000 flower beds and 3,400 trees, including acacia, chestnut, exotic Japanese pagoda trees, roses and lavender, is packed into a modest 23 hectares.

A beekeeping school is reserved for the serious study of apiculture, and the hives, which date back to 1856, are for use by students. But those in search of a honey fix and sugar rush can seek out the Jardin du Luxembourg's annual Fête du Miel during the last weekend in September, a harvest festival for honey gathered in spring and summer, which attracts everyone from the connoisseur to the curious to taste the honey and tour the hives.

And it's no low-grade offering, either. According to experts, the combination of warm inner-city temperatures, the limited use of pesticides and the ample variety of pollen means that these city bees produce vintage honey in high doses.

Ecole Nationale Supérieure des Beaux-Arts (Ensb-a)

14 rue Bonaparte, 6th (01.47.03. 50.00/www.ensba.fr). Mº St-Germain-des-Prés. **Open** *Courtyard* 9am-5pm Mon-Fri. *Exhibitions* 1-5pm Tue-Sun. **Admission** €4; €2 reductions. *Exhibitions* prices vary. **Map** p131 C1 ❶

The city's most prestigious fine arts school resides in what remains of the 17th-century Couvent des Petits-Augustins, the 18th-century Hôtel de Chimay, some 19th-century additions and some chunks of assorted French châteaux that were moved here after the Revolution (when the buildings briefly served as a museum of French monuments, before becoming the art school in 1816). Exhibitions are often held here; the entrance is situated on quai Malaquais.

Eglise St-Germain-des-Prés

3 pl St-Germain-des-Prés, 6th (01.55.42.81.33/www.eglise-sgp.org). Mº St-Germain-des-Prés. **Open** 8am-7.45pm Mon-Sat; 9am-8pm Sun. **Map** p131 C2 ❷

The oldest church in Paris. Childebert, son of Clovis, had a basilica and monastery built here around 543. It was first dedicated to St Vincent, and came to be known as St-Germain-le-Doré ('the gilded') because of its copper roof, then later as St-Germain-des-Prés ('of the fields'). Most of the present structure dates from the 12th century. Tombs include those of Jean-Casimir, the deposed King of Poland who became Abbot of St-Germain in 1669. Under the window in the second chapel is the funeral stone of philosopher/mathematician René Descartes; his ashes have been here since 1819.

Eglise St-Sulpice

Pl St-Sulpice, 6th (01.42.34.59.98/ www.paroisse-saint-sulpice.org). Mº St-Sulpice. **Open** 7.30am-7.30pm daily. **Map** p131 C3 ❸

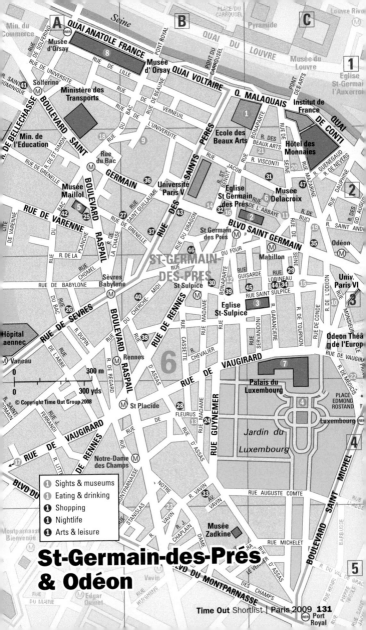

St-Germain-des-Prés & Odéon

It took 120 years (starting in 1646) and six architects to finish the church of St-Sulpice. The grandiose façade was designed by Jean-Baptiste Servandoni. He died in 1766 before the second tower was finished, leaving one tower a good five metres (16 feet) shorter than the other. The trio of murals by Delacroix in the first chapel – *Jacob's Fight with the Angel, Heliodorus Chased from the Temple* and *St Michael Killing the Dragon* – create a sombre atmosphere.

Jardin & Palais du Luxembourg

Pl Auguste-Comte, pl Edmond-Rostand or rue de Vaugirard, 6th (01.42.34. 23.89/www.senat.fr/visite). M° Odéon/ RER Luxembourg. **Open** *Jardin* summer 7.30am-dusk daily; winter 8am-dusk daily. **Map** p131 C4 ④

The palace was built in the 1620s for Marie de Médicis, widow of Henri IV. Reworked by Chalgrin in the 18th century, the palace now houses the French parliament's upper house, the Sénat.

The gardens, though, are the real draw: part formal, part 'English garden', they are the quintessential Paris park. The place is crowded with sculptures: a looming Cyclops, queens of France, a miniature Statue of Liberty, wild animals, busts of literary giants Flaubert and Baudelaire, and a monument to Delacroix. There are orchards and an apiary too. The park attracts a mixture of *flâneurs* and *dragueurs*, chess players and martial-arts practitioners, as well as children on ponies, in sandpits, on roundabouts and playing with sailing boats on the pond. See also box p130.

Musée Maillol

59-61 rue de Grenelle, 7th (01.42.22. 59.58/www.museemaillol.com). M° Rue du Bac. **Open** 11am-6pm (last admission 5.15pm) Mon, Wed-Sun. **Admission** €8; free-€6 reductions. **Map** p131 A2 ⑤

Dina Vierny was 15 when she met Aristide Maillol (1861-1944) and became his principal model for the next decade, idealised in such sculptures as *Spring, Air and Harmony*. In 1995, she opened this delightful museum, exhibiting Maillol's drawings, engravings, pastels, tapestry panels, ceramics and early Nabis-related paintings, as well as the sculptures and terracottas that epitomise his calm, modern classicism. There are also works by Picasso,

Boucherie Roulière p135

Rodin, Gauguin, Degas and Cézanne, a whole room of Matisse drawings, rare Surrealist documents and works by naïve artists.

Musée National Delacroix

6 pl de Furstemberg, 6th (01.44.41. 86.50/www.musee-delacroix.fr). M° St-Germain-des-Prés. **Open** 9.30am-4.30pm Mon, Wed-Sun. **Admission** €5; free reductions. **Map** p131 C2 ⑥
Romantic painter Eugène Delacroix moved to this apartment and studio in 1857 in order to be near the Eglise St-Sulpice, where he was painting murals. The Louvre and the Musée d'Orsay house his major canvas works, but this collection includes small oil paintings (among them *Madeleine au Désert*), free pastel studies of skies, sketches and lithographs, as well as his palette. Exhibits include correspondence between Baudelaire and George Sand.

Musée National du Luxembourg

19 rue de Vaugirard, 6th (01.42.34. 25.95/www.museeduluxembourg.fr). M° Cluny La Sorbonne or Odéon/RER Luxembourg. **Open** 10.30am-10pm

Mon, Fri, Sat; 10.30am-7pm Tue-Thur; 9am-7pm Sun. **Admission** €11; free-€9 reductions. **Map** p131 C3 ⑦
When it opened in 1750, this small museum was the first public gallery in France. Its current stewardship by the national museums and the French Senate has brought some imaginative touches and impressive coups. Book ahead to avoid queues.

► Musée d'Orsay

1 rue de la Légion-d'Honneur, 7th (01.40.49.48.14/recorded information 01.45.49.11.11/www.musee-orsay.fr). M° Solférino/RER Musée d'Orsay. **Open** 9.30am-6pm Tue, Wed, Fri-Sun; 9.30am-9.45pm Thur. **Admission** €7.50; free-€5.50 reductions. **Map** p131 A1 ⑧
The building was originally a train station, designed by Victor Laloux to coincide with the Exposition Universelle in 1900. Now it's a huge museum spanning the fertile art period between 1848 and 1914. It follows a chronological route, from the ground floor to the upper level and then to the mezzanine, showing links between Impressionist painters and their forerunners: here you'll find a profusion of paintings by Delacroix, Corot, Manet, Renoir,

Star in the making

Chef Philippe Belissent on life at Le Restaurant.

It's several hours before dinner in the boudoir-style **Le Restaurant at L'Hôtel** (p137, Oscar Wilde's last residence), but young chef Philippe Belissent is already busy preparing for the evening ahead. 'It's important for me that everything is ready before the first clients arrive because you only get one chance to impress a guest,' says the jovial 30-year-old, who has even more reason to smile since he was awarded his first Michelin star in March 2008, after just two years as head chef at Le Restaurant.

'When a restaurant gains a Michelin star, it is not unusual for business to improve by 30 per cent. When it loses one, business can drop by 50 per cent – that's a huge difference. Customers consider Michelin stars to be a guarantee of excellence. As a chef, I always dreamed of being awarded one, and now that I have, I feel my team and I have finally become guardians of that excellence.'

Belissent knows what he's talking about. Before Le Restaurant, he worked at Joël Robuchon's former restaurant, Laurent, and Pavillon LeDoyen – both Michelin-starred. This is where he says he learned many of the techniques required in the kitchen. 'I enjoy the rigours in maintaining consistently fine cuisine. At Le Restaurant, I've been able to put into action all I learned before. I'd describe my cuisine as classically French with a twist of modernity. The classical element comes from my training, and the twist is my own touch.

'There are two main schools of thought: those who defend adventurous, modern cuisine and those who revive and rework the classics. Both schools have their place in France today. I, for one, am very happy to play around with the classics, and I would be even happier if this meant we could keep our Michelin star and perhaps one day be awarded another one.'

Pissarro, Gauguin, Monet, Caillebotte, Cézanne, Van Gogh, Toulouse-Lautrec and many others.

A central sculpture aisle takes in monuments and maidens by Rude, Barrye and Carrier-Belleuse, but the outstanding pieces are by Carpeaux. The sculpture terraces include busts by Rodin, heads by Rosso and bronzes by Bourdelle and Maillol.

Eating & drinking

L'Atelier de Joël Robuchon

5 rue de Montalembert, 7th (01.42.22.56.56/www.robuchon.com). Mº Rue du Bac. **Open** 11.30am-3.30pm, 6.30pm-midnight daily. €€. **International**. Map p131 B2 ⑨

This is star chef Joël Robuchon's Paris take on a New York coffee-shop-cum-sushi-and-tapas-bar. The lacquer interior and two U-shaped bars are the epitome of sassy Left Bank chic. The menu is split into three different *formules*: start with caviar, Spanish ham, a large seasonal salad or maybe an assortment of little tasting plates. Then go classic (a steak), fanciful (*vitello tonnato*, veal in tuna and anchovy sauce) or lush (sublime cannelloni of roast Bresse chicken, stuffed with foie gras and served with wild mushrooms). Desserts are less inspired.

Le Bar Dix

10 rue de l'Odéon, 6th (01.43.26.66.83). Mº Odéon. **Open** 6pm-2am daily. No credit cards. **Bar**. Map p131 C3 ⑩

It's been here for ever, this homely cavern of a bar. Generations of students have glugged back jugs of the home-made sangria while squeezed into the cramped upper bar, tattily authentic with its Jacques Brel record sleeves, Yves Montand handbills and pre-war light fittings. Spelunkers negotiate the hazardous stone staircase to drink in the cellar bar.

Le Bar du Marché

75 rue de Seine, 6th (01.43.26.55.15). Mº Mabillon or Odéon. **Open** 8am-2am daily. **Bar**. Map p131 C2 ⑪

The market in question is the Cours des Halles, the bar a convivial corner café opening out on to a pleasing bustle of St-Germain-des-Prés. It's all wonderfully simple, with easy dishes like a ham omelette or a plate of herring in the €7 range, half-decent Brouilly or muscadet at €4-€5 a glass, a few retro posters – Campari, Piaf, the Frères Jacques – and the regular passing of a beret-topped waiter. It couldn't be anywhere else in the world.

Boucherie Roulière

24 rue des Canettes, 6th (01.43.26. 25.70). Mº St-Sulpice, Mabillon or St-Germain-des-Prés. **Open** noon-2.30pm, 7-11.30pm Tue-Thur, Sun; noon-2.30pm, 7pm-midnight Fri, Sat. €€. **Bistro**. Map p131 B3 ⑫

This is not somewhere to take your vegetarian friends – Boucherie Roulière glorifies the art of meat preparation. The blackboard menu offers a simple collection of grilled meat and fish. Main courses include a perfectly grilled *rognon de veau* (veal kidney) with a separate pot of sauce and some seriously good mash. Thick tuna steak is pink and moist. Desserts and the single house cheese keep up the standard.

Bread & Roses

7 rue de Fleurus, 6th (01.42.22.06.06). Mº St-Placide. **Open** 8am-8pm Mon-Sat. Closed Aug & 1wk Dec. €€. **Café**. Map p131 B4 ⑬

Come for a morning croissant and you might find yourself staying on for lunch, so tempting are the wares at this Anglo-influenced *boulangerie/épicerie/café*. Giant wedges of cheesecake sit alongside French pastries, while huge puff-pastry tarts are perched on the counter. Prices reflect the quality of the often organic ingredients, but that doesn't seem to deter any of the moneyed locals.

Café de Flore

172 bd St-Germain, 6th (01.45.48. 55.26/www.cafe-de-flore.com). Mº St-Germain-des-Prés. **Open** 7.30am-1.30am daily. €€. **Café**. Map p131 B2 ⑭

Le Rostand

Bourgeois locals crowd the terrace at lunch, eating club sandwiches with knives and forks, as anxious waiters frown at couples with pushchairs or single diners occupying tables for four. This historic café, former HQ of the Lost Generation intelligentsia, attracts tourists, and, yes, celebs have been known to alight here from time to time. But a *café crème* is €4.60, a Perrier €5 and the omelettes and *croques monsieur* are best passed over for better dishes on the menu (€15-€25).

Le Comptoir

Hôtel Le Relais Saint-Germain, 9 carrefour de l'Odéon, 6th (01.44.27. 07.50). M° Odéon. **Open** noon-6pm, 8.30-midnight (last orders 9pm) Mon-Fri; noon-11pm Sat, Sun. Closed 3wks Aug. €. **Brasserie**. **Map** p131 C3 ⑮
Yves Camdeborde runs the bijou 17th-century Hôtel Le Relais Saint-Germain, whose art deco dining room, modestly dubbed Le Comptoir, serves brasserie fare from noon to 6pm and on weekend nights, and a five-course *prix fixe* feast on weekday evenings. You might find dishes like an iced cream of chicken soup spiked with *vin jaune du Jura* and dotted with chanterelle mushrooms, or rolled saddle of lamb with vegetable-stuffed 'Basque ravioli'. The prix fixe dinner is booked up months in advance.

Les Deux Magots

6 pl St-Germain-des-Prés, 6th (01.45. 48.55.25/www.lesdeuxmagots.com). M° St-Germain-des-Prés. **Open** 7.30am-1am daily. Closed 1wk Jan. €€. **Café**. **Map** p131 B2 ⑯
A former haunt of Sartre, de Beauvoir et al now draws a less pensive crowd that can be all too '*m'as-tu vu?*', particularly on weekends. The hot chocolate is still good (and the only item served in generous portions) – but, like everything else, it's pricey. Visit on a weekday afternoon when the editors return, manuscripts in hand, to the inside tables, leaving enough elbow room to engage in serious discussion.

La Ferrandaise

8 rue de Vaugirard, 6th (01.43.26. 36.36). M° Odéon/RER Luxembourg. **Open** noon-2.30pm, 7-10.30pm Tue-Thur; noon-2.30pm, 7pm-midnight Fri; 7pm-midnight Sat. €€. **Bistro**. **Map** p131 A4 ⑰
This bistro with stone walls, a giant chandelier and portraits of cows on the walls has quickly established a

faithful clientele. A platter of excellent ham, sausage and terrine arrives as you study the blackboard menu, and the bread is crisp-crusted, thickly sliced sourdough. Almost every dish is a variation on standards: two specialities are the potato stuffed with escargots in a camembert sauce, and a wonderfully flavoured, slightly rosé slice of veal. Desserts might include chocolate with rum-soaked bananas.

Gaya Rive Gauche

44 rue du Bac, 7th (01.45.44.73.73).
M° Rue du Bac. **Open** 12.15-2.30pm,
7.15-11pm Mon-Sat; Closed Aug &
1wk Dec. €€€€. **Seafood**.
Map p131 A2 ⑱

Pierre Gagnaire, a chef known for his individuality, runs this Left Bank seafood restaurant, redecorating with a fish-scale wall and cloth-less white tables. Given Gagnaire's renown, it's a relief to see starters at around €20 and main courses at less than €50, even if the great man himself is not in the kitchen. Typical of his style is a seafood jelly with neatly arranged *coco de Paimpol* white beans and Spanish ham, followed by strips of wild sea bass simply sautéed and deglazed with manzanilla sherry.

Orestias

4 rue Grégoire de Tours, 6th (01.43.54.
62.01/www.orestias.com). M° Odéon.
Open noon-3pm, 8-11.30pm Mon-Sat.
€. **Greek**. **Map** p131 C2 ⑲

Opened in 1928, Orestias is one of the few good deals left in St-Germain. But more than this, it provides a night of banter second to none. As you enter waiter number one will try to seat you on the right. Resist, because waiter number two who handles the left hand side of the room is a comedian with an operatic voice and you will then witness the Punch and Judy stand-off that ensues. Copious Greek mezze are followed by enormous steaming knuckles of lamb, wild boar stew or steaks. It's amazing value, but you pay the price the next day as the wines are universally foul. But that's all part of the fun.

La Palette

43 rue de Seine, 6th (01.43.26.68.15).
M° Odéon. **Open** 9am-2am Mon-Sat.
Closed Aug. €. **Café**. **Map** p131 C2 ⑳

La Palette is the café-bar of choice for the very beau Beaux-Arts students who study at the venerable institution around the corner. Its prime location and majestic bar have attracted such luminaries as Jim Morrison, Picasso and Ernest Hemingway. The back room, decorated with art deco illustrations, is usually packed. Or you can get a Chablis for €6 or a *demi* at €4.50 and grab a spot on the leafy terrace – but be prepared for competition for seats.

Le Restaurant at L'Hôtel

NEW *13 rue des Beaux Arts, 6th*
(01.44.41.99.01/www.l-hotel.com).
M° St-Germain-des-Prés. **Open** 12-
2pm, 7-10pm Tue-Sat. €€€. **Haute**
cuisine. **Map** p131 C2 ㉑

See box p134.

Le Rostand

6 pl Edmond-Rostand, 6th (01.43.54.
61.58). RER Luxembourg. **Open** 8am-
2am daily. **Bar**. **Map** p131 C3 ㉒

Le Rostand has a truly wonderful view of the Jardin du Luxembourg from its classy interior, decked out with oriental paintings, a long mahogany bar and wall-length mirrors. It's a terribly well-behaved place – consider arriving draped in furs or sporting the latest designer eyewear if you want to fit in with the well-heeled clientele. Whiskies and cocktails are pricey, but not as steep as the brasserie menu.

Le Timbre

3 rue Ste-Beuve, 6th (01.45.49.10.40).
M° Vavin. **Open** noon-1.30pm, 7.30-
10.30pm Tue-Sat. Closed Aug & 1wk
Dec. €. **Bistro**. **Map** p131 B4 ㉓

Chris Wright's restaurant might be the size of a student garret, but this Mancunian aims high. Typical of his cooking is a spring-like plate of fresh green asparagus elegantly cut in half lengthwise and served with dabs of anise-spiked sauce and balsamic vinegar, and a little crumbled parmesan.

PARIS BY AREA

Main courses are also pure in presentation and flavour – a thick slab of pork, pan-fried but not the least bit dry, comes with petals of red onion.

Shopping

APC

4 rue de Fleurus, 7th (01.42.22.12.77/ www.apc.fr). M° St-Placide. **Open** 11am-7.30pm Mon-Sat. **Map** p131 B4 ㉔

The look here is simple but stylish; think perfectly cut basics in muted tones. Hip without being remotely try-hard, its jeans are a big hit with denim aficionados – the skinny version caused a stampede when they came out. Womenswear is at No.3.

L'Artisan Parfumeur

24 bd Raspail, 7th (01.42.22.23.32). M° Rue du Bac. **Open** 10.30am-7.30pm Mon-Sat. **Map** p131 A2 ㉕

Among scented candles, potpourri and charms, you'll find the best vanilla perfume Paris can offer – Mûres et Musc, a bestseller for two decades.

Le Bon Marché

24 rue de Sèvres, 7th (01.44.39.80.00/ www.bonmarche.fr). M° Sèvres Babylone. **Open** 9.30am-7pm Mon-Wed, Fri; 10am-9pm Thur; 9.30am-8pm Sat. **Map** p131 A3 ㉖

The city's oldest department store, opened in 1848, is also its most swish and user-friendly. Luxury boutiques, Dior and Chanel among them, take pride of place on the ground floor; escalators designed by Andrée Putman take you up to the fashion floor, which has an excellent selection of global designer labels, from Lanvin to APC. The adjoining Grande Epicerie food hall (01.44.39.81.00, 8.30am-9pm Mon-Sat) has a café and restaurant.

Bruno Frisoni

34 rue de Grenelle, 6th (01.42.84. 12.30/www.brunofrisoni.fr). M° Rue du Bac. **Open** 10.30am-7pm Tue-Sat. **Map** p131 B2 ㉗

Innovative Frisoni's shoes have a cinematic, pop edge: modern theatrics not for the conventional.

Christian Constant

37 rue d'Assas, 6th (01.53.63.15.15). M° Rennes or St-Placide. **Open** 8.30am-9pm Mon-Fri; 8.30am-8pm Sat, Sun. **Map** p131 B4 ㉘

A master chocolate-maker and *traiteur*, Constant scours the globe for ideas. His *ganaches* are subtly flavoured with verbena, jasmine or cardamom.

Gérard Mulot

76 rue de Seine, 6th (01.43.26.85.77). M° Odéon. **Open** 6.45am-8pm Mon, Tue, Thur-Sun. Closed Easter & Aug. **Map** p131 C3 ㉙

Mulot rustles up stunning pastries. A popular example is *mabillon*: caramel mousse with apricot marmalade.

Hervé Chapelier

1bis rue du Vieux-Colombier, 6th (01.44.07.06.50/www.hervechapelier.fr). M° St-Germain-des-Prés or St-Sulpice. **Open** 10.15am-7pm Mon-Sat. **Map** p131 B3 ㉚

Tops for chic, hard-wearing, bicoloured totes, from a dinky purse at €22 to a weekend bag at €130.

Huilerie Artisanale Leblanc

6 rue Jacob, 6th (01.46.34.61.55/ www.huile-leblanc.com). M° St-Germain-des-Prés. **Open** noon-7pm Tue-Fri; 10am-7pm Sat. Closed 2wks Aug. No credit cards. **Map** p131 C2 ㉛

The Leblancs started out making walnut oil from the family tree in Burgundy before branching out to press pure oils from hazelnuts, almonds, pine nuts, grilled peanuts, pistachios and olives.

La Hune

170 bd St-Germain, 6th (01.45.48. 35.85). M° St-Germain-des-Prés. **Open** 10am-11.45pm Mon-Sat; 11am-7.45pm Sun. **Map** p131 B2 ㉜

This Left Bank institution boasts a global selection of art and design books, and a magnificent collection of French literature and theory.

Jean-Paul Hévin

3 rue Vavin, 6th (01.43.54.09.85/ www.jphevin.com). M° Notre-Dame-des-Champs or Vavin. **Open** 10am-7pm Tue-Sat. Closed Aug. **Map** p131 B4 ㉝

La Hune

Jean-Paul Hévin fills his chocolates with potent cheeses, and loyal customers serve them with wine as an aperitif. Aphrodisiac chocolates are another favourite.

Marie Mercié

*23 rue St-Sulpice, 6th (01.43.26.45.83).
M° Odéon.* **Open** 11am-7pm Mon-Sat.
Map p131 C3 ❸❹
Mercié's creations make you wish you lived in an era when hats were de rigueur. Step out in one shaped like curved fingers (complete with shocking-pink nail varnish and pink diamond ring) or a beret like a face with red lips and turquoise eyes. Ready-to-wear starts at €30; *sur mesure* takes ten days.

Le Mouton à Cinq Pattes

*138 bd St-Germain, 6th (01.43.26.
49.25/www.mouton-a-cinq-pattes.info).
M° Odéon.* **Open** 10am-7pm Mon-Sat.
Map p131 C2 ❸❺
High-end labels including Chanel and Lagerfeld, and vintage in mint condition, can be sought out here, but you have to know what you're buying as this shop is strictly *dégriffé* (the labels are cut out).

Patrick Roger

*108 bd St-Germain, 6th (01.43.29.
38.42/www.patrickroger.com). M°
Odéon.* **Open** 10.30am-7.30pm
Tue-Sat. **Map** p131 B2 ❸❻
Sceaux-based Roger is shaking up the art of chocolate-making. While other *chocolatiers* aim for gloss, Roger may create a brushed effect on hens so realistic you almost expect them to lay eggs.

Paul & Joe

*64 rue des Sts-Pères, 7th (01.42.22.
47.01/www.paulandjoe.com). M° Rue
du Bac or St-Germain-des-Prés.* **Open**
10am-7pm Mon-Sat. **Map** p131 B2 ❸❼
Fashionistas have taken a shine to Sophie Albou's retro-styled creations. The latest collection dresses leggy young things and their intellectual paramours in what look like pristine 1960s couture pieces from the back of *maman*'s and *papa*'s wardrobe.

Peggy Huyn Kinh

*9-11 rue Coëtlogon, 6th (01.42.84.83.
83/www.phk.fr). M° St-Sulpice.* **Open**
10am-7pm Mon-Sat. **Map** p131 B3 ❸❽
Once creative director at Cartier, Peggy Huyn Kinh now makes bags of boar skin and python, plus silver jewellery.

PARIS BY AREA

Pierre Hermé

72 rue Bonaparte, 6th (01.43.54. 47.77). Mº Mabillon, St-Germain-des-Prés or St-Sulpice. **Open** 10am-7pm Tue-Fri, Sun; 10am-7.30pm Sat. Closed 1st 3wks Aug. **Map** p131 B3 **39**
Pastry superstar Hermé attracts connoisseurs from St-Germain and afar with his seasonal collections.

Poilâne

8 rue du Cherche-Midi, 6th (01.45.48. 42.59/www.poilane.com). Mº Sèvres Babylone or St-Sulpice. **Open** 7.15am-8.15pm Mon-Sat. **Map** p131 B3 **40**
Apollonia Poilâne runs the family shop, where locals queue for fresh country *miches*, flaky-crusted apple tarts and buttery shortbread biscuits.

Richart

258 bd St-Germain, 7th (01.45.55. 66.00/www.richart.com). Mº Solférino. **Open** 10am-7pm Mon-Sat. **Map** p131 A1 **41**
Each chocolate *ganache* has an intricate design, packages look like jewel boxes, and each purchase comes with a tract on how best to savour the stuff.

Ryst Dupeyron

79 rue du Bac, 7th (01.45.48.80.93/ www.dupeyron.com). Mº Rue du Bac. **Open** 12.30-7.30pm Mon; 10.30am-7.30pm Tue-Sat. Closed 2wks Aug. **Map** p131 A2 **42**
The Dupeyrons have been selling armagnac for four generations, and still have bottles from 1868. Treasures here include 200 fine Bordeaux wines and an extensive range of vintage port.

Sonia Rykiel

175 bd St-Germain, 6th (01.49.54. 60.60/www.soniarykiel.com). Mº St-Germain-des-Prés or Sèvres Babylone. **Open** 10.30am-7pm Mon-Sat. **Map** p131 B2 **43**
The queen of stripes produces skinny rib knitwear evoking the Left Bank babes of yore. Menswear is across the street, while two newer boutiques stock the younger, more affordable Sonia by Sonia Rykiel (59 rue des Sts-Pères, 6th, 01.49.54.61.00) and kids' togs (4 rue de Grenelle, 6th, 01.49.54.61.10). Also on

rue de Grenelle, on the site of Sonia's original 1966 shop, the Rykiel Woman store at No.6 (01.49.54.66.21) stocks a range of designer sex toys.

Vanessa Bruno

25 rue St-Sulpice, 6th (01.43.54.41.04/ www.vanessabruno.com). Mº Odéon. **Open** 10.30am-7.30pm Mon-Sat. **Map** p131 C3 **44**
Mercerised cotton tanks, flattering trousers and feminine tops have a Zen-like quality that stems from Bruno's stay in Japan, and they look good on any figure. She also makes great bags; the ample Lune was created to mark ten years in the business.

Yves Saint Laurent

6 pl St-Sulpice, 6th (01.43.29.43.00/ www.ysl.com). Mº St-Sulpice. **Open** 11am-7pm Mon; 10.30am-7pm Tue-Sat. **Map** p131 C3 **45**
Yves Saint Laurent retired in 2002 after a 40-year career that began at Dior and continued with the androgynous revolution he fomented in the 1960s under his own name. This is the main women's store; you'll find menswear at No.12 (01.43.26.84.40).

Nightlife

Le Sabot

6 rue du Sabot, 6th (01.42.22.21.56). Mº St-Germain-des-Prés or St-Sulpice. **Open** noon-3pm, 6pm-2am Mon-Sat. Concerts 9pm. **Admission** free (drink compulsory). **Map** p131 B2 **46**
Another tasty jazz-while-you-eat spot, where *gigotin d'agneau* and jam sessions are on the menu and the owner plays along with guests.

Wagg

62 rue Mazarine, 6th (01.55.42.22.00/ www.wagg.fr). Mº Odéon. **Open** 11.30pm-6am Fri, Sat; 3pm-midnight Sun. **Admission** €15 Fri, Sat; €10 Sun. **Map** p131 C2 **47**
Refurbished as part of the makeover of La Mezzanine upstairs, Wagg went through a period of attracting big name DJs, but has settled down to be home to a well-to-do Left Bank crowd.

Jardin des Plantes p144

The Latin Quarter & the 13th

The Latin Quarter

The section of the Left Bank east of boulevard St-Michel is said to have earned its name because the students here spoke Latin until the Revolution. Another theory is that the title alludes to the fact that this area was the heart of Roman Lutetia. Whatever the truth of the matter, the Latin Quarter is the site of the city's most important Roman remains: the Cluny baths, now part of the **Musée National du Moyen Age**, and the **Arènes de Lutèce** amphitheatre. The first two Roman streets were on the site of modern-day rue St-Jacques (later the pilgrims' route to Compostela) and rue Cujas. The forum was probably underneath what is now rue Soufflot. The area has been the university quarter since medieval times and, despite spiralling property prices, it still has a distinctly intellectual edge.

Sights & museums

Arènes de Lutèce

Rue Monge, rue de Navarre or rue des Arènes, 5th. M° Cardinal Lemoine or Place Monge. **Open** *Summer* 8am-10pm daily. *Winter* 8am-5.30pm daily. **Admission** free. **Map** p143 B4 ①
This Roman arena, where wild beasts and gladiators fought, could once seat 10,000 people. It was still visible during the reign of Philippe-Auguste in the 12th century, then disappeared under rubble. The site was rediscovered in

1869 and now incorporates a romantically planted garden. These days, it attracts skateboarders, footballers and boules players.

Eglise St-Etienne-du-Mont

Pl Ste-Geneviève, 5th (01.43.54. 11.79). M° Cardinal Lemoine/RER Luxembourg. **Open** 10am-7pm Tue-Sun. **Map** p143 B4 ②

Geneviève, patron saint of Paris, is credited with having miraculously saved the city from the ravages of Attila the Hun in 451, and her shrine has been a popular site of pilgrimage ever since. The present church was built in an amalgam of Gothic and Renaissance styles between 1492 and 1626, and the interior is wonderfully tall and light, with soaring columns and a classical balustrade. The stunning Renaissance rood screen, with its double spiral staircase and ornate stone strapwork, is the only surviving one in Paris, and was possibly designed by Philibert Delorme.

Eglise St-Séverin

3 rue des Prêtres-St-Séverin, 5th (01.42.34.93.50). M° Cluny La Sorbonne or St-Michel. **Open** 11am-7.30pm daily. **Map** p143 A3 ③

This lovely Flamboyant Gothic edifice was long the parish church of the Left Bank. It was rebuilt on various occasions to repair damage after ransacking by Normans and to meet the needs of the city's growing population. The church dates from the 15th century, though the doorway, carved with foliage, was added in 1837 from the demolished Eglise St-Pierre-aux-Boeufs on Ile de la Cité. The double ambulatory is famed for its forest of 'palm tree' vaulting, which meets at the end in a unique spiral column that inspired a series of paintings by Robert Delaunay. The bell tower, a survivor from one of the earlier churches on the site, has the oldest bell in Paris (1412). Next door, around the former cemetery, is the only remaining charnel house in Paris.

Eglise de Val-de-Grâce

Pl Alphonse-Laveran, 5th (01.40.51. 47.28). RER Luxembourg or Port-Royal. **Open** noon-6pm Tue, Wed, Sat, Sun. **Admission** €5; free-€2.50 reductions. No credit cards. **Map** p143 A5 ④

Anne of Austria, the wife of Louis XIII, vowed to erect 'a magnificent temple' if God blessed her with a son. She got two. The resulting church and surrounding Benedictine monastery – these days a military hospital and the Musée du Service de Santé des Armées – were built by François Mansart and Jacques Lemercier. This is the most luxuriously Baroque of the city's 17th-century domed churches. In contrast, the surrounding monastery offers the perfect example of François Mansart's classical restraint. Phone in advance if you're after a guided visit.

Grande Galerie de l'Evolution

36 rue Geoffroy-St-Hilaire, 2 rue Bouffon or pl Valhubert, 5th (01.40.79.54.79/56.01). M° Gare d'Austerlitz or Jussieu. **Open** *Grande Galerie* 10am-6pm Mon, Wed-Fri, Sun; 10am-8pm Sat. *Other galleries* 10am-5pm Mon, Wed-Fri; 10am-6pm Sat, Sun. **Admission** *Grande Galerie* €8; free-€7 4-18s. *Other galeries* (each) €6; free-€4 reductions. No credit cards. **Map** p143 C5 ⑤

One of the city's most child-friendly attractions. Located within the Jardin des Plantes, this 19th-century iron-framed, glass-roofed structure has been modernised with lifts, galleries and false floors, and filled with life-size models of tentacle-waving squids, open-mawed sharks, tigers hanging off elephants and monkeys swarming down from the ceiling. The centrepiece is a procession of African wildlife across the first floor that resembles the procession into Noah's Ark.

Institut du Monde Arabe

1 rue des Fossés-St-Bernard, 5th (01.40.51.38.38/www.imarabe.org). M° Jussieu. **Open** *Museum* 10am-6pm Tue-Sun. *Library* 1-8pm Tue-Sat. *Café* noon-

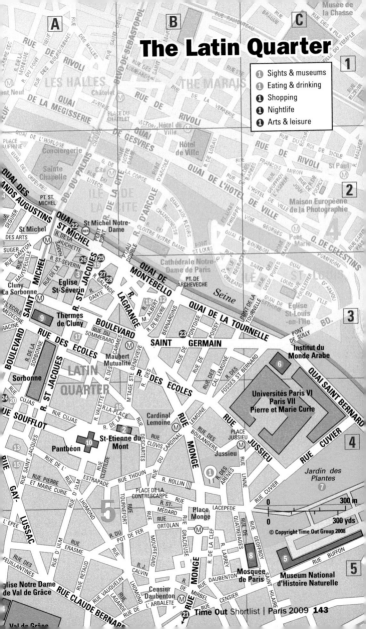

Le Panthéon

6pm Tue-Sun. *Tours* 3pm Tue-Fri; 3pm & 4.30pm Sat, Sun. **Admission** *Roof terrace, library* free. *Museum* €5; free-€4 reductions. *Exhibitions* varies. *Tours* €8. **Map** p143 C3 ⑥

A clever blend of high-tech and Arab influences, this Seine-side *grand projet* was constructed between 1980 and 1987 to a design by Jean Nouvel. Shuttered windows, inspired by the screens of Moorish palaces, act as camera apertures, contracting or expanding according to the amount of sunlight. A museum covering the history and archaeology of the Islamic Arab world occupies the upper floors: start at the seventh with Classical-era finds and work down via early Islamic dynasties to the present day. The views from the roof terrace (to which access is free) are fabulous.

Jardin des Plantes

36 rue Geoffroy-St-Hilaire, 2 rue Bouffon, pl Valhubert or 57 rue Cuvier, 5th. Mº Gare d'Austerlitz, Jussieu or Place Monge. **Open** *Main garden* Winter 8am-dusk daily. Summer 7.30am-8pm daily. *Alpine garden* Apr-Sept 8am-4.30pm Mon-Fri; 1-5pm Sat,

Sun. Closed Oct-Mar. *Ménagerie* Apr-Sept 9am-5pm daily. **Admission** *Alpine Garden* free Mon-Fri; €1 Sat, Sun. *Jardin des Plantes* free. *Ménagerie* €7; free-€5 reductions. **Map** p143 C4 ⑦

Although small and slightly dishevelled, the Paris botanical garden – which contains more than 10,000 species and includes tropical greenhouses and rose, winter and Alpine gardens – is enchanting. Ancient trees on view include a false acacia planted in 1636 and a cedar from 1734. A plaque on the old laboratory declares that this is where Henri Becquerel discovered radioactivity in 1896.

La Mosquée de Paris

2 pl du Puits-de-l'Ermite, 5th (01.45.35. 97.33/tearoom 01.43.31.38.20/baths 01.43.31.18.14/www.mosquee-de-paris.net). Mº Monge. **Open** *Tours* 9am-noon, 2-6pm Mon-Thur, Sat, Sun (closed Muslim hols). *Tearoom* 10am-11.30pm daily. *Restaurant* noon-2.30pm, 7.30-10.30pm daily. *Baths* (women) 10am-9pm Mon, Wed, Sat; 2-9pm Fri; (men) 2-9pm Tue, Sun. **Admission** €3; free-€2 reductions. *Tearoom* free. *Baths* €15-€35. **Map** p143 C5 ⑧

This vast Hispano-Moorish construct is the spiritual heart of France's Algerian-dominated Muslim population. Built from 1922 to 1926, the Paris mosque is dominated by a stunning green-and-white tiled square minaret. In plan and function it divides into three sections: religious (grand patio, prayer room and minaret, all for worshippers and not curious tourists); scholarly (Islamic school and library); and, via rue Geoffroy-St-Hilaire, commercial (café and domed hammam). La Mosquée café (open 9am-midnight daily) is delightful – a modest courtyard with tables shaded beneath green foliage and scented with the sweet smell of sheesha smoke.

Musée National du Moyen Age – Thermes de Cluny

6 pl Paul-Painlevé, 5th (01.53.73.78.00/ www.musee-moyenage.fr). M° Cluny La Sorbonne. **Open** 9.15am-5.45pm Mon, Wed-Sun. **Admission** €7.50; free-€5.50 reductions. **Map** p143 A3 ❾

The national museum of medieval art is best known for the beautiful, allegorical *Lady and the Unicorn* tapestry cycle, but it also has important collections of medieval sculpture and enamels. The building itself, commonly known as Cluny, is also a rare example of 15th-century secular Gothic architecture, with its foliate Gothic doorways, hexagonal staircase jutting out of the façade and vaulted chapel. It was built from 1485 to 1498 – on top of a Gallo-Roman baths complex. The baths, built in characteristic Roman bands of stone and brick masonry, are the finest Roman remains in Paris. The vaulted frigidarium (cold bath), tepidarium (warm bath), caldarium (hot bath) and part of the hypocaust heating system are all still visible. A themed garden fronts the whole complex.

Recent acquisitions include the illuminated manuscript *L'Ascension du Christ* from the Abbey of Cluny, dating back to the 12th century, and the 16th-century triptych *Assomption de la Vierge* by Adrien Isenbrant of Bruges.

Le Panthéon

Pl du Panthéon, 5th (01.44.32.18.00). M° Cardinal Lemoine/RER Luxembourg. **Open** 10am-6pm (until 6.30pm summer) daily. **Admission** €7.50; free-€4.50 reductions. **Map** p143 A4 ❿

Soufflot's neo-classical megastructure, with its huge dome, was the architectural *grand projet* of its day, commissioned by a grateful Louis XV to thank Sainte Geneviève for his recovery from illness. But by the time it was ready in 1790, a lot had changed; during the Revolution, the Panthéon was rededicated as a 'temple of reason' and the resting place of the nation's great men. The austere barrel-vaulted crypt now houses Voltaire, Rousseau, Hugo and Zola. New heroes are installed but rarely: Pierre and Marie Curie's remains were transferred here in 1995; André Malraux, writer, Resistance hero and de Gaulle's culture minister, arrived in 1996; Alexandre Dumas in 2002. Mount the steep spiral stairs to the colonnade encircling the dome for superb views.

Eating & drinking

Allard

41 rue St-André-des-Arts, 6th (01.43.26.48.23). M° Odéon. **Open** noon-2.30pm, 7-11.30pm Mon-Sat. Closed 3wks Aug. €€. **Bistro**. **Map** p143 A2 ⓫

This fine, traditional bistro has a pre-war feel, an impression confirmed by the kitchen, which sends out the sort of glorious Gallic grub you come to Paris for. Start with sliced Lyonnaise sausage studded with pistachios and served with potato salad in delicious vinaigrette, or maybe a sauté of wild mushrooms; then try roast Bresse chicken with sautéed ceps or roast duck with olives. Finish up with the *tarte fine de pommes*.

Atelier Maître Albert

1 rue Maître-Albert, 5th (01.56.81. 30.01/www.ateliermaitrealbert.com). M° St-Michel or Maubert Mutualité. **Open** noon-2.30pm, 6.30-11.30pm Mon-Wed; noon-2.30pm, 6.30pm-1am Thur,

Fri; 6.30pm-1am Sat; 6.30-11.30pm Sun.
€€. Brasserie. Map p143 B3 ⑫
This Guy Savoy outpost in the 5th has
slick decor by Jean-Michel Wilmotte.
The dining room with open kitchen
and rôtisseries on view is attractive but
very noisy at night – book a table in the
quieter bar area if you want to chat.
The short menu lets you have a Savoy
classic or two to start with, including
oysters in seawater *gelée*. Next up, perhaps, a chunk of tuna served with tiny
iron casseroles of dauphinois potatoes,
and cauliflower in béchamel sauce.

Le Crocodile

*6 rue Royer-Collard, 5th (01.43.54.
32.37). RER Luxembourg.* **Open**
10pm-late Mon-Sat. Closed Aug.
Bar. Map p143 A4 ⑬
Ignore the apparently boarded-up windows at Le Crocodile – if you're here
late, it's open. Young friendly regulars
line the sides of this small, narrow bar
and try to decide on a drink: not easy,
given the length and complexity of the
cocktail list. At last count there were
311 choices, each one more potent than
the last. Pen and paper are provided to
note your decision; the pen comes in
handy for point-and-choose decisions
when it all gets hazy.

Lapérouse

*51 quai des Grands-Augustins, 6th
(01.43.26.68.04). M° St-Michel.* **Open**
noon-2.30pm, 7.30-10pm Mon-Fri; 7.30-
10pm Sat. Closed 1wk Jan & Aug. **€€.**
Brasserie. Map p143 A2 ⑭
One of the most romantic spots in Paris,
Lapérouse was formerly a clandestine
rendezvous for French politicians and
their mistresses. Chef Alain Hacquard
does a modern take on classic French
cooking: his beef fillet is smoked for a
more complex flavour; a tender saddle
of rabbit is cooked in a clay crust,
flavoured with lavender and rosemary
and served with ravioli of onions.

Le Pantalon

*7 rue Royer-Collard, 5th (no phone).
RER Luxembourg.* **Open** 5.30pm-
2am Mon-Sat. No credit cards. **€.**
Café. Map p143 A4 ⑮

Le Pantalon is a local café that seems
familiar yet is utterly surreal. It has the
standard fixtures and fittings, including the old soaks at the bar – plus a
strange vacuum-cleaner sculpture,
disco-light toilets and the world's most
prosaic proposal of marriage. Offbeat
decor aside, the regulars and staff are
enough to tip the balance firmly into
eccentricity. Friendly and very funny
French grown-ups and foreign students chat in a mishmash of languages;
drinks are always cheap enough to
make you tipsy without the worry of a
cash-crisis hangover.

Le Piano Vache

*8 rue Laplace, 5th (01.46.33.75.03/
www.lepianovache.com). M° Maubert
Mutualité or Cardinal Lemoine.* **Open**
noon-2am Mon-Fri; 9pm-2am Sat, Sun.
Bar. Map p143 A4 ⑯
A Left Bank drinking haunt for many
a long decade, the Piano Vache has
all the hallmarks of what any beer-
stained, smoky hovel should be: dark,
cramped, filled with a hardcore
drinker/student clientele, walls covered
four times over with posters and inde-
terminate pub grime, and the hits of
alternative 1980s synth-pop on repeat
on the stereo.

Le Pré Verre

*8 rue Thénard, 5th (01.43.54.59.47).
M° Maubert Mutualité.* **Open** noon-
2pm, 7.30-10.30pm Tue-Sat. Closed
3wks Aug & 2wks Dec. **€€. Bistro.**
Map p143 A3 ⑰
Philippe Delacourcelle knows how to
handle spices like few other French
chefs, having lived in Asia for long
enough to master ingredients like cassia bark and tamarind. Salt cod with
cassia bark and smoked potato purée
is a classic: what the fish lacks in size
it makes up for in rich, cinnamon-like
flavour and crunchy texture, while
smooth potato cooked in a smoker
makes a startling accompaniment.

Le Reminet

*3 rue des Grands-Degrés, 5th (01.44.
07.04.24). M° Maubert Mutualité
or St-Michel.* **Open** noon-2.30pm,

7.30-1.30pm Tue, Thur-Sun. Closed 3wks Jan & 3wks Aug. **€**. **Bistro**. **Map** p143 B3 ⑬
This reliable, open-on-Sunday bistro recently changed hands. Although the cooking may lack a little of its former sparkle, some oysters and a melting camembert tart are both up to standard. A chunky steak, rare yet piping hot, comes with potato wedges fried in goose fat, and a moist chicken breast stuffed with wild mushrooms is served on top of a comforting *fricassée* of root vegetables. A creamy combination of berries, chocolate and pears makes the perfect autumn dessert.

Ribouldingue

10 rue St-Julien-le-Pauvre, 5th (01.46.33.98.80). M° St-Michel. **Open** noon-2pm, 7-11pm Mon-Sat. **€**. **Bistro**. **Map** p143 A3 ⑲
This bistro is the creation of Nadège Varigny, who spent ten years working with Yves Camdeborde before opening a restaurant inspired by the food of her childhood in Grenoble. It's full of people, including critics and chefs, who love simple, honest bistro fare, such as *daube de boeuf* (a winey beef stew with macaroni) or seared tuna on a bed of melting aubergine. If you have an appetite for offal, go for the gently sautéed brains with divine new potatoes. For dessert, try the fresh ewe's cheese with bitter honey.

Le Salon

NEW *Cinéma du Panthéon, 13 rue Victor-Cousin, 5th (01.56.24.88.80/ www.cinemadupantheon.fr). RER Luxembourg.* **Open** noon-7pm Mon-Fri. **€€**. **Café**. **Map** p143 A4 ⑳
The latest insider address in the Latin Quarter has quickly been colonised by film people, PR types and ladies who tea, which is hardly surprising when you discover that the eclectic array of old sofas, pouffes, tables and ceramic lamps were picked up at Les Puces by Catherine Deneuve herself. The setting for Deneuve's foray into interior decoration is a vast loft-like space hidden above Paris's oldest arthouse cinema. Food is ideal for a light lunch: soup, smoked salmon, salads.

Atelier Maître Albert p145

A river runs by it

The new Cité de la Mode et du Design.

Cité de la Mode et du Design

The **Cité de la Mode et du Design** (p152), a slinky, green fluorescent tidal wave surging down the Seine near the Gare d'Austerlitz, is the latest element in the huge ZAC Rive Gauche redevelopment of the Paris riverside. In fact it's a clever piece of industrial rehab by architects Dominique Jakob and Brendan Macfarlane. The duo, responsible for the silver globules of restaurant Georges at the Centre Pompidou, are transforming the Magasins Généraux, an early 20th-century concrete warehouse complex, more recently used as a carpet store and examination centre, into a dynamic new creative showcase.

Jakob and Macfarlane have kept the concrete frame and opened out the building's innards to create 'a convivial place ready to be appropriated by Parisians'. New staircases, walkways and spectacular viewpoints have been created thanks to the undulating green skin or 'plug over', a layer of green glass panels clipped on to a tubular steel frame over the existing building.

The architects hope visitors will explore the different levels and wander between interior and exterior in what is the only public building in Paris to open directly on to the river. You'll be able to promenade along the Seine, relax in the central piazza or sunbathe on the planted roof terrace, with its wooden decking, landscaping by Michel Desvignes and groovy illuminations.

However, for a building that has been advancing with great speed – construction only began in December 2006 – and has such high visibility, it's been surprisingly hard to find out what's actually going to be inside; even the name seems to fluctuate between Docks en Seine and the Cité de la Mode et du Design. The Institut Français de la Mode fashion and management school is definitely transferring here from the Champs-Elysées; beyond that we are promised cafés and restaurants, shops, exhibition spaces, riverside kiosks and a club operated by indie music label Naïve. Watch this space…

Shopping

Le Boulanger de Monge

*123 rue Monge, 5th (01.43.37.54.20/
www.leboulangerdemonge.com). M°
Censier Daubenton.* **Open** 7am-8.30pm
Tue-Sun. **Map** p143 B5 ㉑
Dominique Saibron uses spices to give
inimitable flavour to his organic sourdough *boule*. Every day, about 2,000
bread-lovers visit his wonderful boutique, which also produces one of the
city's best baguettes.

Bouquinistes

*Along the quais, especially quai de
Montebello & quai St-Michel, 5th. M°
St-Michel.* **Open** times vary from stall
to stall, generally Tue-Sun. No credit
cards. **Map** p143 A2 ㉒
The green, open-air boxes along the
quais are one of the city's oldest institutions. Most sell second-hand books
– ignore the nasty postcards and
instead have a rummage through
boxes packed with ancient paperbacks
for something suitably Existential.
Feel free to haggle.

Diptyque

*34 bd St-Germain, 5th (01.43.26.45.27/
www.diptyqueparis.com). M° Maubert
Mutualité.* **Open** 10am-7pm Mon-Sat.
Map p143 B3 ㉓
Don't miss Diptyque's divine scented
candles. They come in 48 different
varieties and are probably the best
you'll ever find.

Princesse Tam-Tam

*52 bd St-Michel, 6th (01.42.34.99.31/
www.princessetam-tam.com). M° Cluny
La Sorbonne.* **Open** 1.30-7pm Mon;
10am-7pm Tue-Sat. **Map** p143 A4 ㉔
This inexpensive underwear and
swimwear brand now features plenty
of traffic-stopping promotions. Bright
colours and sexily transparent and
sporty gear are in.

Shakespeare & Co

*37 rue de la Bûcherie, 5th (01.43.25.
40.93/www.shakespeareandcompany.
com). M° St Michel.* **Open** 10am-
11pm Mon-Sat; 11am-11pm Sun.
Map p143 A3 ㉕

Unequivocally the best bookshop in
Paris, the historic and ramshackle
Shakespeare & Co is always packed
with ex-pat and tourist book lovers.
Aside from knowledgeable permanent
staff there is a selection of bookish
travellers who live in the store's upper
rooms in exchange for working there.
There is a large second-hand section,
antiquarian books next door, and just
about anything you could ask for new.
The free Monday night readings
always provide interesting debate and
the shop hosts a big-name literary festival in June.

Nightlife

Caveau de la Huchette

*5 rue de la Huchette, 5th (01.43.26.
65.05/www.caveaudelahuchette.fr).
M° St-Michel.* **Open** 10.15pm-late daily.
Tickets €11-€13; €9 students.
Map p143 A2 ㉖
This medieval cellar has been a Left
Bank mainstay for some 60 years
now. The jazz shows are followed by
early-hours performances in a swing,
rock, soul or disco vein, and attract a
regular student following.

Caveau des Oubliettes

*52 rue Galande, 5th (01.46.34.23.09).
M° Maubert Mutualité or St-Michel/
RER St-Michel Notre-Dame.* **Open**
10pm-late daily. **Admission** free.
Map p143 A3 ㉗
A foot-tapping frenzy thrives in this
medieval dungeon, complete with
instruments of torture and underground
passages. There are jam sessions in the
week if you fancy contributing a note or
two to the merry-making.

Arts & leisure

Studio Galande

*42 rue Galande, 5th (01.43.54.72.71).
M° Cluny La Sorbonne or St-Michel.*
Admission €7.80; €6 Wed, students.
No credit cards. **Map** p143 A3 ㉘
Some 20 different films are screened in
subtitled versions at this venerable
Latin Quarter venue every week:
international arthouse fare, combined

with the occasional instalment from the *Matrix* series. On Fridays and Saturdays, fans of *The Rocky Horror Picture Show* turn up in drag, equipped with rice and water pistols.

The 13th

It's all happening in the 13th – particularly in the new ZAC Rive Gauche development zone. This is where you'll find the newest bridge in Paris, the Passerelle Simone-de-Beauvoir, and next to it a floating swimming pool and sundeck, both inaugurated in 2006. Coming next are the **Cité de la Mode et du Design** and a university complex that will eventually house 30,000 students and staff.

Sights & museums

Bibliothèque Nationale de France François Mitterrand

10 quai François-Mauriac, 13th (01.53.79.59.59/www.bnf.fr). M° Bibliothèque François Mitterrand. **Open** 2-7pm Mon; 9am-7pm Tue-Sat; 1-7pm Sun. **Admission** *1 day* €3.30. *2 weeks* €20. *1 year* €35; €18 reductions. **Map** p151 E2 ㉙
Opened in 1996, the new national library was the last and costliest of Mitterrand's *grands projets*, the first stage in the redevelopment of the 13th arrondissement. Its architect, Dominique Perrault, was criticised for his curiously staid design. The library houses over ten million volumes and can accommodate 3,000 readers. Much of the library is open to the public: books, newspapers and periodicals are accessible to anyone over 18, and you can browse through photographic, film and sound archives in the audiovisual section. There are regular classical music concerts and exhibitions too.

Chapelle St-Louis-de-la-Salpêtrière

47 bd de l'Hôpital, 13th (01.42.16.04.24). M° Gare d'Austerlitz. **Open** 8.30am-6pm Mon-Fri, Sun; 11am-6pm Sat. **Admission** free. **Map** p151 C2 ㉚
This austerely beautiful chapel, designed by Libéral Bruand and completed in 1677, features an octagonal dome in the centre and eight naves in which they used to separate the sick from the insane, the destitute from the debauched. Around the chapel sprawls the vast Hôpital de la Pitié-Salpêtrière, which became a centre for research into insanity in the 1790s, when renowned doctor Philippe Pinel began to treat some of the inmates as sick rather than criminal; Charcot later pioneered neuropsychology here. Salpêtrière is today one of the city's main teaching hospitals, but the chapel is also used for contemporary art installations.

Manufacture Nationale des Gobelins

42 av des Gobelins, 13th (tours 01.43.13.46.46). M° Les Gobelins. **Open** *Tours* 2pm, 3pm Tue-Thur. **Admission** €10; free-€6 reductions. No credit cards. **Map** p151 B2 ㉛
The royal tapestry factory was originally founded by Colbert when he set up the Manufacture Royale des Meubles de la Couronne in 1662; it's named after Jean Gobelin, a dyer who owned the site. Tapestries are still made here (mainly for French embassies), and visitors can watch weavers at work. The tour (in French) through the 1912 factory takes in the 18th-century chapel and the Beauvais workshops. Arrive 30 minutes before the tour starts.

Eating & drinking

L'Avant-Goût

26 rue Bobillot, 13th (01.53.80.24.00). M° Place d'Italie. **Open** noon-2pm, 7.45-10.45pm Tue-Sat. Closed 3wks Aug. **€**. **Bistro**. **Map** p151 B3 ㉜
Self-taught chef Christophe Beaufront has turned this nondescript street on the edge of the villagey Butte-aux-Cailles into a foodie destination. Typical of Beaufront's cooking is his *pot-au-feu de cochon aux épices*. It's

The 13th

Sights & museums
Eating & drinking
Shopping
Nightlife
Arts & leisure

Quai de Bercy

Gare de Paris Bercy

BOULEVARD DE BERCY

Ministère des Finances

Palais Omnisports de Paris Bercy

QUAI DE BERCY

QUAI FRANÇOIS MAURIAC

QUAI DE LA GARE

QUAI DE LA RAPÉE

Seine

QUAI D'AUSTERLITZ

Bibliothèque Nationale de France

Bibliothèque F. Mitterrand

29

QUAI
D'AUSTERLITZ

Gare d'Austerlitz

Hôpital La Pitié Salpêtrière

30

RUE DU CHEVALERET

AVENUE PIERRE MENDÈS FRANCE

RUE DE CHAMBRES

LOUISE WEISS

PLACE JEANNE-D'ARC

RUE NATIONALE

RUE DU CHÂTEAU DES RENTIERS

RUE DE TOLBIAC

BOULEVARD DE L'HÔPITAL

Museum National d'Histoire Naturelle

Jardin des Plantes

Musée de Paris

BOULEVARD SAINT MARCEL

RUE JEANNE D'ARC

BOULEVARD VINCENT AURIOL

Chevaleret

RUE DU CHEVALERET

Campo Formio

BOULEVARD DE L'HÔPITAL

Nationale

RUE R. PINEL

BOULEVARD VINCENT AURIOL

Tolbiac

AVENUE DE CHOISY

AVENUE D'ITALIE

Place d'Italie

Place Monge

RUE CLAUDE BERNARD

AVENUE DES GOBELINS

Les Gobelins

BOULEVARD ARAGO

BOULEVARD AUGUSTE BLANQUI

RUE DE LA BUTTE AUX CAILLES

Glacière

Corvisart

RUE MOUFFETARD

Église Notre Dame de Val de Grâce

Val de Grâce

BOULEVARD DE PORT ROYAL

Hôpital Cochin

Hôpital Broca

BOULEVARD ARAGO

RUE DE LA SANTÉ

500 m
500 yds

0

© Copyright Time Out Group 2008

good, if not earth-shaking – however, a starter of piquillo pepper stuffed with smoked haddock rillettes illustrates his talent. Reluctant cooks will be interested to know that Beaufront's food is available to take away at the *épicerie* across the street.

Chez Paul

22 rue Butte-aux-Cailles, 13th (01.45.89.22.11). M° Place d'Italie. **Open** noon-2.30pm, 7.30-11.30pm daily. **€**. **Bistro**. Map p151 B3 ⓸

Chez Paul's wood and white drapery are a chic alternative to other places along this street. Tradition takes pride of place – *pot-au-feu*, beef knuckle, bone marrow – and you can eat your way from one end of a beast to the other. Seafood makes an appearance on the blackboard menu in the shape of oysters, whelks, and a main of monkfish nuggets in a garlic sauce served with gleaming spinach. Book ahead.

L'Ourcine

92 rue Broca, 13th (01.47.07.13.65). M° Les Gobelins or Glacière. **Open** noon-2pm, 7-10.30pm Tue-Thur; noon-2.30pm, 7-11pm Fri, Sat. Closed 4wks July-Aug. **€**. **Bistro**. Map p151 B2 ⓷

This cream-and-red restaurant near Gobelins is a wonderful destination for anyone who really loves Basque and Béarnais cooking, since the kitchen sends out comforting, delicious and impeccably prepared regional classics. Start with *pipérade*, succulent chorizo or a spread of sliced beef tongue with piquillo peppers; then try the sautéed baby squid with parsley, garlic and Espelette peppers. Homely desserts include *gâteau basque* and ewe's milk cheese with black cherry preserve.

Nightlife

Batofar

Opposite 11 quai François-Mauriac, 13th (recorded information 01.53.60. 17.30/www.batofar.org). M° Quai de la Gare. **Open** 11pm-6am Mon-Sat; 6am-noon 1st Sun of mth. **Admission** €5-€12. Map p151 E2 ⓵

In recent years, the Batofar has gone through a rapid succession of management teams, with varying levels of success. The current management has helped revive the venue's tradition of peddling cutting-edge music, including electro, dub step, techno and dancehall nights featuring international acts. In summer, clubbers chill on the quayside while DJs play on deck. Inside are loads of nooks to hide in, and a robust sound system.

Arts & leisure

Cité de la Mode et du Design

NEW *28-36 quai d'Austerlitz, 13th. M° Gare d'Austerlitz.* **Map** p151 D1 ⓶ See box p148.

MK2 Bibliothèque

128-162 av de France, 13th (08.92.69. 84.84/www.mk2.com). M° Bibliothèque François Mitterrand or Quai de la Gare. **Admission** €9.80; €5.90-€6.80 reductions; €19.80 monthly pass. Map p151 E2 ⓷

The MK2 chain's flagship offers an all-in-one night out: 14 screens, three restaurants, a bar open until 5am at weekends and two-person 'love seats'. A paragon of imaginative programming, MK2 is growing all the time; it has added ten more venues in town, including two along the Bassin de la Villette with waterside cafés.

Piscine Josephine-Baker

Quai François-Mauriac, 13th (01.56.61.96.50). M° Quai de la Gare. **Open** 7-8.30am, 1-3pm, 5-9pm Mon; noon-5pm, 7pm-midnight Tue; 7-8.30am, 1-9pm Wed; noon-3pm, 5-9pm Thur; 7-8.30am, 1-5pm, 7pm-midnight Fri; 10am-8pm Sat, Sun. **Admission** €2.60; €1.50 reductions. Map p151 E2 ⓸

Moored on the Seine by the Bibliothèque Nationale, the Piscine Josephine-Baker opened in 2006. It boasts a 25m main pool, a paddling pool and café – plus a busy schedule of exercise classes. There's a sundeck in summer and a glass roof in winter.

Rue Daguerre

Montparnasse & Beyond

Picasso, Léger and Soutine fled to 'Mount Parnassus' in the early 1900s to escape the rising rents of Montmartre. They were soon joined by Chagall, Zadkine and other refugees from the Russian Revolution, along with Americans such as Man Ray, Henry Miller, Ezra Pound and Gertrude Stein. Between the wars, the neighbourhood was the epitome of modernity: studios with large windows were built by avant-garde architects; artists, writers and intellectuals drank and debated in the quarter's showy bars; and naughty pastimes – including the then risqué tango – flourished.

Sadly, the Montparnasse of today has lost much of its former soul, dominated as it is by the lofty

Tour Montparnasse – the first skyscraper in central Paris. The dismay with which its construction was greeted prompted a change in building regulations in central Paris. For those with a head for heights, there are fabulous panoramic views to be had from the café on the 56th floor.

Sights & museums

Les Catacombes
1 av Colonel Henri-Rol-Tanguy, 14th (01.43.22.47.63/www.catacombes.info). M°/RER Denfert Rochereau. **Open** 9.30am-4pm Tue-Sun. **Admission** €5; free-€3.30 reductions. **Map** p155 C3 ❶
This is the official entrance to the 3,000km (1,864-mile) tunnel network that runs under much of the city. With

public burial pits overflowing in the era of the Revolutionary Terror, the bones of six million people were transferred to the *catacombes*. The bones of Marat, Robespierre and their cronies are packed in with wall upon wall of their fellow citizens. It's not a journey for the faint-hearted: an 85-step spiral staircase takes visitors some 20m (66ft) below ground level to a mass of bones and carvings. Carry a torch with you.

Cimetière du Montparnasse

3 bd Edgar-Quinet, 14th (01.44.10. 86.50). M° Edgar Quinet or Raspail. **Open** *16 Mar-5 Nov* 8am-6pm Mon-Fri; 8.30am-6pm Sat; 9am-6pm Sun. *6 Nov-15 Mar* 8am-5.30pm Mon-Fri; 8.30am-5.30pm Sat; 9.30am-5.30pm Sun. **Admission** free. **Map** p155 B2 ❷
As with much of the Left Bank, the Montparnasse cemetery scores highly for literary credibility: Beckett, Baudelaire, Sartre, de Beauvoir, Maupassant, Ionesco and Tristan Tzara all rest here; the artists include Brancusi, Henri Laurens, Frédéric Bartholdi and Man Ray. The roll-call continues with Serge Gainsbourg, André Citroën (of automobile fame), comic Coluche and actress Jean Seberg.

Fondation Cartier

261 bd Raspail, 14th (01.42.18.56.72/ recorded information 01.42.18.56.51/ www.fondation.cartier.fr). M° Denfert-Rochereau or Raspail. **Open** 10am-10pm Tue; 10am-8pm Wed-Sun. **Admission** €7.50; free-€5.50 reductions. **Map** p155 C2 ❸
Jean Nouvel's glass-and-steel building, an exhibition centre with Cartier's offices above, is as much a work of art as the installations inside. Shows by artists and photographers often have wide-ranging themes, such as 'Birds' or 'Desert'. Live events around the shows are called Nuits Nomades.

Fondation Henri Cartier-Bresson

2 impasse Lebouis, 14th (01.56.80. 27.00/www.henricartierbresson.org). M° Gaîté. **Open** 1-6.30pm Tue-Fri,
Sun; 1-8.30pm Wed; 11am-6.45pm Sat. Closed Aug & between exhibitions. **Admission** €6; €3 reductions. No credit cards. **Map** p155 A2 ❹
Opened back in 2003, this two-floor gallery is dedicated to the acclaimed photographer Henri Cartier-Bresson. It consists of a tall, narrow *atelier* in a 1913 building, with a minutely catalogued archive, open to researchers, and a lounge area on the fourth floor screening films. In the spirit of Cartier-Bresson, who assisted on three Jean Renoir films and drew and painted all his life, the *fondation* throws opens its doors to other disciplines with three annual shows.

Musée Bourdelle

16-18 rue Antoine-Bourdelle, 15th (01.49.54.73.73/www.bourdelle. paris.fr). M° Falguière or Montparnasse Bienvenüe. **Open** 10am-6pm Tue-Sun. **Admission** free. *Exhibitions* prices vary. **Map** p155 A1 ❺
The sculptor Antoine Bourdelle (1861-1929), pupil of Rodin, produced monumental works including the Modernist relief friezes at the Théâtre des Champs-Elysées, inspired by Isadora Duncan and Nijinsky. Set around a small garden, the museum includes the artist's apartment and studios, which were also used by Eugène Carrière, Dalou and Chagall. A 1950s extension tracks the evolution of Bourdelle's equestrian monument to General Alvear in Buenos Aires, and his masterful *Hercules the Archer*. A new wing houses bronzes.

Musée du Montparnasse

21 av du Maine, 15th (01.42.22.91.96/ www.museedumontparnasse.net). M° Montparnasse Bienvenüe. **Open** 12.30-7pm Tue-Sun. **Admission** €6; free-€5 reductions. No credit cards. **Map** p155 A1 ❻
Set in one of the last surviving alleys of studios, this was home to Marie Vassilieff, whose own academy and cheap canteen welcomed poor artists Picasso, Cocteau and Matisse. Trotsky

and Lenin were also guests. Shows focus on the area's creative past and present-day artists.

Tour Montparnasse

33 av du Maine, 15th (01.45.38. 52.56/www.tourmontparnasse56.com). M° Montparnasse Bienvenüe. **Open** 1 Oct-31 Mar 9.30am-10.30pm daily. 1 Apr-30 Sept 9.30am-11.30pm daily. **Admission** €9.50; free-€6.80 reductions. **Map** p155 A1 ❼

Built in 1974 on the site of the old station, this 209m (686ft) steel-and-glass monolith is shorter than the Eiffel Tower, but better placed for fabulous views of the city – including, of course, the Eiffel Tower itself. A lift whisks you up in 38 seconds to the 56th floor, where you'll find a display of aerial scenes of Paris, an upgraded café-lounge, a souvenir shop – and plenty of sky. On a clear day you can see up to 40km (25 miles). Another lift takes you up to the roof. Classical concerts are held on the terrace.

Eating & drinking

Apollo

3 pl Denfert-Rochereau, 14th (01.45.38. 76.77). M°/RER Denfert Rochereau. **Open** noon-3pm, 7pm-11pm daily. **€. Bistro. Map** p155 C3 ❽

From the same team that conceived Quai Ouest, this high-design restaurant in the former RER offices at Denfert Rochereau brings a breath of novelty into a staid part of Paris. The decor fits nicely with the original design, but the menu is firmly 21st-century. Modern takes on classic comfort food include herring caviar and potatoes, *blanquette de coquilles St-Jacques* and braised beef with carrots. Desserts include pineapple and bananas sautéed in rum.

La Cerisaie

70 bd Edgar Quinet, 14th (01.43. 20.98.98). M° Edgar Quinet or Montparnasse. **Open** noon-2pm, 7-10pm Mon-Fri. Closed Aug & 1wk Dec. **€€. Brasserie. Map** p155 A1 ❾

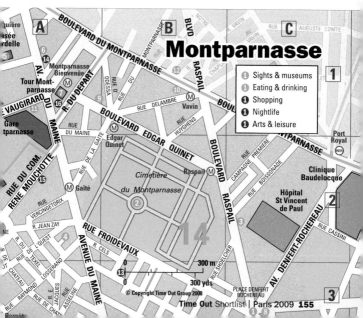

© Copyright Time Out Group 2008

Fondation Cartier p154

Nothing about La Cerisaie's unprepossessing red façade in the shadow of the Montparnasse Tower hints at the talent that lurks inside. With a simple starter of white asparagus served with preserved lemon and drizzled with bright green parsley oil, chef Cyril Lalanne proves his ability to select and prepare the finest produce. On the daily changing blackboard menu you might find *bourride de maquereau*, a thrifty take on the garlicky southern French fish stew, or *cochon noir de Bigorre*, an ancient breed of pig that puts ordinary pork to shame.

La Coupole

102 bd du Montparnasse, 14th (01.43.20.14.20). Mº Vavin. **Open** 8am-1am Mon-Fri; 8.30am-1am Sat, Sun. **€€. Brasserie. Map** p155 B1 ⑩
Though Montparnasse today is a far cry from its avant-garde heyday when this restaurant opened in 1927 – as a *bar américain* with cocktails and dancing – La Coupole still glows with some of the old glamour. The opportunities for people-watching remain superb, both inside and out, while the long ranks of linen-covered tables, 32 art deco columns and sheer scale of the operation still make coming here an event. The set menu offers steaks, foie gras, fish and autumn game stews, but the real treat is the shellfish, displayed along a massive counter.

L'Ostreade

11 bd de Vaugirard, 15th (01.43.21. 87.41/www.ostreade.com). Mº Montparnasse-Bienvenüe. **Open** noon-3pm, 7-10pm daily. **€€.** **Brasserie. Map** p155 A1 ⑪
From the outside, L'Ostreade (sandwiched between Gare Montparnasse and a Quick fast-food joint), might look like a tourist trap, but is in fact a chic address, dressed up like a luxury yacht, coveted by seafood aficionados hooked on big 'n' juicy oysters and perfect fish. If in season, try the Part-Ar-Cum oysters, fresh from the Finistère in Brittany, renowned for their hazelnut-like flavour; then the sea bass served with saffron sauerkraut; and a crackly-topped passionfruit crème brûlée.

Le Select

99 bd du Montparnasse, 6th (01.42. 22.65.27). Mº Vavin. **Open** 7am-2am Mon-Thur, Sun; 7am-4am Fri, Sat. **€€. Brasserie. Map** p155 B1 ⑫

For a decade between the wars, the junction of boulevards Raspail and du Montparnasse was where Man Ray, Cocteau and Lost Generation Americans hung out in the vast glass-fronted cafés. Eight decades on, Le Select is the best of these tourist haunts. Sure, its pricey menu is big on historical detail and short on authenticity, but by and large Le Select manages to hold on to its heyday with dignity.

Shopping

Paris Accordéon

80 rue Daguerre, 14th (01.43.22. 13.48/www.parisaccordeon.com). M° Denfert Rochereau or Gaîté. **Open** 9am-noon, 1-7pm Tue-Fri; 9am-noon, 1-6pm Sat. **Map** p155 B3 ⓭

Accordions, ranging from simple squeezeboxes to beautiful tortoiseshell models, both second-hand and new.

Nightlife

Club Mix

24 rue de l'Arrivée, 15th (01.56.80.37. 37/www.mixclub.fr). M° Montparnasse Bienvenüe. **Open** 11pm-6am Wed-Sat; 5pm-1am Sun. **Admission** €12-€20. **Map** p155 A1 ⓮

The Mix, formerly Amnesia, has one of the city's biggest dancefloors and DJ booths. Regular international visitors include Erick Morillo's Subliminal and Ministry of Sound parties.

Le Petit Journal Montparnasse

13 rue du Commandant-René-Mouchotte, 14th (01.43.21.56.70/ www.petitjournal-montparnasse.com). M° Gaîté or Montparnasse-Bienvenüe. **Open** *Concerts* 10pm Mon-Sat. **Admission** (incl 1 drink) €20. **Map** p155 A2 ⓯

Two-level jazz brasserie in the shadow of the Tour Montparnasse with Latin sounds, R&B and soul-gospel. Dinner (€55-€85) starts at 8pm.

Red Light

34 rue du Départ, 15th (01.42.79. 94.53). M° Edgar Quinet or Montparnasse Bienvenüe. **Open** midnight-11am Fri, Sat. **Admission** (incl 1 drink) €20. **Map** p155 A1 ⓰

The former Enfer ('Hell') remains a trance, techno and house mecca with DJs spinning tunes to a young, up-for-it, often gay, well-groomed crowd. Expect a top-class mix of local and international DJs.

PARIS BY AREA

Château de Versailles p160

Worth the Trip

West

Bois de Boulogne

16th. Mº Les Sablons or Porte Dauphine.
Covering 865 hectares, the Bois was
once the Forêt de Rouvray hunting
grounds. It was landscaped in the 1860s,
when artifical grottoes and waterfalls
were created. The Jardin de Bagatelle is
famous for roses, daffodils and water
lilies, and contains an orangery that
rings to the sound of Chopin in summer.
The Jardin d'Acclimatation is a children's amusement park, complete with
a miniature train, farm, rollercoaster
and boat rides. The Bois also boasts two
racecourses (Longchamp and Auteuil),
sports clubs and stables, and restaurants. It attracts picnickers and dog
walkers, with boats rented on the lake.
But by night it's transformed into a
parade ground for transsexuals and
swingers of every stripe.

Musée Marmottan – Claude Monet

*2 rue Louis-Boilly, 16th (01.44.96.
50.33/www.marmottan.com). Mº La
Muette.* **Open** 10am-5.30pm Tue-Sun
(last entry 5pm). **Admission** €8;
free-€4.50 reductions.
This old hunting pavilion has become
a famed holder of Impressionist art
thanks to two bequests: the first by the
daughter of the doctor of Manet,
Monet, Pissarro, Sisley and Renoir; the
second by Monet's son Michel. Its
Monet collection, the largest in the
world, numbers 165 works – including
the seminal *Impression Soleil Levant* –
plus sketchbooks, palette and photos.
A circular room was created for the
breathtaking late water lily canvases;
upstairs are works by Renoir, Manet,
Gauguin and Caillebotte.
Event highlights Mémoire de la
vision 'Claude Monet' (15 Oct 2008-
15 Feb 2009).

East

104

NEW *104 rue d'Aubervilliers, 19th (01.
40.05.51.71/www.104.fr). M° Riquet.*
See box p161.

Cité des Sciences
et de l'Industrie

*La Villette, 30 av Corentin-Cariou, 19th
(01.40.05.70.00/www.cite-sciences.fr).
M° Porte de la Villette.* **Open** 10am-
6pm Tue-Sat; 10am-7pm Sun.
Admission €8; free-€6 reductions.
The ultra-modern science museum at
La Villette pulls in five million visitors
every year. Explora, the permanent
show, occupies the upper two floors,
whisking visitors through 30,000sq m
(320,000sq ft) of space, life, matter and
communication: scale models of satel-
lites including the Ariane space shuttle,
planes and robots, plus the chance to
experience weightlessness, make for an
exciting journey. In the Espace Images,
try the delayed camera and other opti-
cal illusions, draw 3D images or lend
your voice to the *Mona Lisa*.
Event highlights 60 ans de la Citroën
2CV (until 30 Nov 2008).

Disneyland Paris/Walt
Disney Studios Park

*Marne-la-Vallée (08.25.30.60.30/from
UK 0870 503 0303/www.disneyland
paris.com). 32km E of Paris. RER A or
TGV Marne-la-Vallée-Chessy. By car
A4 exit 14.* **Open** *Disneyland Paris*
Sept-mid July 10am-8pm Mon-Fri; 9am-
8pm Sat, Sun. Mid July-Aug 9am-11pm
daily. *Studios Park* Winter 10am-6pm
Mon-Fri; 9am-6pm Sat, Sun. Summer
9am-6pm daily. **Admission** 1 park
€43; €35 3-11s; free under-3s. 1-day
hopper (both parks) €53; €45 3-11s;
free under-3s.
Now 15 years old, the theme park is a
familiar part of the flat Ile de France
landscape. Radiating out from sugary
Main Street USA are Fantasyland,
Adventureland, Frontierland and
Discoveryland. Fantasyland, with its
Alice maze, Sleeping Beauty's castle
and teacup and Dumbo rides, is most
suitable for small children; the splashy

Pirates of the Caribbean and Phantom
Manor provide spooky fun; and dare-
devils can experience the bone-shaking
Indiana Jones and le Temple de Péril and
Space Mountain. The adjacent Studios
Park takes you into animation studios
and on a tram tour through a film set.

Musée de la Musique

*Cité de la Musique, 221 av Jean-Jaurès,
19th (01.44.84.44.84/www.cite-
musique.fr).* M° Porte de Pantin. **Open**
noon-6pm Tue-Sat; 10am-6pm Sun.
Admission €7; free-€5.60 reductions.
Alongside the concert hall, this innovative museum houses a restored collection of instruments from the old
Conservatoire, interactive computers
and scale models of opera houses and
concert halls. The musical commentary
is a joy, playing the appropriate instrument as you approach each exhibit.
Alongside the trumpeting brass, curly
woodwind instruments and precious
strings are more unusual items, such
as the Indonesian gamelan orchestra.

Parc de la Villette

*Av Corentin-Cariou, 19th (01.40.03.
75.75/www.villette.com). M° Porte de
la Villette. Av Jean-Jaurès, 19th.
M° Porte de Pantin.*
Once the city's main cattle market, La
Villette now contains the Cité des
Sciences et de l'Industrie, the spherical
La Géode IMAX cinema and the
Argonaute submarine. Dotted with red
pavilions, or *folies*, the park was
designed by Swiss architect Bernard
Tschumi. The *folies* serve as glorious
giant climbing frames, as well as a
first-aid post, burger bar and children's
art centre. An undulating suspended
path follows the Canal de l'Ourcq.
South of the canal are the Zénith, used
for rock concerts, and the Grande Halle
de la Villette – now used for trade fairs,
exhibitions and September's high pro-
file jazz festival. It is flanked by the
Conservatoire de la Musique and the
Cité de la Musique. This is also the site
of a new concert hall for the Orchestre
de Paris, due to open in 2012.

PARIS BY AREA

South

Parc André Citroën

Rue Balard, rue St-Charles or quai Citroën, 15th. M° Balard or Javel.
Open 8am-dusk Mon-Fri; 9am-dusk Sat, Sun, public hols.
This park is a fun, postmodern version of a French formal garden, designed by Gilles Clément and Alain Prévost. It comprises glasshouses, computerised fountains, waterfalls, a wilderness and themed gardens featuring different coloured plants and even sounds. Stepping stones and water jets make it a garden for pleasure as well as philosophy. The tethered Eutelsat helium balloon takes visitors up for marvellous views over the city. If the weather looks unreliable, call 01.44.26.20.00 to check the day's programme.

Versailles

Centuries of makeovers have made Versailles the most sumptuously clad château in the world – a brilliant cocktail of extravagance. Architect Louis Le Vau first embellished the original building – a hunting lodge built during Louis XIII's reign – after Louis XIV saw Vaux-le-Vicomte, the impressive residence of his finance minister, Nicolas Fouquet. The Sun King had the unlucky minister jailed, and stole not only his architect but also his painter, Charles Le Brun, and his landscaper, André Le Nôtre, who turned the boggy marshland into terraces, parterres, fountains and lush groves.

After Le Vau's death in 1670, Jules Hardouin-Mansart took over as principal architect, transforming Versailles into the château we know today. He dedicated the last 30 years of his life to adding the two main wings, the Cour des Ministres and the Chapelle Royale. In 1682, Louis moved in, accompanied by his court; thereafter, he rarely set foot in Paris. In the 1770s, Louis XV commissioned Jacques-Ange Gabriel to add the sumptuous Opéra Royal. The expense of building and running Versailles cost France dear. With the fall of the monarchy in 1792, most of the furniture was lost – but the château was saved from demolition after 1830 by Louis-Philippe.

Versailles has hosted the official signings of many historic treaties – European recognition of the United States, the unification of Germany in 1871, the division of Europe after 1918 – and it is still used by the French government for summits. In the gardens, the Grand Trianon accommodates heads of state.

The gardens are works of art in themselves, their ponds and statues once again embellished by a fully working fountain system. On summer weekends, the spectacular jets of water are set to music, a prelude to the occasional fireworks displays of the Fêtes de Nuit.

Versailles is currently undergoing a major overhaul, so expect a little chaos for the next few years. As well as sprucing up Marie-Antoinette's residence (see below), the French state and several sponsors have funded a restoration of the Hall of Mirrors – a 73-metre (240-foot) gallery overlooking the garden, hung with chandeliers. Commissioned in 1678 by Louis XIV and decorated by Le Brun, it is lined with 357 mirrors.

► Château de Versailles

78000 Versailles (01.30.83.78.00/ advance tickets 08.92.68.46.94/www. chateauversailles.fr). **Open** *Apr-Oct* 9am-6.30pm Tue-Sun. *Nov-Mar* 9am-5.30pm Tue-Sun. **Admission** €13.50; free-€10 reductions.
Versailles is a masterpiece – and it's almost always packed with visitors. Allow yourself a whole day to appreciate the sumptuous State Apartments and the Hall of Mirrors, the highlights

Art for all at 104

104

It is more than a hundred years since photogenic, tourist-choked Montmartre was the centre of artistic activity in Paris. But now the north of Paris is again where the action is – albeit a couple of kilometres east of the Place du Tertre, in a previously neglected area of bleak railway goods yards and dilapidated social housing.

104 (p159), described as a 'space for artistic creation', occupies a vast 19th-century building on the rue d'Aubervilliers that used to house Paris's municipal undertakers. The site was saved from developers by the mayor of the 19th arrondissement, Roger Madec, who has made its renovation the centrepiece of a massive project of cultural and urban renewal.

The directors of 104 hope that established international stars and talented unknowns alike will be attracted to this corner of north-east Paris by generously funded residencies that will include use of individual studios. There won't be any constraints on the kind of work the resident artists do – 104 is open to 'all the arts' – but they will be expected to show finished pieces in one of four annual 'festivals'. And they'll also be required to get involved in projects with the public, the fruits of which will be exhibited in a dedicated space next door.

There'll be an international dimension to the work of 104 too: it belongs to a network of similar reclaimed art spaces across Europe and has established a partnership with the California Institute of the Arts. 104 will also contribute to the commercial life of the area. It will be home to a café, restaurant and shop selling books, CDs and other 'cultural goods'. All of which suggests that the rue d'Aubervilliers will soon be on the itinerary of any discerning visitor to Paris.

of any visit – and mainly accessible with just a day ticket. The Grand Appartement, where Louis XIV held court, consists of six gilded salons (Venus, Mercury, Apollo and so on), all opulent examples of Baroque craftsmanship. No less luxurious, the Queen's Apartment includes her bedroom, where royal births took place in full view of the court. Hardouin-Mansart's showpiece, the Hall of Mirrors, where a united Germany was proclaimed in 1871 and the Treaty of Versailles signed in 1919, is flooded with natural light from its 17 vast windows. Designed to catch the last of the day's rays, it was here that the Sun King would hold extravagant receptions. Other private apartments can be seen only as part of a guided tour.

Domaine de Versailles

Gardens **Open** *Apr-Oct* 7am-dusk daily. *Nov-Mar* 8am-dusk daily. **Admission** *Winter* free (statues covered over). *Summer* €3; free-€1.50 reductions. *Grandes Eaux Musicales* (01.30.83.78.88). **Open** *Apr-Sept* Sat, Sun. **Admission** €7; free-€5.50 reductions. *Park* **Open** dawn-dusk daily. **Admission** free.

Sprawling across 8sq km (3sq miles), the carefully planned gardens consist of formal parterres, ponds, elaborate statues – many commissioned by Colbert in 1674 – and a spectacular series of fountains, served by an ingenious hydraulic system only recently restored to working order. On weekend afternoons in the spring and autumn, the fountains are set in action to music for the Grandes Eaux Musicales – and also serve as a backdrop, seven times a year, for the extravagant Fêtes de Nuit, capturing the regal splendour of the Sun King's celebrations with fireworks, music and theatre.

Grand Trianon/Petit Trianon/Domaine de Marie-Antionette

Open *Apr-Oct* noon-6.30pm daily. *Nov-Mar* noon-5.30pm daily. **Admission** *Summer* €9; €5 after 4pm; free under-18s. *Winter* €5; free under-18s.

In 1687, Hardouin-Mansart built the pink marble Grand Trianon in the north of the park, away from the protocol of the court. Here Louis XIV and his children's governess and secret second wife, Madame de Maintenon, could admire the intimate gardens from the colonnaded portico. It retains the Empire decor of Napoleon, who stayed here with his second Empress, Marie-Louise. The Petit Trianon, built for Louis XV's mistress Madame de Pompadour, is a wonderful example of neo-classicism. It later became part of the Domaine de Marie-Antoinette, an exclusive hideaway located beyond the canal in the wooded parkland. Given to Marie-Antoinette as a wedding gift by her husband Louis XVI in 1774, the domain also includes the chapel adjoining the Petit Trianon, plus a theatre, a neo-classical 'Temple d'Amour', and Marie-Antoinette's fairy-tale farm and dairy, known as the Hameau de la Reine. Here, the queen escaped from the discontent of her subjects and the revolutionary fervour of Paris by pretending to be a humble milkmaid. A stroll can be enlivened by hiring hand-held digital PDA or iPod guides.

Getting there

By car

20km (12.5 miles) from Paris by the A13 or D10.

By train

For the station nearest the château, take the RER C5 (VICK or VERO trains) to Versailles-Rive Gauche; or take a Transilien SNCF train from Gare St-Lazare to Versailles-Rive Droit (from where it's 10mins on foot to the château).

Tourist information

Office de Tourisme

2bis av de Paris, 78000 Versailles (01.39.24.88.88/www.versailles-tourisme.com). **Open** 11am-5pm Mon, Sun; 9am-6pm Tue-Sat.

Essentials

Kube Rooms & Bar p172

Hotels

Last year, some 27 million tourists came to have a peek at the Eiffel Tower, between them occupying over 76,000 rooms in more than 1,450 hotels. The long-established luxury palaces now face a challenge from smaller, cosier newcomers such as the exclusive **Hôtel Particulier Montmartre** and **Jays Paris**. Last year saw the opening of several much-awaited hotspots, including the **Five Hôtel** in the Latin Quarter and fashionista paradise the **Bellechasse** – the latest hotel to be 'dressed' by designer Christian Lacroix.

Classification

We've divided the hotels into four categories, according to the price for one night in a double room with en suite shower/bath: Deluxe €350+ **€€€€**; Expensive €220-€350 **€€€**; Moderate €120-€220 **€€**; Budget up to €120 **€**.

In the know

All hotels in France charge a room tax (*taxe de séjour*) of around €1 per person per night, sometimes included in the rate. Hotels are often booked solid during trade fairs (January, May, September), and it's hard to find a quality room in Fashion Weeks (January, March, July and October). At quieter times, including July and August, hotels often offer special deals at short notice; phone ahead or check websites. Same-day reservations can be made in person for a nominal commission at the **Office de Tourisme de Paris** (p188).

Champs-Elysées & Western Paris

Four Seasons George V

31 av George-V, 8th (01.49.52. 70.00/fax 01.49.52.70.10/www.four seasons.com). M° Alma Marceau or George V. **€€€€**.

There's no denying that the George V is serious about luxury: chandeliers, marble and tapestries; very attentive staff; glorious flower arrangements; divine bathrooms; and ludicrously comfortable beds in some of the largest rooms in all of Paris. The Versailles-inspired spa includes whirlpools, saunas and a menu of treatments for an unabashedly metrosexual clientele; non-guests can now reserve appointments. It's worth every euro.

Hôtel le A

4 rue d'Artois, 8th (01.42.56.99.99/fax 01.42.56.99.90/www.paris-hotel-a.com). M° Franklin D. Roosevelt or St-Philippe-du-Roule. €€€€.
The black-and-white decor of this designer boutique hotel provides a fine backdrop for the models, artists and media types hanging out in the lounge bar area; the only splashes of colour come from the graffiti-like artworks by conceptual artist Fabrice Hybert. The 26 rooms all have granite bathrooms, and the starched white furniture slip covers, changed after each guest, make the smallish spaces seem larger than they are. The dimmer switches are a nice touch – as are the lift lights changing colour at each floor.

Hôtel Daniel

8 rue Frédéric-Bastiat, 8th (01.42. 56.17.00/fax 01.42.56.17.01/www. hoteldanielparis.com). M° Franklin D. Roosevelt or St-Philippe-du-Roule. €€€€.
A romantic hideaway close to the Champs-Elysées, the city's new Relais & Châteaux is decorated in chinoiserie and a palette of rich colours, with 26 rooms cosily appointed in *toile de Jouy* and a hand-painted restaurant that feels like a courtyard. At about €50 a head, the gastronomic restaurant Le Lounge, run by chef Denis Fetisson, is a good deal for this neighbourhood; the bar menu is served at all hours.

Hôtel Fouquet's-Barrière

46 av George-V, 8th (01.40.69.60.00/ fax 01.40.69.60.05/www.lucien barriere.com). M° George V. €€€€.

SHORTLIST

Best newcomers
- Le Bellechasse (p177)
- Five Hôtel (p180)
- Mama Shelter (p176)

Best spa options
- Four Seasons George V (p164)
- Hôtel Fouquet's-Barrière (p165)
- Intercontinental Paris Le Grand (p171)

Best alfresco breakfast
- Hôtel des Grandes Ecoles (p181)
- Regents Hotel (p180)

Best bars
- Hôtel Plaza Athénée (p167)
- Kube Rooms & Bar (p172)
- Murano Urban Resort (p176)

Best for fashionistas
- L'Hôtel (p179)
- Le Montalembert (p177)

Best bathrooms
- Hôtel le A (p165)
- Hôtel Edouard VII (p169)
- Hôtel de Vigny (p167)

Best bargain beds
- Grand Hôtel Jeanne d'Arc (p173)
- Hôtel Chopin (p168)
- Hôtel Esmeralda (p181)
- Regents Hotel (p180)

Chic sleeps
- L'Hôtel (p179)
- Hôtel Amour (p171)
- Kube Rooms & Bar (p172)
- Le Sezz (p168)

Lap of luxury
- Four Seasons George V (p164)
- Hôtel de Crillon (p168)
- Le Meurice (p171)
- Hôtel Ritz (p169)

ESSENTIALS

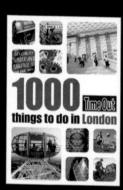

This grandiose five-star is built around the famous fin-de-siècle brasserie Le Fouquet's. Five buildings form the hotel complex, housing 107 rooms (including 40 suites), upmarket restaurant Le Diane, a spa, indoor pool and a rooftop terrace for hire. Jacques Garcia, of Hôtel Costes fame, was responsible for the interior design, which retains the Empire style of the exterior while incorporating luxury modern touches inside – flat-screen TVs and mist-free mirrors in the marble bathrooms, for example. And, of course, it's unbeatable for location.

Hôtel Plaza Athénée

25 av Montaigne, 8th (01.53.67.66.67/ fax 01.53.67.66.66/www.plaza-athenee- paris.com). M° Alma Marceau. €€€€.
This palace is ideally placed for power shopping at Chanel, Vuitton, Dior and other avenue Montaigne boutiques. Material girls and boys will enjoy the high-tech room amenities such as remote-controlled air-con, internet and video-game access on the TV via infrared keyboard, and mini hi-fi. The stylish bar full of rock stars and hotshots has modern decor, matched by a cool cocktail list and staff who know what service is.

Hôtel Regent's Garden

6 rue Pierre-Demours, 17th (01.45.74. 07.30/fax 01.40.55.01.42/www.hotel- paris-garden.com). M° Charles de Gaulle Etoile or Ternes. €€.
This elegant hotel – built for Napoleon III's physician – features appropriately Second Empire high ceilings and plush upholstery, and a lounge overlooking a lovely walled garden. There are 39 large bedrooms, some with gilt mirrors and fireplaces. An oasis of calm ten minutes from the Champs-Elysées.

Hôtel de Sers

41 av Pierre-1er-de-Serbie, 8th (01.53. 23.75.75/fax 01.53.23.75.76/www.hotel desers.com). M° Alma Marceau or George V. €€€€.
Behind its 19th-century façade, the Hôtel de Sers is an ambitious mix of minimalist contemporary furnishings

(often in deep reds and mauves; nothing too austere), with a few pop art touches. Original architectural details such as the grand staircase and reception complete the picture.

Hôtel Square

3 rue de Boulainvilliers, 16th (01.44.14. 91.90/fax 01.44.14.91.99/www.hotel square.com). M° Passy/RER Avenue du Pdt Kennedy. €€€.
This courageously modern hotel has a dramatic yet welcoming interior, and attentive service that comes from having to look after only 22 rooms. These are decorated in amber, brick or slate colours, with exotic woods, quality fabrics and bathrooms seemingly cut from one huge chunk of Carrara marble. View the exhibitions in the atrium gallery or mingle with the media types at the hip Zebra Square restaurant and DJ lounge bar.

Hôtel de Vigny

9-11 rue Balzac, 8th (01.42.99.80.80/ fax 01.42.99.80.40/www.hoteldevigny. com). M° George V. €€€€.
One of only two Relais & Châteaux in the city, this hotel has the feel of a private, plush townhouse. Although it's just off the Champs-Elysées, the Vigny pulls in a discerning, low-key clientele. Its 37 rooms and suites are decorated in tasteful stripes or florals, with marble bathrooms. Enjoy dinner in the art deco Baretto restaurant, or a cup of tea in the library.

Jays Paris

6 rue Copernic, 16th (01.47.04. 16.16/fax 01.47.04.16.17/www. jays-paris.com). M° Kléber or Victor Hugo. €€€€.
Introducing a new concept on the Paris hotel scene, Jays is a luxurious '*boutique-apart*' hotel that trades on a clever blend of antique furniture, modern design and high-tech equipment. The five suites all have a kitchenette, and a cosy salon is available to welcome in-house guests and their visitors. The balcony is the only place for a cigarette since the establishment was made entirely smoke-free.

Le Sezz

Le Sezz

6 av Frémiet, 16th (01.56.75.26.26/
fax 01.56.75.26.16/www.hotelsezz.com).
M° Passy. €€€€.

Le Sezz opened its doors in 2005 with
27 sleek, luxurious rooms and suites –
the work of acclaimed French furniture
designer Christophe Pillet. The understated decor represents a refreshingly
modern take on luxury, with black parquet flooring, rough-hewn stone walls
and bathrooms partitioned off with
sweeping glass façades. The bar and
public areas are equally sleek and chic.

Opéra to Les Halles

Hôtel Brighton

218 rue de Rivoli, 1st (01.47.03.61.61/
fax 01.42.60.41.78/www.esprit-de-
france.com). M° Tuileries. €€€.

With several rooms overlooking the
Tuileries garden, the Brighton is great
value (book well ahead for a good
view). All faux-marble and mosaic
decor, the recently restored hotel was
opened at the start of the 20th century
as the Entente Cordiale got under way.

Hôtel Chopin

10 bd Montmartre or 46 passage
Jouffroy, 9th (01.47.70.58.10/fax

01.42.47.00.70/www.hotel-chopin.com).
M° Grands Boulevards. €.

Handsomely set in a historic, glass-
roofed arcade, the Chopin's original
1846 façade adds to its old-fashioned
appeal. The 36 rooms are quiet and
functional, with salmon walls and
green carpet.

Hôtel Concorde St-Lazare

108 rue St-Lazare, 8th (01.40.08.
44.44/fax 01.42.93.01.20/www.
concordestlazare-paris.com). M°
St-Lazare. €€€€.

Guests here are cocooned in soundproofed luxury. The 19th-century
Eiffel-inspired lobby is a historic landmark: the high ceilings, marble pillars
and sculptures look much as they have
for over a century. Rooms are spacious,
with double entrance doors and exclusive Annick Goutal toiletries; the Belle
Epoque brasserie, Café Terminus, and
sexy Golden Black Bar were designed
by Sonia Rykiel. Guests have access to
a nearby fitness centre.

Hôtel de Crillon

10 pl de la Concorde, 8th (01.44.71.
15.00/fax 01.44.71.15.02/www.
crillon.com). M° Concorde. €€€€.

Hôtel de Crillon

The height of neo-classical European magnificence, the Crillon lives up to its *palais* reputation with decor strong on marble, mirrors and gold leaf. The Michelin-starred Les Ambassadeurs has an acclaimed chef, Jean-François Piège, and a brand new kitchen with a glassed-in private dining area for groups of no more than six people who wish to dine amid the bustle of the 80-strong kitchen staff.

Hôtel Edouard VII

39 av de l'Opéra, 2nd (01.42.61.56.90/ fax 01.42.61.47.73/www.edouard7 hotel.com). M° Opéra. €€€€.
Owned by the same family for five generations, this refined hotel includes some delightfully artful touches such as Murano glass lights, smooth wood features and modern sculptures in the entrance hall. The stylish bar and restaurant Angl'Opéra is decked out in dark mahogany and comfortable stripes. Some of the individually decorated bedrooms offer wonderful balcony views of the Garnier opera house.

Hôtel Langlois

63 rue St-Lazare, 9th (01.48.74.78.24/ fax 01.49.95.04.43/www.hotel-langlois.com). M° Trinité. €€.

Built as a bank in 1870, this Belle Epoque building became the Hôtel des Croisés in 1896. In 2001, after featuring in the Jonathan Demme film *Charade*, it changed its name to Hôtel Langlois in honour of the founder of the Cinémathèque Française. Its 27 spacious, air-conditioned bedrooms are all decorated in art nouveau style; the larger ones feature delightful hidden bathrooms.

Hôtel Madeleine Opéra

12 rue Greffulhe, 8th (01.47.42. 26.26/fax 01.47.42.89.76/www.hotel-madeleine-opera.com). M° Havre-Caumartin or Madeleine. €.
This bargain hotel is located just north of the Eglise Madeleine, right in the heart of the city's theatre and *grands magasins* districts. Its sunny lobby sits behind a 200-year-old façade that was once a shopfront. The 24 bedrooms are perhaps a touch on the basic side, but they are still nice enough, and a continental breakfast is brought to your room every morning.

Hôtel Ritz

15 pl Vendôme, 1st (01.43.16.30.30/ fax 01.43.16.45.38/www.ritzparis.com). M° Concorde or Opéra. €€€€.

ESSENTIALS

The grande dame of Paris hotels has proffered hospitality to Coco Chanel, the Duke of Windsor, Proust, and Dodi and Di. Today's guests have the choice of 162 bedrooms, of which 56 are suites, from the romantic Frédéric Chopin to the glitzy Impérial. There are plenty of corners in which to strike poses or quench a thirst, from Hemingway's elegant cigar bar and the plush Victorian champagne bar to the Ancient Greece-themed poolside hangout.

Hôtel Westminster

13 rue de la Paix, 2nd (01.42.61. 57.46/fax 01.42.60.30.66/www. warwickhotels.com). M° Opéra/ RER Auber. €€€€.
This luxury hotel near place Vendôme has more than a touch of British warmth about it, no doubt owing to the influence of its favourite 19th-century guest, the Duke of Westminster (after whom the hotel was named; the current Duke reportedly still stays here). The hotel fitness centre has a top-floor location, with a beautiful tiled steam room and views over the city, while the cosy bar features deep leather chairs, a fireplace and live jazz at weekends.

InterContinental Paris Le Grand

2 rue Scribe, 9th (01.40.07.32.32/ fax01.42.66.12.51/www.paris. intercontinental.com). M° Opéra. €€€€.
This 1862 hotel is the chain's European flagship – the landmark establishment occupies the entire block (three wings, almost 500 rooms) next to the opera house; some 80 of the honey-coloured rooms overlook the Palais Garnier. The space under the vast *verrière* is one of the best oases in town, while the hotel's restaurant and elegant coffeehouse, the Café de la Paix, poached its chef, Laurent Delarbre, from the Ritz. For a relaxing daytime break, head to the I-Spa for its seawater treatments.

Le Meurice

228 rue de Rivoli, 1st (01.44.58.10.10/ fax 01.44.58.10.15/www.lemeurice. com). M° Tuileries. €€€€.

With its extravagant Louis XVI decor and intricate mosaic tiled floors spruced up in a lengthy facelift, Le Meurice looks absolutely splendid. All its 160 rooms are done up in distinct historical styles; among the 36 suites (25 full and 11 junior), the Belle Etoile on the seventh floor provides 360-degree panoramic views of Paris from its terrace. You can relax by the Winter Garden to the strains of regular live jazz performances; for more intensive intervention, head over to the lavishly appointed spa with its *vinothérapie* treatments – or get grape products into your bloodstream at the gorgeous Bar Fontainebleau.

Montmartre & Pigalle

Blanche Hôtel

69 rue Blanche, 9th (01.48.74.16.94/ fax 01.49.95.95.98). M° Blanche. €.
If you're prepared to forgo frills and don't mind the rather racy aspect of the neighbourhood, this is a good-value bet. The interior is far from palatial and features less-than-luxurious 1970s furniture, but the rooms are a good size and there's a bar in the lobby.

Hôtel Amour

8 rue Navarin, 9th (01.48.78.31.80/fax 01.48.74.14.09/www.hotelamour.com). M° St-Georges. €€.
Opened in 2006, this boutique hotel is a real hit with the in crowd. Each of the 20 rooms is unique, decorated to the theme of love by a coterie of contemporary artists and designers such as Marc Newson, M&M, Stak, Pierre Le Tan and Sophie Calle. Seven of the rooms contain artists' installations, and two others have a private bar and a large terrace on which to hold your own party. The late-night brasserie has a delightful outdoor garden, and the Amour crowd is young, beautiful and loves to entertain.

Hôtel Particulier Montmartre

23 avenue Junot, 18th (01.53.41. 81.40/fax 01.42.58.00.87/www.

ESSENTIALS

Hôtel Concorde St-Lazare p168

the priciest ones enjoy views across to the basilica. Air-conditioned rooms cost an extra €10 per day.

Hôtel Royal Fromentin

11 rue Fromentin, 9th (01.48.74. 85.93/fax 01.42.81.02.33/www.hotel royalfromentin.com). M° Blanche or Pigalle. €€.

Wood panelling, art deco windows and a vintage glass lift echo the hotel's origins as a 1930s cabaret hall; its theatrical feel attracted Blondie and Nirvana. It's just down the road from the Moulin Rouge, and many of its 47 rooms overlook Sacré-Coeur. Rooms have been renovated in French style, with bright fabrics and an old-fashioned feel.

Kube Rooms & Bar

1-5 passage Ruelle, 18th (01.42.05. 20.00/fax 01.42.05.21.01/www.kube hotel.com). M° La Chapelle. €€€€.

The younger sister of the Murano Urban Resort, Kube is an edgier and more affordable design hotel. Like the Murano, it sits behind an unremarkable façade in an unlikely neighbourhood – in this case, the ethnically diverse Goutte d'Or. The Ice Kube bar serves up vodka in glasses that, like the bar itself, are carved from ice; drinkers pay €38 to down all the vodka they like in 30 minutes. Also on the menu: 'apérifood' and 'snackubes' by culinary designer Pierre Auge. The 'art brunch' on Sundays introduces an artist each month, with DJ music and a 35-foot buffet. Access to the 41 rooms is by fingerprint identification technology.

Timhotel Montmartre

11 rue Ravignan, 18th (01.42.55. 74.79/fax 01.42.55.71.01/www. timhotel.fr). M° Abbesses or Pigalle. €€.

The location adjacent to picturesque place Emile-Goudeau makes this one of the most popular hotels in the Timhotel chain. It has 59 nice rooms, comfortable without being plush; try to bag one on the fourth or fifth floor for stunning views over Montmartre. Special offers are often available at quieter times of year; ring for details.

hotel-particulier-montmartre.com). M° Lamarck Caulaincourt. €€€€.

Those lucky (and wealthy) enough to book a suite at the Hôtel Particulier Montmartre will find themselves in one of the city's hidden gems. Nestled in a quiet passage off rue Lepic, in the heart of Montmartre, this sumptuous Directoire-style house is dedicated to art, with each of the five luxurious suites personalised by an avant-garde artist. The private garden conceived by Louis Bénech (famous for the Tuileries renovation) adds the finishing touch to this charming hideaway.

Hôtel Roma Sacré-Coeur

101 rue Caulaincourt, 18th (01.42. 62.02.02/fax 01.42.54.34.92/www. hotelroma.fr). M° Lamarck Caulaincourt. €€.

The Roma Sacré-Coeur is located on the trendier, north side of Montmartre, far from the postcard shops and coach parties, but still within walking distance (uphill) of Sacré-Coeur. From the tiny lobby, a whimsical, AstroTurf-covered staircase leads to the 57 pretty rooms;

The Marais & Eastern Paris

Grand Hôtel Jeanne d'Arc

3 rue de Jarente, 4th (01.48.87.62. 11/fax 01.48.87.37.31/www.hotel jeannedarc.com). Mᵒ Chemin Vert or St-Paul. €.

This hotel's strong point is its location on a quiet road close to pretty place du Marché-Ste-Catherine. Recent refurbishment has made the reception area striking, with a huge mirror adding the illusion of space. Rooms are colourful and, for the price, fairly well sized and comfortable.

Hôtel Beaumarchais

3 rue Oberkampf, 11th (01.53.36. 86.86/fax 01.43.38.32.86/www.hotel beaumarchais.com). Mᵒ Filles du Calvaire or Oberkampf. €.

The contemporary Beaumarchais is situated in the Oberkampf area, not far from the Marais and Bastille action. Its 31 bedrooms are all brightly decorated with colourful walls, bathroom mosaics and wavy headboards; breakfast is served on the tiny garden patio or in your room.

Hôtel Bourg Tibourg

19 rue du Bourg-Tibourg, 4th (01.42. 78.47.39/fax 01.40.29.07.00/www. hotelbourgtibourg.com). Mᵒ Hôtel de Ville. €€€.

The Bourg Tibourg has the same owners as Hôtel Costes and the same interior decorator – but don't expect this jewel box of a boutique hotel to look like a miniature replica. Aside from its enviable location in the heart of the Marais and its fashion-pack fans, here it's all about Jacques Garcia's neo-Gothic-cum-Byzantine decor – both impressive and imaginative. Exotic, scented candles, mosaic-tiled bathrooms, luxurious fabrics in rich colours and the cool contrast of crisp white linens create the perfect escape from the outside world. There's no restaurant or lounge – posing is done in the neighbourhood bars.

Hôtel de la Bretonnerie

22 rue Ste-Croix-de-la-Bretonnerie, 4th (01.48.87.77.63/fax 01.42.77. 26.78/www.bretonnerie.com). Mᵒ Hôtel de Ville. €€.

With its combination of wrought ironwork, exposed stone and wooden beams, the labyrinth of corridors and passages in this 17th-century *hôtel particulier* is full of historic atmosphere. Tapestries, rich colours and the occasional four-poster bed give the 29 suites and bedrooms individuality. The location is convenient too, with the bars, shops and museums of the Marais just a short stroll away.

Hôtel Duo

11 rue du Temple, 4th (01.42.72.72.22/ fax 01.42.72.03.53/www.duoparis.com). Mᵒ Hôtel de Ville. €€€.

Formerly the Axial Beauborg, this stylish boutique hotel, decorated with white marble floors, mud-coloured walls, crushed-velvet sofas and exposed beams, is close to the Centre Pompidou. Rooms are not large, but exude refinement and comfort.

Hôtel du Petit Moulin

29 rue de Poitou, 3rd (01.42.74. 10.10/fax 01.42.74.10.97/www.hotel dupetitmoulin.com). Mᵒ St-Sébastien Froissart. €€€.

Within striking distance of the Musée Picasso and the hip shops around rue Charlot, this turn-of-the-century façade masks what was once the oldest *boulangerie* in Paris, lovingly restored as a boutique hotel by Nadia Murano and Denis Nourry. The couple recruited no lesser figure than fashion designer Christian Lacroix for the decor, and the result is a riot of colour, trompe l'oeil effects and a savvy mix of old and new. Each of its 17 exquisitely appointed rooms is unique, and the walls in rooms 202, 204 and 205 feature swirling, extravagant drawings and scribbles taken from Lacroix's sketchbook.

Hôtel de Roubaix

6 rue Greneta, 3rd (01.42.72.89.91/ fax 01.42.72.58.79/www.hotel-de-roubaix.com). Mᵒ Arts et Métiers. €.

Shelter in style

Mama Shelter

The trend for design on a budget continues with the opening in autumn 2008 of the ground-breaking 172-room Mama Shelter, by Town & Shelter, the company set up by Serge Trigano, former chairman of the Club Med resort group. In eschewing Paris's traditional hotel districts for a vacant plot next to the disused Petite Ceinture railway line in the most picturesque corner of the 20th arrondissement, Trigano is setting his sights on a trendy urban clientele.

At first sight, it's an unlikely collaboration between socially committed architect Roland Castro, best known for his schemes to rehabilitate the mass housing disasters of the 1960s and '70s, and maverick superstar designer Philippe Starck. But the idea, says Trigano, is 'to associate their talents around an innovative project'.

Castro's rectilinear white design features roof gardens and large window areas. Inside, the bedrooms focus on style over size, but its not just a question of going for hip minimalism. Everything has been conceived by Starck to make the most of a compact space, with the bed inserted into the window bay, a desk area, open-plan hanging space, fridge and microwave. Fashionably dark walls are offset by white and orange bed coverings, slinky bedside lamps and specially designed graphic carpets; bathrooms come with jazzy black and white tiling.

Aimed at business clients in Paris for trade shows and 'tourists keen to discover one of the new quarters of Paris that is authentic, amusing and in a state of evolution', success, according to Trigano, is not just about creating a beautiful place but about how the hotel will live. One of the unusual features of Mama Shelter is that it is within a complex incorporating local housing and a multimedia library; its facilities – bar, restaurant, fitness room – will be open to Parisians, while guests will be encouraged to cross the road for a concert at the Flèche d'Or (in which Trigano is now a shareholder) music bar.

ESSENTIALS

You're two blocks from the Centre Pompidou, the Marais and the trendy shops of rue Etienne-Marcel, with an immaculately clean bathroom, television, telephone and even a lift. So why are the rates so low? Could be the granny-friendly decor or the squishy mattresses; but since the hotel's 53 rooms are invariably fully booked, it seems that no one is too discouraged.

Hôtel St-Merry

78 rue de la Verrerie, 4th (01.42.78. 14.15/fax 01.40.29.06.82/www.hotel marais.com). M° Châtelet or Hôtel de Ville. €€.
The Gothic decor of this former presbytery attached to the Eglise St-Merry is ideal for a Dracula set, with wooden beams, stone walls and plenty of iron – behind the door of room No.9 an imposing flying buttress straddles the carved antique bed. On the downside, the historic building has no lift and only the suite has a TV.

Mama Shelter

NEW *rue de Bagnolet, 20th (www.town shelter.com). M° Alexandre Dumas. €.*
See box p175.

Mercure Terminus Est

5 rue du 8-Mai 1945, 10th (01.55.26. 05.05/fax 01.55.26.05.00/www. mercure.com). M° Gare de l'Est. €€.
Located opposite the Gare de l'Est, this great railway hotel combines modern interior design with elements that evoke the classic age of steam: leather luggage handles on the wardrobes, retro bathroom fittings and a library in the lobby. The 200 rooms and public areas all offer Wi-Fi internet access.

Murano Urban Resort

13 bd du Temple, 3rd (01.42.71.20.00/ fax 01.42.71.21.01/www.muranoresort. com). M° Filles du Calvaire or Oberkampf. €€€€.
Behind this unremarkable façade is a super-cool and supremely luxurious hotel, popular with the fashion set for its slick lounge-style design and high-tech flourishes – including coloured light co-ordinators that enable

you to change the mood of your room at the touch of a button. The handsome bar has a mind-boggling 140 varieties of vodka to sample, which can bring the op art fabrics in the lift to life and make the fingerprint access to the hotel's 43 rooms and nine suites (two of which feature private pools) a late-night godsend.

Le Quartier République, Le Marais

39 rue Jean-Pierre Timbaud, 11th (01.48.06.64.97/fax 01.48.05.03.38/ www.lequartierhotelrm.com). M° Parmentier or République. €.
Despite its slightly misleading name (the hotel isn't exactly located in the Marais), the younger sibling of Le Général and Le Quartier Bastille offers the most wallet-friendly rates of Franck Altruie's chain of budget design hotels.

The Seine & Islands

Hôtel des Deux-Iles

59 rue St-Louis-en-l'Ile, 4th (01.43.26. 13.35/fax 01.43.29.60.25/www.deux iles-paris-hotel.com). M° Pont Marie. €€.
This peaceful 17th-century townhouse offers 17 soundproofed, air-conditioned rooms done out in vaguely colonial style. Attractive features include a tiny courtyard off the lobby and a vaulted stone breakfast area. All the rooms were freshened up in 2007, with new decoration and refurbished bathrooms. The equally pleasant Hôtel le Lutèce, which is located at nearby No.65 (01.43.26.23.52), is run by the same management team.

Hôtel du Jeu de Paume

54 rue St-Louis-en-l'Ile, 4th (01.43. 26.14.18/fax 01.40.46.02.76/www. jeudepaumehotel.com). M° Pont Marie. €€€€.
With a discreet courtyard entrance, 17th-century beams, private garden and a unique timbered breakfast room that was once a real tennis court built under Louis XIII, this is a charming and romantic hotel. These days, it is

filled with an attractive array of modern and classical art. A dramatic glass lift and catwalks lead to the rooms, which are simple and tasteful, the walls hung with Pierre Frey fabric.

The 7th & Western Paris

Le Bellechasse

NEW *8 rue de Bellechasse, 7th (01.45.50.22.31/fax 01.45.51. 52.36/www.lebellechasse.com). M° Assemblée Nationale or Solferino/ RER Musée d'Orsay.* €€€€.
A former *hôtel particulier*, the Bellechasse fell into the hands of Christian Lacroix. It reopened in July 2007, duly transformed into a trendy boutique hotel. Only a few steps away from the Musée d'Orsay, it offers 34 splendid – though rather small – rooms, in seven different decorative styles. It's advisable to book up early as the Bellechasse promises to be *the* hit of 2008/9.

Hôtel Duc de Saint-Simon

14 rue de St-Simon, 7th (01.44.39. 20.20/fax 01.45.48.68.25/www.hotel ducdesaintsimon.com). M° Rue du Bac. €€€.
A lovely courtyard leads the way into this popular hotel situated on the edge of St-Germain-des-Prés. Of the 34 romantic bedrooms, four have terraces over a closed-off, leafy garden. It's perfect for lovers, though if you can do without a four-poster bed, there are more spacious rooms than the Honeymoon Suite.

Hôtel Eiffel Rive Gauche

6 rue du Gros-Caillou, 7th (01.45.51. 24.56/fax 01.45.51.11.77/www.hotel-eiffel.com). M° Ecole Militaire. €.
The provençal decor and warm welcome make this a nice retreat. For the quintessential Paris view at a bargain price, ask to stay on one of the upper floors: you can see the Eiffel Tower from nine of the 29 rooms. All feature Empire-style bedheads and modern bathrooms. Outside, there's a tiny, tiled courtyard with a bridge. A nearby sister hotel in the 15th, the Hôtel Eiffel Villa Garibaldi (01.56.58.56.58), has equally modest rates.

Hôtel Lenox

9 rue de l'Université, 7th (01.42.96. 10.95/fax 01.42.61.52.83/www. lenoxsaintgermain.com). M° St-Germain-des-Prés. €€.
The location may be the 7th, but this venerable literary and artistic haunt is unmistakeably part of St-Germain-des-Prés. The art deco-style Lenox Club Bar, open to the public, features comfortable leather club chairs and jazz instruments on the walls. Bedrooms, reached by an astonishing glass lift, have more traditional decor and city views.

Le Montalembert

3 rue Montalembert, 7th (01.45.49. 68.68/fax 01.45.49.69.49/www. montalembert.com). M° Rue du Bac. €€€€.
Grace Leo-Andrieu's impeccable boutique hotel opened in 1990 and is a benchmark of quality and service. It has everything that *mode* maniacs (who flock here for Fashion Week) could want: bathrooms stuffed with Contemporel toiletries, a set of digital scales and 360° mirrors to check out that all-important figure. Decorated in pale lilac, cinnamon and olive tones, the entire hotel is equipped with Wi-Fi access and each room is equipped with a flat-screen TV. Clattery two-person stairwell lifts are a nice nod to old-fashioned ways in a hotel that is otherwise *tout moderne*.

St-Germain-des-Prés & Odéon

Le Clos Médicis

56 rue Monsieur-le-Prince, 6th (01.43.29.10.80/fax 01.43.54.26.90/ www.closmedicis.com). M° Odéon/ RER Luxembourg. €€€.
Designed more like a stylish, private townhouse than a hotel, Le Clos Médicis is located by the Luxembourg

www.parisaddress.com

Short term apartment rental in Paris

Live in Paris like a true Parisian!
You wish to live Paris from "within", like a true Parisian?
Saint-Germain-des-Prés, the Latin Quarter, the Marais…

Paris Address invites you to discover picturesque
and lively central apartments.

Prices all included, instant availability and
easy-booking on the website.

gardens: perfect if you fancy starting the morning with a stroll among the trees. The hotel's decor is refreshingly modern chic, with bedrooms done out in taffeta curtains and chenille bedcovers, and antique floor tiles in the bathrooms. The cosy lounge has a working fireplace.

Grand Hôtel de l'Univers

6 rue Grégoire-de-Tours, 6th (01. 43.29.37.00/fax 01.40.51.06.45/ www.hotel-paris-univers.com). M° Odéon. **€€**.
Making the most of its 15th-century origins, this hotel features exposed wooden beams, high ceilings, antique furnishings and toile-covered walls. Manuel Canovas fabrics lend a posh touch, but there are also some useful services such as a laptop for hire. The same helpful team runs the Hôtel St-Germain-des-Prés nearby, which has a medieval-themed room and the sweetest attic in Paris.

L'Hôtel

13 rue des Beaux-Arts, 6th (01.44.41. 99.00/fax 01.43.25.64.81/www. l-hotel.com). M° St-Germain-des-Prés or Mabillon. **€€€€**.
Guests at the sumptuously decorated L'Hôtel are more likely to be models and film stars than the starving writers who frequented it during Oscar Wilde's last days. Under Jacques Garcia's careful restoration, each room has its own theme: Mistinguett's *chambre* retains its art deco mirror bed, and Oscar's deathbed room has, appropriately, been decorated with green peacock murals. Don't miss the cellar swimming pool or *fumoir*.

Hôtel de l'Abbaye

10 rue Cassette, 6th (01.45.44.38.11/ fax 01.45.48.07.86/www.hotelabbaye paris.com). M° Rennes or St-Sulpice. **€€€**.
A monumental entrance opens the way through a courtyard into this tranquil hotel, originally part of a convent. Wood panelling, well-stuffed sofas and an open fireplace in the drawing room make for a relaxed atmosphere, but,

best of all, there's a surprisingly large garden where breakfast is served in the warmer months. The 44 rooms are tasteful and luxurious, and the suites have rooftop terraces.

Hôtel des Académies et des Arts

NEW *15 rue de la Grande Chaumière, 6th (01.43.26.66.44/fax 01.40.46. 86.85/www.hotel-des-academies. com). M° Notre-Dame des Champs, Raspail or Vavin.* **€€€**.
Reopened in early 2007 after a full refurbishment, this small boutique hotel scores highly on style. There are cosy salons, fireplaces and an extensive collection of art books. The 20 immaculate rooms are individually designed around four themes (Paris, Actor, Man Ray or Rulhmann), and offer some wonderful views over the city rooftops or down on to the spectacular Jérôme Mesnager mural in the courtyard.

Hôtel du Globe

15 rue des Quatre-Vents, 6th (01.43. 26.35.50/fax 01.46.33.62.69/www. hotel-du-globe.fr). M° Odéon. **€€**.
The Hôtel du Globe has managed to retain much of its 17th-century character – and very pleasant it is too. Gothic wrought-iron doors take you through into the florid corridors, while an unexplained suit of armour supervises guests from the tiny salon. The bedrooms with baths are somewhat larger than those with showers – all 14 of them underwent complete renovation in 2004. There's even a four-poster bed to be had if you ask for it upon reservation.

Hôtel Lutetia

45 bd Raspail, 6th (01.49.54.46.46/fax 01.49.54.46.00/www.lutetia-paris.com). M° Sèvres Babylone. **€€€€**.
This historic Left Bank hotel is a masterpiece of art nouveau and early art deco architecture that dates from 1910. It has a plush jazz bar and lively brasserie with views of the chic Bon Marché store across the street. Its 250 rooms, revamped in purple, gold and

ESSENTIALS

pearl grey, maintain a 1930s feel. Big-name guests in years gone by have included Pablo Picasso, Josephine Baker and Charles de Gaulle. It also functioned as Abwehr HQ during the Nazi occupation.

Hôtel des Saints-Pères

65 rue des Sts-Pères, 6th (01.45.44. 50.00/fax 01.45.44.90.83/www. espritfrance.com). M° St-Germain-des-Prés. €€.

Built in 1658 by one of Louis XIV's architects, this discreet hotel now occupies an enviable location near St-Germain-des-Prés' designer boutiques. It boasts a charming garden and a sophisticated, if small, bar. The most coveted room is No.100 (€325), with its fine 17th-century ceiling by painters from the Versailles School; it also has an open bathroom, so you can gaze at scenes from the myth of Leda and the Swan while you scrub.

Regents Hôtel

44 rue Madame, 6th (01.45.48.02.81/ fax 01.45.44.85.73). M° St-Sulpice. €.

This discreet hotel located in a quiet street is a lovely surprise, its courtyard garden used for breakfast in the warmer months. The reception rooms are painted a sunny provençal blue and yellow, and the bedrooms are comfortable, with new bathrooms. Some have small balconies.

Relais Saint-Germain

9 carrefour de l'Odéon, 6th (01.43.29.12.05/fax 01.46.33. 45.30/www.hotel-paris-relais-saint-germain.com). M° Odéon. €€€.

The rustic, wood-beamed ceilings remain intact at the Hotel Relais Saint-Germain, a 17th-century hotel bought and renovated by much-acclaimed chef Yves Camdeborde (originator of the *bistronomique* dining trend) and his wife Claudine. Each of the 22 rooms offers a different take on eclectic provençal charm, and the marble bathrooms are huge by Paris standards. Guests get first dibs on a highly sought-after seat in the 15-table restaurant Le Comptoir next door.

The Latin Quarter & the 13th

Familia Hôtel

11 rue des Ecoles, 5th (01.43.54. 55.27/fax 01.43.29.61.77/www.hotel-paris-familia.com). M° Cardinal Lemoine or Jussieu. €.

This old-fashioned Latin Quarter hotel has balconies hung with tumbling plants and walls draped with replica French tapestries. Owner Eric Gaucheron offers a warm welcome, and the 30 rooms have personalised touches such as sepia murals, cherry-wood furniture and stone walls. The Gaucherons also own the Minerve next door – book in advance for both.

Five Hôtel

3 rue Flatters, 5th (01.43.31.74.21/fax 01.43.31.61.96/www.thefivehotel.com). M° Les Gobelins or Port Royal. €€.

The rooms in this stunning boutique hotel may be small, but they're all exquisitely designed, with Chinese lacquer paint and velvety fabrics. Fibre optics built into the walls create the illusion of sleeping under a starry sky, and you can choose among four different fragrances to perfume your room (the hotel is entirely non-smoking).

Hôtel les Degrés de Notre-Dame

10 rue des Grands-Degrés, 5th (01.55.42.88.88/fax 01.40.46. 95.34/www.lesdegreshotel.com). M° Maubert-Mutualité or St-Michel. €€.

On a tiny street across the river from Notre-Dame, this vintage hotel is a gem. Its ten rooms are full of character, with original paintings, antique furniture and exposed wooden beams (Nos.47 and 501 have views of the cathedral). It has an adorable restaurant and, a few streets away, two studio apartments that the owner rents to preferred customers only.

Hôtel la Demeure

51 bd St-Marcel, 13th (01.43.37.81.25/ fax 01.45.87.05.03/www.hotel-paris-lademeure.com). M° Les Gobelins. €€.

This comfortable, modern hotel on the edge of the Latin Quarter is run by a friendly father and son. It has 43 air-conditioned rooms with internet access, plus suites with sliding doors to separate sleeping and living space. The wrap-around balustrades of the corner rooms offer lovely views of the city, and bathrooms feature either luxurious tubs or shower heads.

Hôtel Esmeralda

4 rue St-Julien-le-Pauvre, 5th (01.43.54.19.20/fax 01.40.51.00.68). M° Maubert Mutualité or St-Michel. **€**.

An offbeat piece of historic Paris, the Esmeralda has 19 floral rooms with antique furnishings and aged wallpaper, as well as the uneven floors and wonky staircase you'd expect in a building that's been here since 1640. Book ahead: the rooms overlooking Notre-Dame are popular with honeymooners.

Hôtel des Grandes Ecoles

75 rue du Cardinal-Lemoine, 5th (01.43.26.79.23/fax 01.43.25.28.15/ www.hotel-grandes-ecoles.com). M° Cardinal Lemoine. **€€**.

A breath of fresh air in the heart of the Latin Quarter, this country-style hotel has 51 old-fashioned rooms set around a leafy garden where breakfast is served in the summer. The largest of the three buildings houses the reception area and a stylish breakfast room.

Hôtel du Panthéon

19 pl du Panthéon, 5th (01.43.54.32.95/fax 01.43.26.64.65/www.hoteldupantheon.com). M° Cluny La Sorbonne or Maubert Mutualité/ RER Luxembourg. **€€**.

The 36 rooms of this elegant hotel are beautifully decorated with *toile de Jouy* fabrics, antique furniture and painted woodwork. Some enjoy impressive views of the Panthéon; others squint out on to a romantic courtyard.

Hôtel Résidence Henri IV

50 rue des Bernardins, 5th (01.44.41.31.81/fax 01.46.33.93.22/www.residencehenri4.com). M° Cardinal Lemoine. **€€**.

This Belle Epoque style hotel has a mere eight rooms and five apartments, so guests are assured of the staff's full attention. Peacefully situated next to leafy square Paul-Langevin, it's minutes away from Notre-Dame. The four-person apartments come with a handy mini-kitchen featuring a hob, fridge and microwave – although you may be reduced to eating on the beds in the smaller ones.

Hôtel de la Sorbonne

6 rue Victor-Cousin, 5th (01.43.54.58.08/fax 01.40.51.05.18/www.hotelsorbonne.com). M° Cluny La Sorbonne/RER Luxembourg. **€€**.

This cosy hotel features wooden floors, beams and a fireplace in the salon. The 39 rooms are pale green or lavender, with cheerful geranium-filled window boxes. Bathrooms are tiny; those with shower are preferable to those with a gnome-sized tub.

Montparnasse

Hôtel Aviatic

105 rue de Vaugirard, 6th (01.53.63.25.50/fax 01.53.63.25.55/www.aviatic.fr). M° Duroc, Montparnasse Bienvenüe or St-Placide. **€€**.

This historic hotel has tons of character, from the Empire-style lounge and garden atrium to the bistro-style breakfast room. The polished floor in the lobby and the hints of marble and brass lend an impressive touch of glamour.

Hôtel Istria Saint-Germain

29 rue Campagne-Première, 14th (01.43.20.91.82/fax 01.43.22.48.45/www.istria-paris-hotel.com). M° Raspail. **€€**.

Behind this unassuming façade is the place where the artistic royalty of Montparnasse's heyday – the likes of Man Ray, Marcel Duchamp and Louis Aragon – once lived. The Istria Saint-Germain has been modernised since then, but it still has plenty of charm, with 26 bright, simply furnished rooms, a cosy cellar breakfast room and a comfortable communal area.

ESSENTIALS

Getting Around

Airports

Roissy-Charles-de-Gaulle
*01.48.62.22.80/www.paris-cdg.com.
30km (19 miles) north-east of Paris.*
For most international flights. The
two main terminals are some way
apart; check which one you need for
your flight back. The **RER B** line
(08.91.36.20.20) is the quickest way
to central Paris (40mins to Gare du
Nord; 45mins to RER Châtelet-Les
Halles; €8.20 single). A new station
gives direct access from Terminal 2;
from Terminal 1 take the free
shuttle. Trains run every 15mins,
5.24am-11.56pm daily.

Air France buses (08.92.35.08.20,
www.cars-airfrance.com; €13 single,
€20 return) leave every 15mins,
5.45am-11pm daily, from both
terminals, and stop at Porte Maillot
and place Charles-de-Gaulle (35-
50mins trip). Buses also run to Gare
Montparnasse and Gare de Lyon
(€14 single, €22 return) every 30mins
(45-60mins trip), 7am-9pm daily; a
bus between Roissy and Orly (€16)
runs every 30mins, 6am-10.30pm
Mon-Fri, 7am-10.30pm Sat, Sun.

RATP Roissybus (08.92.68.77.14;
€8.60) runs every 15mins, 5.45am-
11pm daily, between the airport
and the corner of rue Scribe/
rue Auber (at least 45mins); buy
your tickets on the bus.

Paris Airports Service is a
24-hour door-to-door minibus service
between airports and hotels, seven
days a week. Roissy prices go from
€25 for one to €12.40 each person
for eight people, 6am-8pm (minimum
€34, 5-6am, 8-10pm); you can reserve
a place on 01.55.98.10.80, www.
parisairportservice.com.

A **taxi** into central Paris from
Roissy-Charles-de-Gaulle airport
should take 30-60mins and cost
€30-€50, plus €1 per luggage item.

Orly
*01.49.75.15.15/www.paris-orly.com.
About 18km (11 miles) south of Paris.*
Orly-Sud terminal is international
and Orly-Ouest domestic. **Orlyrail**
(€5.65) runs to Pont de Rungis, for
the RER C into central Paris. Trains
run every 15mins, 6am-11pm daily;
50mins trip.

Air France buses (08.92.35.08.20,
www.cars-airfrance.com; €9 single,
€14 return) leave both terminals
every 15mins, 6am-11pm daily,
and stop at Invalides and
Montparnasse (30-45mins).

The **RATP Orlybus** (08.92.68.
77.14) runs to Denfert-Rochereau
every 15mins, 5.35am-11.05pm daily
(30mins trip); buy tickets (€5.80) on
the bus. High-speed **Orlyval** shuttle
trains run every 7mins (6am-11pm
daily) to RER B station Antony
(shuttle and RER together is €17.05;
allow 35mins for central Paris.

Orly prices for the Paris Airports
Service (*see left*) are €24 for one and
€9-€14 per passenger depending on
the number. A **taxi** takes 20-40mins
and costs €16-€26.

Paris Beauvais
*08.92.68.20.66/www.aeroportbeauvais.
com. 70km (43 miles) north of Paris.*
Budget hub. **Buses** (€13) to Porte
Maillot leave 20mins after each
arrival and 3hr 15mins before each
departure. Tickets from Arrivals or
1 bd Pershing, 17th (01.58.05.08.45).

Arriving by car

Options for crossing the Channel
include: **Eurotunnel** (08.10.63.
03.04, www.eurotunnel.com);
Brittany Ferries (08.25.82.88.28,
www.brittanyferries.com), **P&O
Ferries** (08.25.12.01.56, www.
poferries.com) and **SeaFrance** (08.
25.04.04.45, www.seafrance.com).

Arriving by coach

International coaches arrive at **Gare Routière Internationale Paris-Galliéni** at Porte de Bagnolet, 20th. For tickets (in English) call Eurolines on 08.92.89.90.91 or (UK) 01582 404 511, or visit www.eurolines.fr.

Arriving by rail

The Eurostar from London St Pancras International (01233 617575, www.eurostar.com) to Paris Gare du Nord (08.92.35.35.39) takes 2hrs 15mins direct. You must check in at least 30mins before departure.

Maps

Free maps of the métro, bus and RER systems are available at airports and métro stations.

Public transport

RATP (08.92.68.41.14, www.ratp.fr) runs the bus, métro and suburban tram routes, as well as lines A and B of the RER express railway, which connects with the métro inside Paris. State rail **SNCF** (08.92.35.35.39, www.sncf.com) runs RER lines C, D and E for the suburbs.

Fares & tickets

Paris and its suburbs are divided into eight concentric travel zones, with 1 and 2 covering the city centre. RATP tickets and passes are valid on the métro, bus and RER. Tickets and carnets can be bought at métro stations, tourist offices and tobacconists; single tickets can be bought on buses. Retain your ticket in case of spot checks; you'll also need it to exit from RER stations.

A ticket is €1.50, a carnet of ten €11.10. A Mobilis day pass is €5.60 for zones 1 and 2 and €18.70 for zones 1-8 (not including airports).

A one-day Paris Visite pass for zones 1-3 is €8.50; a five-day pass is €27.20, with discounts on sights.

Métro & RER

The Paris **métro** is the best way of getting around. Trains run daily 5.30am-12.40am. Numbered lines have their direction named after the last stop. Follow the orange *Correspondance* signs to change lines. The five **RER** lines run 5.30am-1am daily across Paris and into commuterland. Métro tickets are valid for RER zones 1-2.

Buses

Buses run 6.30am-8.30pm, with some routes continuing until 12.30am, Mon-Sat; limited services operate on selected lines Sun and public holidays. You can use a métro ticket, a ticket bought from the driver (€1.50) or a travel pass. Tickets should be punched in the machine next to the driver; passes should be shown to the driver.

Night buses

The 18 **Noctambus** lines run from place du Châtelet to the suburbs (hourly 1.30am-5.35am Mon-Thur; half-hourly 1am-5.35am Fri, Sat); look out for the owl logo. A ticket is €2.70 and allows one change.

River transport

Batobus

08.25.05.01.01/www.batobus.com. Feb-Mar, Oct-Dec 10am-7pm daily; Apr-Sept 10am-10pm daily. One-day pass €11 (€5, €7).
River buses stop every 15-25mins at the Eiffel Tower, Musée d'Orsay, St-Germain-des-Prés (quai Malaquais), Notre-Dame, Jardin des Plantes, Hôtel de Ville, the Louvre, Champs-Elysées (Pont Alexandre III). Tickets are available from Batobus stops, RATP and tourist offices.

ESSENTIALS

Rail travel

Versailles and Disneyland Paris are served by the RER. Most locations out of the city are served by the SNCF railway; the TGV high-speed train has slashed journey times and is steadily being extended to all the main regions. Tickets can be bought at any SNCF station (not only the one from which you'll travel), SNCF shops and travel agents. If you reserve online or by phone, you can pay and pick up your tickets from the station or have them sent to your home. SNCF automatic machines (*billeterie automatique*) only work with French credit/debit cards. Buy tickets in advance to secure the cheaper fare. Before you board any train, stamp your ticket in the orange *composteur* machines on the platforms, or you might have to pay a hefty fine.

SNCF
08.92.35.35.39/www.sncf.com.
Open 7am-10pm daily.
The line can also be reached (inside France) by dialling 3635 and saying '*billet*' at the prompt.

Taxis

Taxis are hard to find at rush hour or early in the morning. Ranks are indicated with a blue sign. A white light on a taxi's roof means it's free; an orange one means it's busy. You also pay for the time it takes your radioed taxi to arrive. Payment by credit card – mention this when you order – is €15 minimum.

Airportaxis
01.41.50.42.50/www.taxiparisien.fr.
Alpha
01.45.85.85.85/www.alphataxis.fr.
G7
01.47.39.47.39/www.taxis-g7.fr.

Taxis Bleus
01.49.36.29.48/08.91.70.10.10/www.taxis-bleus.com.

Driving

If you bring your car to France, you must bring its registration and insurance documents. An insurance green card, available from insurance companies and the AA and RAC in the UK, is not compulsory but is useful. Traffic information for Ile-de-France is given at 08.26.02.20.22, www.securiteroutiere.gouv.fr.

Breakdown services

The AA or RAC do not have reciprocal arrangements with an equivalent organisation in France, so it's advisable to take out additional breakdown insurance cover, for example with Europ Assistance (0870 737 5720, www.europ-assistance.co.uk). If you don't have insurance, you can use its service (01.41.85.85.85), but it will charge you the full cost. Other 24-hour breakdown services in Paris include: Action Auto Assistance (01.45.58.49.58); Dan Dépann Auto (01.40.06.06.53).

Parking

There are still a few free on-street parking areas in Paris, but they're often full. If you park illegally, your car may be clamped or towed away. Don't park in zones marked for deliveries (*livraisons*) or taxis. *Horodateurs*, pay-and-display machines, which take a special card (*carte de stationnement* at €10 or €30, from tobacconists). Parking is often free at weekends, after 7pm in the evening and in August. Underground car parks cost around €2.50 per hour, €22 for 24 hours. Some have lower rates after 6pm. See www.parkingsdeparis.com.

Vehicle removal

If your car is impounded, contact
the nearest police station. There
are eight car pounds (*préfourrières*)
in Paris; to find out where your car
might be, contact 01.53.73.53.73,
08.91.01.22.22 or www.prefecture-
police-paris.interieur.gouv.fr.

Car hire

To hire a car you must be 25 or
over and have held a licence for at
least a year. Some agencies accept
drivers aged 21-24, but a day fee of
€20-€25 is usual. Take your licence
and passport. There are often good
weekend offers. Weekly deals are
better at bigger companies: around
€300 a week for a small car with
insurance and 1,750km included.
Costlier hire companies allow the
return of a car in other French cities
and abroad. Cheaper ones may
have a high charge for damage:
read the small print before signing.

Ada
08.25.16.91.69/www.ada.fr.
Avis
08.20.05.05.05/www.avis.fr.
Budget
08.25.00.35.64/www.budget.fr.
EasyRentacar
www.easycar.com.
Europcar
08.25.82.55.13/www.europcar.fr.
Hertz
01.41.91.95.25/www.hertz.fr.
Rent-a-Car
08.91.70.02.00/www.rentacar.fr

Cycling

In 2007, the mayor launched
a free bike scheme – Vélib
(www.velib.paris.fr). There
are now over 20,000 bicycles
available 24 hours a day, at nearly
1,500 'stations' across the city. Just
swipe your travel card to release
the bikes from their stands. The
mairie actively promotes cycling

in the city and the Vélib scheme is
complemented by the 353km (220
miles) of bike lanes snaking their
way around Paris.

A free *Paris à Vélo* map can be
picked up at any *mairie* or from
bike shops. Cycle lanes (*pistes
cyclables*) run mostly N–S and E–W.
N–S routes include rue de Rennes,
av d'Italie, bd Sébastopol and av
Marceau. E–W routes take in the
rue de Rivoli, bd St-Germain, bd
St-Jacques and av Daumesnil.
You could be fined (€22) if you
don't use them, which is a bit rich
considering the lanes are often
blocked by delivery vans and the
€135 fine for obstructing a cycle
lane is barely enforced. Cyclists are
also entitled to use certain bus
lanes (especially the new ones,
which are set off by a strip of kerb
stones); look out for traffic signs
with a bike symbol.

Cycle hire

Note that bike insurance may not
cover theft: make sure you check
before you sign.

Maison Roue Libre

*1 passage Mondétour, 1st (08.10.
44.15.34). M° Châtelet. Also Mar-Oct
four RATP cyclobuses at Stalingrad,
pl du Châtelet, porte d'Auteuil and
parc Floral in the Bois de Vincennes
(01.48.15.28.88/www.rouelibre.fr).*
Open 9am-7pm daily.
Bike hire is €4 an hour, €10-€15 a
day, €28 a weekend. Helmets free.
Passport and €200 deposit required.
*Other locations: 37 bd Bourdon, 4th
(01.42.71.54.54).*

Paris-Vélo

*2 rue du Fer-à-Moulin, 5th (01.43.
37.59.22/www.paris-velo-rent-a-bike.fr).
M° Censier-Daubenton.* **Open** 10am-
7pm daily.
Mountain bikes and 21-speed models
for hire. Five hours is €12, a weekend
€30. Valid passport and €300 deposit
are required.

Resources A-Z

Accident & emergency

Most of the following services operate 24 hours a day. In a medical emergency, you should call the Sapeurs-Pompiers, who have trained paramedics.

Ambulance (SAMU)	**15**
Police	**17**
Fire (Sapeurs-Pompiers)	**18**
Emergency	
(from a mobile phone)	**112**

Credit card loss

In case of credit card loss or theft, call one of the following 24hr services that have English-speaking staff.

American Express
01.47.77.70.00
Diners Club
01.49.06.17.50
MasterCard/Visa
08.36.69.08.80

Customs

Non-EU residents can claim a tax refund or *détaxe* (around 12%) on VAT if you spend over €175 in any one purchase and if you live outside the EU for more than six months in the year. At the shop make sure you ask for a *bordereau de vente à l'exportation*.

Dental emergencies

Look in the *Pages Jaunes* (www. pagesjaunes.fr) under *Dentistes*. For emergencies contact:

Hôpital de la Pitié-Salpêtrière
47-83 bd de l'Hôpital, 13th (01.42. 16.00.00). Mº Gare d'Austerlitz. **Open** 24hrs.

SOS Dentaire
87 bd Port-Royal, 13th (01.43.36.36. 00). Mº Les Gobelins/RER Port-Royal. **Open** by phone 9am-midnight.

Disabled

General information (in French) is available on the Secrétaire d'Etat aux Personnes Handicapées website: www.handicap.gouv.fr.

Electricity

France uses the standard 220-240V, 50-cycle AC system. Visitors with 240V British appliances need an adapter (*adaptateur*). US 110V appliances need an adapter and a transformer (*transformateur*).

Embassies & consulates

See also the *Pages Jaunes* under 'Ambassades et Consulats'.

Australian Embassy
4 rue Jean-Rey, 15th (01.40.59.33.00/ www.france.embassy.gov.au). Mº Bir-Hakeim. **Open** *Consular services 9.15am-noon, 2-4.30pm Mon-Fri. Visas 10am-noon Mon-Fri.*
British Embassy
35 rue du Fbg-St-Honoré, 8th (01.44. 51.31.00/www.amb.grandebretagne.fr). Mº Concorde. Consular services 18bis rue d'Anjou, 8th. Mº Concorde. **Open** 9.30am-12.30pm, 2.30-4.30pm Mon-Fri. *Visas 16 rue d'Anjou, 8th (01.44.51. 31.01).* **Open** 9.30am-noon Mon-Fri. *By phone 2.30-4.30pm Mon-Fri.* British citizens wanting consular services (such as new passports) should ignore the long queue along rue d'Anjou for the visa department and walk straight in at No.18bis.
Canadian Embassy
35 av Montaigne, 8th (01.44.43. 29.00/www.amb-canada.fr). Mº

Franklin D Roosevelt. Consular services (01.44.43.29.02). **Open** 9am-noon Mon-Fri. *Visas 37 av Montaigne (01.44.43.29.16).* **Open** 8.30-11am Mon-Fri.

Irish Embassy
12 av Foch, 16th. Consulate 4 rue Rude, 16th (01.44.17.67.00). Mº Charles de Gaulle Etoile. **Open** *Consular/visas* 9.30am-noon Mon-Fri. *By phone* 9.30am-1pm, 2.30-5.30pm Mon-Fri.

New Zealand Embassy
7ter rue Léonard-de-Vinci, 16th (01.45.01.43.43/www.nzembassy.com/ france). Mº Victor Hugo. **Open** *Sept-June* 9am-1pm, 2-5.30pm Mon-Thur; 9am-1pm, 2-4pm Fri. *July, Aug* 9am-1pm, 2-4.30pm Mon-Thur; 9am-2pm Fri. *Visas* 9am-12.30pm Mon-Fri. Visas for travel to New Zealand can be applied for on the website www. immigration.govt.nz.

South African Embassy
59 quai d'Orsay, 7th (01.53.59.23.23/ www.afriquesud.net). Mº Invalides. **Open** 8.30am-5.15pm Mon-Fri. *Consulate and visas* 8.30am-noon Mon-Fri.

US Embassy
2 av Gabriel, 8th (01.43.12.22.22/ www.amb-usa.fr). Mº Concorde. Consulate and visas 4 av Gabriel, 8th (01.43.12.22.22). Mº Concorde. **Open** *Consular services* 9am-12.30pm, 1-3pm Mon-Fri. *Visas* 08.92.23.84.72.

Internet

More and more public spaces are becoming Wi-Fi hotspots.

Milk
31 bd de Sébastopol, 1st (08.20.00. 10.00/www.milkinternethall.com). Mº Châtelet or Rambuteau/RER Châtelet Les Halles. **Open** 24hrs daily.

Opening hours

Standard opening hours for shops are generally 9am/10am-7pm/8pm Mon-Sat. Some close on Mondays, some for lunch (usually between midday-2pm) and some in August.

Pharmacies

All French *pharmacies* sport a green neon cross. If closed, a pharmacy will have a sign indicating the nearest one open. Staff can provide basic medical services like disinfecting and bandaging wounds (for a small fee) and will indicate the nearest doctor on duty. These stay open late:

Pharmacie des Champs-Elysées
84 av des Champs-Elysées, 8th (01.45.62.02.41). Mº George V. **Open** 24hrs daily.

Matignon
2 rue Jean-Mermoz, 8th (01.43.59. 86.55). Mº Franklin D Roosevelt. **Open** 8.30am-2am daily.

Pharmacie Européenne de la Place de Clichy
6 pl de Clichy, 9th (01.48.74.65.18). Mº Place de Clichy. **Open** 24hrs daily.

Pharmacie des Halles
10 bd de Sébastopol, 4th (01.42.72. 03.23). Mº Châtelet. **Open** 9am-midnight Mon-Sat; 9am-10pm Sun.

Police

The French equivalent of 999/911 is **17** (**112** from a mobile), but don't expect a speedy response. If you're assaulted or robbed, report the incident as soon as possible. Make a statement (*procès verbal*) at the *point d'accueil* closest to the crime. To find it, contact the Préfecture Centrale (08.91.01.22.22) or www.prefecture.police.paris. interieur.gouv.fr. You'll need a statement for insurance purposes.

Post

Post offices (*bureaux de poste*) are open 8am-7pm Mon-Fri; 8am-noon Sat, apart from the 24hr one listed below. All are listed in the phone book: under *Administration des PTT* in the *Pages Jaunes*; under *Poste* in the *Pages Blanches*.

Most post offices have machines that weigh your letter, print out a stamp and give change, saving you from queuing. You can also buy stamps at a tobacconist.

Main Post Office
52 rue du Louvre, 1st (01.40.28.76.00). M° Les Halles or Louvre Rivoli. **Open** 24hrs daily.

Smoking

Smoking is banned in all enclosed public spaces. Hotels can still offer smoking rooms.

Telephones

All French phone numbers have ten digits. Paris and Ile-de-France numbers begin with 01; the rest of France is divided into four zones, 02 to 05. Mobile phone numbers start with 06. Numbers beginning with 08 can only be reached from inside France. The France country code is 33; leave off the first 0 at the start of the ten-digit number. Most public phones use *télécartes* (phonecards). Sold at post offices and tobacconists, they are €7.50 for 50 units and €15 for 120 units.

Tickets

For events tickets, go to a **Fnac** store (www.fnac.com). **Virgin** and **Ticketnet** have created an online ticket office, www.virginmega.fr.

Time

France is one hour ahead of GMT and uses the 24hr system.

Tipping

A service charge of ten to 15% is legally included in your bill at all restaurants, cafés and bars. It's polite to round up the final amount.

Tourist information

Espace du Tourisme d'Ile de France
Carrousel du Louvre, 99 rue de Rivoli, 1st (08.26.16.66.66/www.paris-ile-de-france.com). M° Pyramides. **Open** 8.30am-7pm Mon-Fri.
For Paris and the Ile-de-France.

Maison de la France
20 av de l'Opéra, 1st (01.42.96.70.00/www.franceguide.com). M° Opéra. **Open** 10am-6pm Mon-Fri; 10am-5pm Sat.
The state organisation for tourism in France: information galore.

Office de Tourisme et des Congrès de Paris
Carrousel du Louvre, 99 rue de Rivoli, 1st (08.92.68.30.00/www.parisinfo.com). M° Palais Royal Musée du Louvre. **Open** 9am-7pm daily.
Info on Paris and the suburbs; tickets. **Other locations** *Gare de Lyon, 20 bd Diderot, 12th. Gare du Nord, 18 rue de Dunkerque, 10th. Montmartre, 21 pl du Tertre, 18th. Opéra, 11 rue Scribe, 9th. Pyramides, 25 rue des Pyramides, 1st. Tour Eiffel, Champ de Mars, 7th.*

Visas

European Union nationals do not need a visa to enter France, nor do US, Canadian, Australian or New Zealand citizens for stays of up to three months. Nationals of other countries should enquire at the nearest French Consulate before leaving home. If you are travelling to France from one of the countries included in the Schengen agreement (most of the EU, but not Britain or Ireland), the visa from that country should be sufficient.

What's on

Two small publications compete for consumers of Wednesday-to-Tuesday listings information: *L'Officiel des Spectacles* (€0.35) and *Pariscope* (€0.40).

Vocabulary

General expressions

good morning/hello *bonjour*; good evening *bonsoir*; goodbye *au revoir*; hi *salut*; OK *d'accord*; yes *oui*; no *non*; how are you? *comment allez-vous?*; how's it going? *comment ça va?/ça va?*; sir/Mr *monsieur* (M); madam/Mrs *madame* (Mme); miss *mademoiselle* (Mlle); please *s'il vous plaît*; thank you *merci*; thank you very much *merci beaucoup*; sorry *pardon*; excuse me *excusez-moi*; do you speak English? *parlez-vous anglais?*; I don't speak French *je ne parle pas français*; I don't understand *je ne comprends pas*; speak more slowly, please *parlez plus lentement, s'il vous plaît*; good *bon/bonne*; bad *mauvais/mauvaise*; small *petit/petite*; big *grand/grande*; beautiful *beau/belle*; well *bien*; badly *mal*; a bit *un peu*; a lot *beaucoup*; very *très*; with *avec*; without *sans*; and *et*; or *ou*; because *parce que*; who? *qui?*; when? *quand?*; what? *quoi?*; which? *quel?*; where? *où?*; why? *pourquoi?*; how? *comment?*; at what time? *à quelle heure?*; forbidden *interdit/défendu*; out of order *hors service* (HS)/*en panne*; daily *tous les jours* (tlj)

Getting around

where is the (nearest) métro? *où est le métro (le plus proche)?*; when is the next train for… ? *c'est quand le prochain train pour..?*; ticket *un billet*; station *la gare*; platform *le quai*; entrance *entrée*; exit *sortie*; left *gauche*; right *droite*; straight on *tout droit*; far *loin*; near *pas loin/près d'ici*; street map *le plan*; bank *la banque*; is there a bank near here? *est-ce qu'il y a une banque près d'ici?*

Accommodation

do you have a room (for this evening/for two people)? *avez-vous une chambre (pour ce soir/pour deux personnes)?*; full *complet*; room *une chambre*; bed *un lit*; double bed *un grand lit*; (a room with) twin beds *(une chambre à) deux lits*; with bath(room)/shower *avec (salle de) bain/douche*; breakfast *le petit déjeuner*; included *compris*

At the restaurant

I'd like to book a table (for three/at 8pm) *je voudrais réserver une table (pour trois personnes/à vingt heures)*; lunch *le déjeuner*; dinner *le dîner*; coffee (espresso) *un café*; white coffee *un café au lait/café crème*; tea *du thé*; wine *du vin*; beer *la bière*; mineral water *eau minérale*; fizzy *gazeuse*; still *plate*; tap water *eau du robinet/une carafe d'eau*; the bill, please *l'addition, s'il vous plaît*

Numbers

0 *zéro*; 1 *un, une*; 2 *deux*; 3 *trois*; 4 *quatre*; 5 *cinq*; 6 *six*; 7 *sept*; 8 *huit*; 9 *neuf*; 10 *dix*; 11 *onze*; 12 *douze*; 13 *treize*; 14 *quatorze*; 15 *quinze*; 16 *seize*; 17 *dix-sept*; 18 *dix-huit*; 19 *dix-neuf*; 20 *vingt*; 21 *vingt-et-un*; 22 *vingt-deux*; 30 *trente*; 40 *quarante*; 50 *cinquante*; 60 *soixante*; 70 *soixante-dix*; 80 *quatre-vingts*; 90 *quatre-vingt-dix*; 100 *cent*; 1000 *mille*; 1,000,000 *un million*

Index

Sights